# CORPORATE MAKEOVER

# HARVEY H. SEGAL

# CORPORATE MAKEOVER

## The Reshaping of the American Economy

VIKING

VIKING
Published by the Penguin Group
Viking Penguin Inc., 40 West 23rd Street,
New York, New York 10010, U.S.A.
Penguin Books Ltd, 27 Wrights Lane, London W8 5TZ, England
Penguin Books Australia Ltd, Ringwood, Victoria, Australia
Penguin Books Canada Ltd, 2801 John Street,
Markham, Ontario, Canada L3R 1B4
Penguin Books (N.Z.) Ltd, 182–190 Wairau Road,
Auckland 10, New Zealand

Penguin Books Ltd, Registered Offices:
Harmondsworth, Middlesex, England

First published in 1989 by Viking Penguin Inc.

1 3 5 7 9 10 8 6 4 2

Library of Congress Cataloging in Publication Data
Segal, Harvey.
Corporate makeover: The reshaping of the American economy / Harvey Segal.
p.   cm.
Includes index.
ISBN 0-670-82099-7
1. Corporations—United States.   I. Title.   II. Title: Corporate makeover.
HD2785.S4127   1989
338.7′4′0973—dc20        88-40419

Printed in the United States of America
Set in Times Roman

*For Eloise*
*who made it all happen.*

# PREFACE

In its customary context, "makeover" denotes an effort to improve our body: new cosmetics, a new hairstyle, and, most importantly—far more often than not—a rigid regime of diet and exercise to effect a sharp loss of weight. Cutting the fat—increasing efficiency by the elimination of what is redundant or extravagant and the adoption of what is painful but salutary—is, or should be, the principal objective of what I call the corporate makeover. It embraces the gamut of recent change: hostile takeovers (whether by tender offer or proxy contest), friendly mergers and acquisitions, leveraged buyouts, divestitures, and corporate recapitalizations.

My purpose is not yet another account of what's happening, one that exposes the avarice of raiders, the felonies of insider traders, or the hardship endured by people displaced in the shuffle. Rather it is to explain, to analyze the corporate makeover. I look beyond the foibles and troubles of individuals to tell you why it's happening, what it means for us as investors, consumers, employees, and managers. And, finally, where the corporate makeover is going and how it's likely to change the shape of the American economy in the next century. In that endeavor, I draw on history and use what is valuable in the economist's analytical toolkit.

The issues that I confront are hardly academic. Publicly held corporations—those with freely traded shares of stock—account for more than nine-tenths of the dollar value of what the private sector of the American economy produces. Incorporated businesses embrace virtually all activities: from the production of motor vehicles, computers, jet aircraft, and food to the provision of services by banking, insurance, securities, and retail-trade establishments. And just as the fate of a football team hinges on the performance of each player, the performance of the American economy is critically affected by the efficiency of its constituent corporate parts. In these times of increasingly intensive international competition, American living standards cannot rise unless our corporations achieve higher efficiency, which means supplying quality goods and services at prices as low as, if not lower, than those set by the competition.

Americans used to look to a doubling of living standards from one generation to the next. But over the last fifteen years, the real median family income in the United States hardly increased at all. What that means, after allowance for inflation, is a standstill in the purchasing power of families which are neither rich nor poor but are in the middle. It is a stagnation of economic well-being that will not end unless corporations, which are the backbone of the American economy, become much more efficient.

Because I opine on so many controversial issues, the reader may sometimes think me in error but never in doubt.

# ACKNOWLEDGMENTS

Joe Spieler, my supportive agent, saw me through the formative stages. Dan Frank applied his impressive skills in the editing phase. And my wife, Eloise, provided help for which there is no adequate recompense.

I'm also grateful to the following people for information or suggestions: Roger E. Alcaly, John Anderson, Susan Azrati, Patricia Beardsley, Charlotte R. Boschan, Ann Carolyn, Peter H. Crawford, the late Salomon J. Flink, Horace J. De Podwin, Nicole Ernsberger, David Glasner, Fred Heiter, Arnold Hoffman, Michael C. Jensen, Alex Ladias, the late Robert Lekachman, Frank R. Lichtenberg, Leonard Lieberman, Robert E. Lipsey, Jane S. Little, Alan P. Murray, Bernard D. Nossiter, Conchita Pineda, Susan Rose-Ackerman, Jed Rubenfeld, Linda Sandler, Anna J. Schwartz, Emma F. Segal, Harry G. Segal, Penny Simon, the late Ephraim Stern, Susan E. Woodward, Walter B. Wriston, and Frederick Yohn.

# CONTENTS

# CORPORATE MAKEOVER

# 1

# WITH NEITHER A BODY TO KICK NOR A SOUL TO DAMN:

## The Publicly Held Corporation

"**C**orporation" is one of those words that are now used with little or no thought about their proper meaning. In casual conversation, "corporation" denotes a business, a company, a firm, or an eleemosynary institution, such as a university, a church, or a research foundation. But the unique character of the corporation is highlighted in *The American Heritage Dictionary,* where it is defined as "a body of persons granted a charter legally recognizing them as a separate entity having its own rights, privileges, and liabilities distinct from those of its members."

This implies that people, with the blessing of the state, form a body corporate to shield themselves from hazards to which they would otherwise be exposed; and for those engaged in business enterprise, the corporation offers protections that are denied proprietorships and partnerships. Because it is a "separate entity," people who invest their wealth in a business corporation—its shareholders—are not personally liable for debts that the corporation incurs. This limited liability means that the individual investor's risk in the event of bankruptcy will not exceed the price paid for the shares, a decisive edge over an interest in a partnership or proprietorship, in which liability is unlimited. Another advantage is the unlimited—if not perpetual—life of a corporation. Unlike the partnership, the demise of a principal owner or manager need not threaten a corporate enterprise with extinction or necessitate radical change, as often happens with a partnership.

1

Together, limited liability and unlimited duration are decisively conducive to the growth of publicly held corporations, companies with shares owned by thousands—in some instances by millions—of investors which are continuously traded so that their prices may be followed minute by minute. Because of this liquidity—the ease and certainty with which its stocks and bonds can be sold for cash in organized markets—the publicly held corporation is able to raise large sums of capital, quickly and at minimal cost.

Corporations now account for more than 98 percent of the private sector's output of the U.S. economy, everything from a truck produced by Ford (one of the publicly held companies with which this book is concerned) to services rendered by the personal corporation of a physician (one of a number of privately held entities that it will ignore). But the overwhelming dominance of the business corporation is of rather recent origin. It was not until the second decade of this century—about one hundred and thirty-five years after independence—that corporations outstripped proprietorships and partnerships to produce more than half of the country's output of goods and services, or what is known as the gross national product.[1]

The concept of a shielded or privileged body can be traced to the early history of state power. Rulers or ruling bodies in ancient Athens and Rome, feudal lords in the medieval period, and petty princes and national monarchs in more recent times all made a practice of bestowing sovereign power on chosen groups. The basic privilege of perpetual life was conferred on corporate entities so that the endeavor, whether sacred or secular, would survive the lives of its founders. Other powers were fashioned to the needs of the particular enterprise, be it a cathedral, a monastery, a college, a trade guild, or a newly chartered town.

## The Rise of the Corporation: Some Natural History

By the early Middle Ages, legists and canonists were beginning to draw subtle distinctions between a real person and what they called the *persona ficta,* a group treated as a fictive person who, having been created by the fist of the prince rather than by God, had no soul and hence no will of his own. Difficult questions were posed, some of which foreshadowed the problems of contemporary business corporations. If the corporation had no will of its own, how could the wills of its individual members be adequately reflected in a corporate decision? Since the corporation was comprised of a head and members, how were lines of authority to be drawn between them? Issues such as these were not very likely to disturb the tranquility of the medieval monastery, but they did surface in the newly incorporated boroughs and towns.[2]

The precursors of the modern business corporation were the British and Dutch joint-stock companies chartered in the sixteenth and seventeenth centuries to engage in foreign trade and banking.[3] In 1602, the Dutch East India Company—said to be the first stock corporation—was organized with permanent capital, shares of unlimited duration; and in 1612, the British East India Company, formed in 1600, began gradually increasing the life of its shares. While the issuance of shares of unlimited duration to raise capital is distinctly modern, the early stock companies were very much creatures of their times, organizations that were granted trading and other monopolies in efforts to achieve the ends of European states engaged in a spirited rivalry for the domination of the Americas.

The growth of business corporations was sharply retarded by the collapse of the "South Sea Bubble" in 1720, a part of the first international financial crash of modern times. Robert Harley—the first earl of Oxford, a Tory leader, and a great bibliophile—got the South Sea Company chartered in 1711 to gain support for efforts to end the War of Spanish Succession. Holders of £9 million of government bonds could exchange them for stock—paying 6 percent—in the new company, which had a monopoly on trade with the islands of the South Seas and South America. Five years later John Law, a Scot who understood the profit potential of paper money, did Harley one better: he persuaded the prince regent of France to allow him not only to form the Mississippi Company—which soon secured a monopoly of trade with French colonies in North America—but at the same time to establish a royal bank. Like its British counterpart, the Mississippi Company assumed French debt in exchange for its shares and also served as the crown's tax collector. Expectations of large dividends—and in France, Law's "system" of monetary expansion and then foreign-exchange controls—caused prices of both South Sea and Mississippi Company stocks to rise sharply. Soon there was a frenzy of activity in which Frenchmen and Englishmen speculated both at home and abroad, a fever to which the Dutch also succumbed. The sad end came with the bursting of the twin bubbles in 1720: the South Sea in September and the Mississippi in October. A spate of litigation by injured British investors led Parliament to pass the Bubble Act of 1720, which forbade unchartered companies to issue stock. But although the way was still clear for duly chartered companies, memories of the South Sea fiasco lingered on, and few businesses were incorporated during the rest of the eighteenth century.[4]

## American Corporations—Soulless Yet Contentious

Corporations were prime movers in the original settlement of North America, and before independence the colonies, following British legal precedents, had chartered seven business corporations with the approval of Parliament or the king. One was a fire insurance company in Pennsylvania and the others—in Massachusetts, Rhode Island, and Connecticut—were chartered to build docks and waterworks. After 1780, the number of business corporations increased rapidly as the newly independent state legislatures exercised their charter-granting authority. By the beginning of the nineteenth century, 337 charters had been granted and their scope was expanded to embrace banking, speculative land development, and bridge, canal, and turnpike construction as well as manufacturing. In fact, throughout U.S. history there have been waves or cycles of incorporations, reflecting the underlying optimism or pessimism of entrepreneurs.[5]

But in an insightful passage of *The Wealth of Nations,* first published in 1776, Adam Smith declared that the future held little hope for the survival of the corporation:

> The directors of such companies, however, being the managers of other people's money rather than their own, it cannot well be ex-

pected, that they should watch over it with the same anxious vigilance with which the partners in a private copartnery frequently watch over their own. Like the stewards of a rich man, they are apt to consider attention to small matters as not for their master's honour, and very easily give themselves a dispensation from having it. Negligence and profusion, therefore, must always prevail, more or less in the management of the affairs of such a company. It is upon this account that joint stock companies for foreign trade have seldom been able to maintain the competition against private adventurers. They have, accordingly, very seldom succeeded without exclusive privilege; and frequently have not succeeded with one. Without an exclusive privilege they have commonly mismanaged the trade. With an exclusive privilege they have both mismanaged and confined it.[6]

Despite similar sentiments—especially those voiced by hard-pressed middle-western farmers who fought the railroads over high freight rates in the years of falling prices and hard times that followed the Civil War—the American business corporation flourished. And in a landmark decision handed down in 1889 by Justice Stephen J. Field, the Supreme Court ruled that "corporations can invoke the benefits of provisions of the Constitution and laws which guarantee to persons the enjoyment of property, or afford to them the means for its protection."[7] What the Court embraced, after a long struggle, was the proposition that a corporation is a person in the eyes of the law and that its rights are protected by the celebrated clause in the first section of the Fourteenth Amendment, adopted in 1868: "nor shall any State deprive any person of life, liberty or property, without due process of law." After some fifteen hundred years, the *persona ficta* got still another lease on life.

At the same time that the courts were bestowing new rights on existing corporations, state legislatures were gradually removing the barriers to the formation of new ones. In the beginning, corporations were created by special acts, a process that invited bribery and corruption since it involved negotiating specific charter provisions with legislators—among others, the purpose of the enterprise, the location of its activities, the amount of capital to be raised by stock sales, and the power of its directory. As early as 1811, New York enacted a general incorporation statute that was restricted to manufacturing enterprises; and in 1837 Connecticut passed the first modern law that permitted incorporation "for any lawful business," a category from which banking and public utilities were excluded. Other states followed suit in the 1840s and 1850s, but the path to achieving a working corporate enterprise was still full of hurdles. Applications had to be approved by the state secretary, or by some other high official, who enforced firm rules such as the requirement that a minimum of capital had to be paid in before an enterprise could be launched and that delinquent shareholders would be held personally liable—up to the unpaid balances on their stock subscriptions—for any corporate debts. High taxes were levied, and there were also severe constraints on the kinds of securities—common stocks, preferred stocks, and bonds—that a corporation could issue. When newly issued, shares of common stocks had a minimum price or par value, and existing shareholders usually had a preemptive right to purchase them. New York in 1912 led the way by permitting no par stock, but the practice did not become common until after the First World War.

A radical relaxation of standards for incorporation began in the 1880s, a reaction to two ineluctable forces: first, the states' needs for new, politically palatable sources of tax revenue, and second, businessmen's determination to check the fall of prices and the erosion of profits, through the formation first of trusts and then of holding companies.

Business first responded to the price deflation that followed the Civil War by forming pricing pools: companies in the same industry sat down together and agreed to bolster prices by restricting their output and taking punitive action against producers who refused to participate in the collusion.[8] But maintaining cartel discipline through voluntary trade associations proved difficult, and the next stage was the development of the trust, an arrangement under which independent companies turned shares of their stock over to a trustee in return for an agreed-upon number of trust certificates. The trustee then managed the combined operations—closing down or expanding facilities—with a view to raising prices or at least checking their decline.

In wielding such broad discretionary power, the trustees established important precedents for the control of corporations by professional managers rather than dominant shareholders.

The Standard Oil Trust, in force from 1882 until its replacement by a holding company in 1899, was perhaps the most predatory of the species, a combination of drillers, pipelines, and refiners that demanded and got rebates on rail shipments by its competitors.

Congress outlawed trusts together with other conspiracies or combinations "in restraint of trade or commerce" in the Sherman Act of 1890. That set the stage for outright mergers and consolidations in the form of the holding company, a corporation that held shares in other companies. A classic case in the growth of a new industry is General Motors, the brainchild of William Crapo Durant, a former carriage builder who in 1908 began acquiring stakes in independent auto makers—Cadillac, Oldsmobile, and Chevrolet—as well as in such suppliers of components as Fisher Body, Hyatt Roller Bearing, and Dayton Engineering Laboratory, or Delco. Durant converted General Motors to an operating company in 1917, at which time the various car, parts, and accessories subsidiaries became GM divisions.

In some of the consolidations—notably the United States Steel Corporation, created through mergers by J. P. Morgan & Co. in 1901 with an eye to softening competition and firming prices—there was considerable "stock watering," a term borrowed from cattle drovers' practice of taking their livestock to drink just before weighing in at sale. Corporate stock is watered when the total capitalization—the par, or face, value of the new stocks and bonds issued—exceeds the market value of the tangible assets: buildings, equipment, inventories, and the like. In the formation of U.S. Steel, the excess—or what many other companies carried on their balance sheets as an intangible asset of "goodwill"—came to $508.2 million, or more than 36 percent of the total capitalization.[9]

In 1888, New Jersey became the "cradle of trusts" when it permitted its chartered companies to hold stock in other corporations, a privilege that other states conferred only under special circumstances. Even more radical changes came in 1896, when New Jersey corporations were expressly authorized to do business anywhere, had their taxes sharply reduced, and restrictions on amending their charters by majority votes of the shareholders eased. Later, in 1902, penalties for distributing unearned dividends were softened. Other states—"charter mongers" eager for revenues—responded by offering even broader corporate powers: fewer restraints, lower corporate taxes, and broader discretionary power for managers in their relations with shareholders. In 1913 Governor Woodrow Wilson persuaded the New Jersey legislature to outlaw trusts; and although that law was largely repealed in 1917, the damage was done. Delaware became the "mother of corporations," and by 1929 more than 42 percent of the state's revenues were derived from corporate fees and taxes. Lawyers who appeared before the Court of Chancery in Wilmington—of whom the most prominent was Aaron Finger of Richards, Layton & Finger—became richer if not wiser.[10]

## Corporate Ownership and Control:
## The Great Separation

By 1926, William Z. Ripley, a Harvard economist and a leading authority on corporations, noted with consternation that corporate managements had arrogated "sole responsibility" for the issuance of new securities, that they had "practically unrestrained" authority to dispose of new shares on terms that they might think fit, and that they were empowered to sell assets or enter into new businesses.[11]

The triumph of the corporation in the face of strong agrarian-populist antipathy is a tribute to its functional superiority. It clearly was the most efficient way to organize and finance large undertakings. And while other unpopular economic institutions—chattel slavery and a feudal land tenure system in the Hudson River valley—were violently dismantled, Americans learned to live with the corporation. Even the first Henry Ford (1863–1947)—a Michigan farmer turned engineer who shared the populists' prejudices—had to form a corporation, the Ford Motor Company, in 1903 and grudgingly endure outside shareholders, the original investors, whom he denounced as "parasites," until he froze them out by withholding dividends and forcing them to sell out to him at low prices in 1919.[12]

As a founding entrepreneur, Henry Ford had reason to fear that his minority shareholders—among them the Dodge brothers, auto body builders and later competitors—posed a threat to his control of the company. But, as Adam Smith was probably the first to point out, there were other corporate situations in which ownership was cleanly separated from control by tacit agreement.

> The trade of a joint stock company is always managed by a court of directors. The court, indeed, is frequently subject, in many respects, to the controul of a general court of proprietors. But the greater part of those proprietors seldom pretend to understand any thing of the business of the company; and when the spirit of faction happens not to prevail among them, give themselves no trouble about it, but receive contentedly such half yearly or yearly dividend, as the directors think proper to make them. This total exemption from trouble and from risk, beyond a limited sum, encourages many people to become adventurers in joint stock companies, who would, upon no account, hazard their fortunes in any private copartnery.[13]

Early in this century, Smith's neglected insight was rediscovered. Thorstein Veblen—a great American economist whose analysis centered on a populist dichotomy between "industrial and pecuniary employments," making goods and making money—wrote in 1904 that "management is separated from the ownership of the property, more and more widely as the scope of corporate finance widens."[14] In Austria, Rudolf Hilferding, a Marxist economist who later served twice as finance minister of the Weimar Republic, observed in 1910 that "as a result of the transformation of property into share ownership the rights of the property owner are curtailed. . . . The real control of productive capital rests with people who have only contributed part of it."[15] Some of the consequences of the separation of property from control were spelled out in the 1913 report of the Pujo Committee, which held a celebrated series of hearings on the "money trust"—the "concentration of control of money and credit"—in the U.S. House of Representatives:

> None of the witnesses called was able to name an instance in the history of the country in which the stockholders had succeeded in overthrowing an existing management in any large corporation, nor does it appear that the stockholders have ever even succeeded in so far as to secure the investigation of an existing management of a corporation to ascertain whether it has been well or honestly managed . . . The situation that exists with respect to the control of the so-called mutual companies is in a modified way illustrative of all great corporations with numerous and widely scattered shareholders. *The management is virtually self-perpetuating and is able through the power of patronage, the indifference of the stockholders and other influences to control a majority of stock.*[16]

Another insight into the nature of the modern corporation came from Walther Rathenau (1867–1922), an enormously powerful German industrialist. He headed the *Allgemeine Elektrizitatsgesellschaft* (AEG), founded by his father, Emil, and, in addition to being an investment banker with numerous other holdings, was the man who planned and effectively coordinated Germany's economic mobilization during the First World War. Rathenau was also the author of books on economic and political issues that had a wide international readership.

In 1916 Rathenau wrote that in the modern corporation:

> The claims to ownership are subdivided in such a fashion, and are so mobile, that the enterprise assumes an independent life, as if it belonged to no one; it takes on an objective existence, such as in earlier days was embodied only in state and church, in a municipal corporation, in the life of a guild or religious order. . . .
>
> In the ultimate analysis, the economic meaning of the whole movement grows clear. It is no longer the wealthy capitalist's desire for gain which shapes the enterprise. The undertaking itself, now grown into an objective personality, maintains itself, creates its own means just as much as it creates its own tasks. It is ready to provide these means out of its own profits, by the temporary issue of de-

bentures, out of state loans, out of foundations, out of the savings of its staff and its workmen . . .

Thus, between the domain of state organisations and the domain of private businesses, there arises a domain of intermediate structures. In this we find autonomous enterprises, arising out of and conducted by private initiative, subject to state regulation, and leading an independent life. Essentially, they are transitional varieties between private economy and state economy.[17]

Rathenau, a mystic, an ascetic, and a radical reformer who eschewed luxury, inherited wealth, and avarice, was strongly opposed to socialism in general and the German Social Democratic party in particular, but he was a strong proponent of peacetime planning. So it was the interplay of two institutions with which he was intimately acquainted—the "autonomous" corporation and industrial planning by extensive state intervention—that would shape the future. In his vision the corporation was not merely a form of business enterprise but one of the twin pillars of a new, totalitarian economy.[18]

Rathenau's view of the corporation as a harbinger of social revolution made a strong impression—stronger than they acknowledged—on two Americans, Adolf A. Berle, Jr., and Gardiner C. Means. In 1932, at the very nadir of the Great Depression, they gained prominence with the appearance of their instantly successful book, *The Modern Corporation and Private Property*. Originally it was brought out in a small edition by a law-book house, which withdrew it from circulation at the behest of General Motors; the plates were then sold to a major trade book house that was better able to promote it.[19]

Berle, a young Columbia Law School professor and Wall Street practitioner who as a Harvard student knew William Z. Ripley, served in Franklin Delano Roosevelt's original "brains trust," where in much the spirit of Rathenau, he urged policies that resulted in the effort, declared unconstitutional by the Supreme Court, to cartelize U.S. industry through the price, production, and labor "codes" of the National Recovery Administration.[20] Means, an economist, later attracted much attention with his "administered price" thesis, the

11

belief—contradicted by the statistical evidence—that prices in industries dominated by a few corporations are "inflexible," that they tend to rise faster or fall more slowly than the overall price level, thus aggravating both inflations and deflations.[21]

What made *The Modern Corporation* so striking were Means's data. Where the Pujo Committee offered only case studies of concentration and casual evidence of the separation of ownership from control, Berle and Means came up with hard and alarming numbers at a time of massive unemployment, when people were prepared to believe the worst about big business. After reviewing an impressively detailed body of evidence, they concluded that at the beginning of 1930: (1) the two hundred largest corporations outside of banking controlled about half of the country's corporate wealth; and (2) eighty-eight of those two hundred companies, accounting for 58 percent of their combined wealth, were controlled by managers rather than by substantial shareholders; those managers' self-perpetuated power was in large part the result of a remarkable dispersion of stock ownership, with the biggest investors holding only minute fractions of the total shares of some of the country's largest corporations.[22] Finally, unsupported by any sort of statistical evidence or analysis, Berle and Means assert that "the interests of control are different from and often radically opposed to those of ownership."[23]

Although subsequent research modified their statistical findings—particularly on the extent of managerial control in 1930—it did not overturn them.[24] But even if the numbers on the concentration of assets in the two hundred largest corporations are accepted at face value, the inferences drawn from them cannot withstand scrutiny. Berle and Means clearly looked toward increasing concentration. It would, they write, take "only thirty years at 1924–29 rates for all corporate activity and practically all industrial activity to be absorbed by two hundred giant companies." And they added that if the then current trends continued until 1950, "half of the national wealth would be under control of big companies at the end of that period."[25]

But what Berle and Means took to be a long-term, irreversible trend toward greater concentration was actually the ephemeral result of the groundswell of mergers in the 1920s. The concentration of assets in the two hundred largest nonfinancial corporations peaked at 57 percent in 1933—a year of numerous business failures and consolidations—and then plummeted to less than 35 percent in 1975.[26] So Berle and Means's fears—that competition "has changed in character" or that "production is carried on under the ultimate control of a handful of individuals" rather than "blind economic forces"[27]—were not very substantive. And this judgment is not based solely on hindsight. Their own data indicate that forty-seven of the two hundred biggest companies in 1919 failed to make the list in 1928,[28] a 23.5 percent turnover rate, which hardly squares with the thesis of an increasing concentration of power.

Far more important for our purposes is Berle and Means's impact on subsequent thinking about the nature of the corporation. Thanks to Berle's historical analysis of the legal cases—set forth in more than two hundred pages of heavy reading in Book II of *The Modern Corporation*—the thesis of the separation of ownership from control is solidly buttressed. Over the years state and federal courts greatly strengthened the hand of managers in control of corporations and weakened that of the shareholders. Today boards of directors exercise virtually unlimited discretion in the conduct of corporations because, under what's called the business judgment rule, the courts presume that they are acting in the interests of the shareholders unless there is explicit evidence of fraud or self-dealing.

In his preface—and elsewhere—Berle asks whether the corporation "will dominate the state or be regulated by the state or whether the two will coexist with relatively little connection." His answer: "It is obvious that the corporate system not only tends to be the flower of our industrial organization, but that the public is in a mood to impose on it a steadily growing degree of responsibility for our economic welfare."[29] That sentiment was the basis of much of the federal legislation—specifically the Securities and Exchange Act—that regulated business in the 1930s. Business was held responsible for a devastating depression that was in fact precipitated and deepened by flawed monetary, trade, and fiscal policies, a tragedy in which the managers of the two hundred largest corporations played no significant role. What Berle and Means created was an intellectual rationale for turning on a conspicuous scapegoat.

Another of Berle and Means's legacies survived the Depression and continued to cloud thinking about the corporation: the thesis that the separation of ownership from control somehow insulates the corporation from all external influences save possibly the power of the state. Shareholders, powerless to assert their interests, become "mere recipients of the wages of capital," accepting whatever the controlling managers deign to pay out in dividends. Managers of corporations with widely dispersed ownership, for their part, hold so few shares as to make them rather indifferent to profits or at least not likely to pursue them with anything like the zest of the old-fashioned, individual entrepreneur.[30]

Berle continued to play those themes for the rest of his life. In 1959 he asserted that

> Corporation executives as individuals are not capitalists seeking profit. They are men seeking careers, in a structure offering rewards of power and position rather than profit or great wealth. Probably an exactly similiar situation prevails within any Communist commissariat.

Then he went on to say: "Theoretically it is possible for someone outside management to mobilize the army of small stockholders, aggregate their votes, and displace the existing directors. But the task is huge, the expense great, and the results problematic. It has happened so rarely that the possibility may be discarded."[31]

From the perspective of the late 1980s—when communist commissars emulate capitalists and incumbent U.S. managers quake in fear of corporate raiders—Berle is hopelessly anachronistic. But the fact of the matter is that he had—and still has—plenty of company.

## Demystifying the Separation—The Agency Theory

It is clear that the emergence of large corporations and the separation of ownership from control has not resulted in the revolutionary changes anticipated by Rathenau or Berle and Means. Big corporations, once regarded as omnipotent, are increasingly vulnerable to the very forces of competition they were said to have superseded, and their managements, far from being self-perpetuating, are frequently overturned in pitched battles for control. What Berle and Means took to be an ineluctable economic trend was in fact a temporary phenomenon. U.S. industrial concentration increased in the Great Depression of the 1930s as many existing businesses failed and the bleak outlook damped the growth of new firms in emerging industries. And in the years following the Second World War, the dominant position of the unscathed American economy in a largely ruined industrial world reinforced the impression that our corporations were invulnerable. But U.S. dominance was effectively broken by the mid-1960s; and in the turbulently competitive world of the 1970s and 1980s, the biggest one hundred, two hundred, or five hundred U.S. corporations lost their awesomeness. General Motors, our biggest company in 1987 with $101.8 billion of sales, had only 36 percent of the U.S. auto market, down from about a 50 percent share in 1940. A consequence of that decline as well as of poor earnings in recent years is that the market value of GM's stock was $27.2 billion while General Electric—on a little more than $35 billion in sales, but with profits of $2.5 billion, only $400 million less than GM's—was valued by the market at nearly $60 billion.

But while incumbent corporate managers are vulnerable—though as we shall see in chapter 3, they are working furiously to thwart hostile takeovers—that vulnerability does not resolve the problems created by the separation of ownership from control. Peter F. Drucker, whose perspective is that of a European political theorist and historian, once viewed the problem of the managerially controlled corporation as one of illegitimate power, rule without the consent of the governed. In the best of his many books, *The Future of Industrial Man,* published in 1942, he wrote:

> Managerial power today is illegitimate power. It is in no way based upon a fundamental principle accepted by society as a legitimate basis of power. It is not controlled by such a principle or limited

15

by it. And it is responsible to no one. Individual property was a fundamental principle accepted by society as a legitimate basis of social and political power. But today managerial power is independent of, uncontrolled by, and not responsible to the shareholders. And there is no other fundamental principle to take the place of individual property rights as a legitimate basis for the power which management actually wields. . . .

Lest I be misunderstood: this is *not* an attack upon modern management. On the contrary, there has never been a more efficient, a more honest, a more capable and conscientious group of rulers than the professional management of the great American corporations today. The power is theirs not because they usurped it, but because the stockholder has relinquished his rights and duties. . . .

However, honesty, efficiency and capability have never been and never will be good titles to power. The questions whether power is legitimate or illegitimate, whether a ruler is a constititutional ruler or a despot lie altogether on a plane different from that of personal qualities. Bad qualities can vitiate a good title. But good qualities can never remedy the lack of title. . . . A good man on a usurper's throne will probably rule for a shorter time than the bandit who does not care about the title as long as he has the power. . . .

It was this insight which earned Machiavelli most of the opprobrium which has been heaped upon him.[32]

Forty-four years later, at the peak of the takeover wave in the autumn of 1986, Drucker penned an epitaph for "corporate capitalism"—what he had called "managerial power" in 1942—which has fallen victim to "speculator's capitalism." "Corporate capitalism," he wrote, "failed primarily because under it management was accountable to no one and for nothing. In this the corporate raiders are absolutely right."[33]

If Drucker is right about the illegitimacy of corporate capitalism—as I think he is—two questions have to be answered. First, if managerial power is illegitimate, if it's comparable to government without the explicit consent of the governed, then how could it have persisted for so long? Second, what can be done to legitimize managerial control or, barring that, to replace it?

Managerial control did not just happen but is the end product of an evolution. Its origins are in the early banks and railroads, two enterprises in which specialized knowledge and professional skills were essential for success. The historian Thomas C. Cochran reports that in 1846 John Murray Forbes, the Boston investor, thought that he could run the Michigan Central Railroad in his spare time, but soon was disabused of the idea and turned over the presidency to a full-time career executive. Cochran concludes that because of "the capitalist's lack of knowledge necessary to make decisions . . . the control of policy by salaried officers . . . became the rule in railroading in the nineteenth century."[34]

In 1959 Adolf Berle identified four stages of corporate control. The first is absolute shareholder control, massive concentration of stock ownership, as in Ford, Du Pont, A&P, and Alcoa, each of which was dominated by members of a founding family—the Fords, the Du Ponts, the Hartfords, and the Mellons. The second is working control, where an individual or group has far less than an absolute majority of the shares of voting stock but sufficient influence over— or an affinity with—other shareholders to control the board of directors and hence the company. The Du Pont family's common stock holding of 30 percent—acquired with profits made in the First World War—was ample enough, in conjunction with those of W. C. Durant and others, to control General Motors in the early 1920s. Berle estimated that at the end of the 1950s there were about fifty thousand large shareholders who were survivors of the working control phase. The third stage is management control, one into which many corporations entered during the expansion of the 1920s, where ownership is so dispersed that no shareholder or group of shareholders accounts for more than a minute fraction of the outstanding issue. And finally there is a fourth, and still unfolding stage, in which shareholding is becoming more concentrated, this time in financial institutions— pension plans, mutual funds, and insurance companies. But bear in mind that those distinctions are not very cleanly delineated.[35]

Now to explain the prevalence of managerial control. With the rapid growth of personal incomes and savings in the first three decades of this century, and a dearth of safe federal and state government bonds, there was a sharp rise in the demand for high-grade corporate stocks and bonds by members of a new middle class—prosperous farmers, shopkeepers, salespeople, and professionals—who had never before bought them. Wall Street came to Main Street. An ever-broadening securities market—spurred by a network of banks and brokerage houses that underwrote and marketed securities— made it possible for wealthy members of founding families to diversify their investment portfolios by selling off portions of their holdings at attractive prices; and at the same time businesses, growing ever larger, tapped the capital markets to finance an increasing volume of investment. The result, as already noted, was a radical dispersion of stock ownership and greater liquidity, or ease of cashing in securities, as the efficiency of the markets was enhanced by a growing number of savers and the development of financial intermediaries— securities underwriters, brokers, and other financial institutions that matched investors with issuers. At the end of 1929 the Pennsylvania Railroad's largest shareholder—its employees' credit union—held only 0.34 percent of the total shares, and the twenty largest held only 2.7 percent.[36] With such dispersion, control of the proxy machinery, the lists of shareholders and the holding of elections, is the key to incumbency, and that same control guarantees the perpetuation of managerial rule: it allows the retiring chief executive to anoint his successor with the approval of a board of directors, most or all of whom he has appointed. And barring only the most egregious of scandals, management's slate is almost certain to carry the board election.

So long as earnings and stock prices were rising in the 1920s, only a few critics, the likes of Thorstein Veblen and W. Z. Ripley, raised their voices against managerial control. Even though big business was on the defensive in the 1930s, a shrunken and dispirited army of securities holders did not rise up in revolt against the incumbent managers. The profit pies, if any, were too small to quarrel over. Then, in the decades immediately following the Second World War, the United States' role as the world's dominant supplier assured fat order books and—after a spell of uncertainty and reconversion to civilian production—a rising stock market. So there was little reason for shareholders to be unhappy, and good reason for Peter Drucker to forget, for forty-four years after the appearance of *The Future of Industrial Man* in 1942, that managerial power is illegitmate power.[37] Recollecting it now, when the vulnerability of managers is so painfully apparent, calls to mind Machiavelli's cautionary tale. Maximinus—a "very warlike" and hence admired man, but of "base origin, having herded sheep once in Thrace"—was for a time acclaimed as Emperor only to be reviled and murdered when the Romans, enraged by intrigues and crimes another man might have committed with impunity, remembered who he really was.[38]

To discern the future of managerial control, some questions about the role of property and property rights must be resolved. Berle—and he is not alone in this common misconception—identifies property with physical possession of the *res,* the thing.[39] He contends that there is a basic change in the nature of property because the shareholders, the "owners" of the corporation, can't come onto the premises and touch or feel a robotic arm, a computer, or the steering wheel of a fork lift. That distancing is a practical consequence of the divisibility and dispersion of ownership. But the essence of property is not the physical possession of things—or, more abstractly, real assets—but the services that things provide. I don't need title to an automobile to secure transportation service because I can rent one. By analogy, if I buy shares of Exxon, what I've purchased, at some risk in an uncertain world, is a claim on a stream of future payments— dividends, which I believe the company will continue to pay—and the possibility of capital appreciation if the share price rises.

Now, my desire to achieve income and capital appreciation— rather than to lay claim to a piece of an oil rig—doesn't make me any less an owner of Exxon. And while matters are a bit more complicated if the pension plan of which I am a participant holds Exxon in its portfolio, there is still a nexus of ownership. What I own as a pensioner is my claim on income from a pool of invested capital in an amount that is usually, though not always, specified. It's thus the duty of the pension-fund manager to take care that the yield of the fund's portfolio covers the pensioners' claims. In his fiduciary capacity he must follow the fortunes of each of the companies in which the fund is invested with an eye to either selling the securities of those doing badly or—if the losses would be too large—putting pressure on their managers to improve earnings. So Berle and more recent writers are wrong when they assert that no one really owns the corporation. The corporation has owners, and, contrary to Drucker, its preservation as a "going concern" does not transcend the interests of shareholders.[40]

What, then, is the relationship between shareholder-owners and highly autonomous corporate managers? The answer, in a nutshell, is that the managers are agents of the owners.

The term agency—in law and more recently in economics—covers the complex of relationships and transactions that results when an agent deals with third parties on behalf of a principal.[41] When a commercial bank acts as a transfer agent for an oil company, it carries on thousands of transactions with third parties on behalf of a principal. It keeps the records of stock and debenture holders, noting all changes in ownership, and it makes dividend and interest payments that may at times be in excess of the oil company's deposit balance. It's a relationship in which the agent bank hasn't much autonomy, save for discipline it might exert as a creditor. But the principal-agency relationship between a small, undercapitalized company that wants to issue more stock and a strong securities underwriter is quite another matter. In addition to deciding whether to do the deal in the first place, the underwriter can pretty much call the shots on fees and the pricing of the shares, decisions that determine the net capital that the issuer will realize. Operators of grain elevators are agents of the farmers who own the grain that is stored, and they too have great autonomy because they can decide how much credit to extend farmers and when and at what price to sell grain. The agent, in short, is sometimes far more powerful than the principal.

Thus, when the executive officers of a corporation, agents acting on behalf of shareholder-principals, attain a critical measure of autonomy—notably discretion over the use of retained earnings and power to name their own successors—we say that that corporation is managerially controlled. The current preponderance of managerially controlled companies is sometimes dubbed "managerial capitalism."

This way of thinking about the corporation—what economists call the agency theory of the firm—was originated some fifty years ago in an article by the Anglo-American economist Ronald H. Coase.[42] Coase, presently at the University of Chicago, wanted to explain the existence of the firm or establishment that produces in house all sorts of goods and services that could be purchased from outside suppliers in the marketplace. More concretely, what Coase was driving at is the economic rationale by which a specialty chemical producer prints package labels in house and employs legal counselors and computer programmers as regular staffers rather than purchasing all of those services from outside vendors. Citing English common law, Coase drew a distinction between employees of the firm, whose work is tightly controlled, and agents who have a good deal more freedom.[43] Nearly four decades later, delving into the implications of that distinction led to agency theory.

Michael C. Jensen, a leading exponent of this new approach to the corporation who teaches at Harvard, explains: "Corporate managers are the agents of shareholders, a relationship fraught with conflicting interests. Agency theory [is] the analysis of such conflicts."[44] It does what Berle and Means failed to do in their *obiter dictum* that the interests of managers are antithetical to those of owners.

To understand those conflicts of interest, let us begin with a successful founder—the one and only shareholder of a successful enterprise—who sells 70 percent of his stock to the public, which now freely trades it. As the largest single shareholder, the founder retains working control of the company and continues as chief executive officer. Before he went public, any of the founder's acts of omission or commission that reduced profitability—a bad pricing decision, failure to push aggressively with a new product, or laxity in controlling labor and material costs—directly affected his purse. If, with a million shares issued, the company earned 50 cents less per share, the pie from which our founder could have sliced himself a dividend was $500,000 smaller. But now, with outsiders holding 70 percent of the stock, the founder would bear only 30 percent of the costs of his own derelictions, or $150,000. With shirking on the job now much more harmful to the interests of outside shareholders than to those of the founder, there is a basis for a conflict of interest. What's more, by virtue of controlling the company, the founder can partially offset the decline of his dividends with expanded perquisites.

Perquisites befitting a chief executive officer, most of which are not federally taxed as income in kind, include a company plane in addition to a car and a driver, use of resort homes maintained by the company, and trips to distant places, with or without spouse, on which business and pleasure can be deftly intermingled. But perquisites increase costs and hence depress both a company's earnings— the capital needed to generate that same earnings stream—and its present value.[45] So there are narrow limits beyond which the founder, as a dominant shareholder, can't push without threatening his own wealth. That constraint, however, is progressively weakened—and the stage correspondingly widened for more perquisites and sharper conflicts of interest—as the founder's shareholdings diminish and as the corporation passes from working control to managerial control.

In large managerially controlled corporations, perquisites and the attendant conflicts of interest are in evidence at levels far below that of chief executive. When I joined what is now Citibank in 1971, the size and the kind of furnishings of offices assigned vice-presidents— there were many gradations of same—were carefully specified. Mine, carpeted and accoutered with a long sofa, several comfortable armchairs, and a coffee table, occupied some 256 square feet of prime Manhattan space, just off Park Avenue, and was lighted by three panel windows, a set of amenities that Michael Jensen calls a "non-pecuniary benefit."[46] The costs of those benefits came out of the shareholders' pockets—bear in mind that I was then one of several hundred vice-presidents worldwide, a number subsequently increased to several thousand—and there's no evidence that those posh offices contributed to productivity. In fact, I and my wordsmithing minions would have accomplished more in less time had we been packed, cheek by jowl, into a single small space, much like old newspaper city rooms. Among my other perquisites were a full-time secretary, trips, an expense account, and a daily lunch—at no direct cost to me—in the senior officers' dining room.

But the costs of perquisites are only a part—and by no means the largest part—of the conflict between the interests of owner-shareholders and those of their agent-managers. The fact of the matter is that objectives of most publicly held corporations, and the policies adopted in pursuing them, are fashioned with an eye to serving the interests of managers and subordinate employees rather than those of the shareholders.

Support for that assertion comes from an authoritative source, a monograph called *Managing Corporate Wealth*[47] by Gordon Donaldson, a professor at the Harvard Business School. The "B School"—as it's respectfully known by both graduates and those who only aspired to attend—is no ordinary institution of higher learning. It is America's principal fountainhead of managerial wisdom, and those awarded its Master of Business Administration degrees occupy positions of power and influence throughout the corporate structure. It is the symbiotic relationship between the B School and its loyal, highly placed alumni that made Donaldson's unique project possible.

A number of "mature" industrial corporations (no banks or other regulated financial institutions)—all among the first 250 on the *Fortune* 500 list, with minimum annual sales in the early 1980s of $1 billion and minimum assets of $600 million—agreed to open their books to a team of B School researchers and, through in-depth interviews, to reveal their operating strategies. In return, the B School agreed to write nothing by which a company or its managers could be identified. Companies could review "all relevant manuscript sections" and although each of them exercised that right, none requested "modifications or deletions." Twelve "major industrial companies," no two from the same industry, were finally selected.[48]

Now to the findings. The goals that motivate managers are:

1. *Survival:* "the . . . vitality of the organization as an effective . . . corporate presence, with incumbent managers fully in charge

. . . organizational survival means that management must always command sufficient corporate purchasing power."

2. *Independence:* "freedom to make decisions and take action without consulting parties external to the enterprise. . . . Even insiders such as shareholders and board members may become an object of concern . . . if they seem disposed to challenge management's real or assumed prerogatives."

3. *Self-sufficiency:* "they are reluctant to be dependent on other, equally self-interested external parties for their vital needs."

4. *Self-fulfullment:* "given to likening themselves to professional athletes engaged in the game of business, they look for specific visible measures of achievement."[49]

Those motives, Donaldson explains, are consistent

with the financial objective of the companies studied: the maximization of corporate wealth. Corporate wealth is *that wealth over which management has effective control* and which is an assured source of funds, at least within the limits of meaningful strategic planning. In practical terms it is cash, credit and other corporate purchasing power by which management commands goods and services. In this way corporate wealth differs considerably from the shareholder value which is central to much financial theory.[50]

## Why Profits and Present Values Should Be Maximized

The distinction that Donaldson draws between "corporate wealth" and "shareholder value" is crucial to the arguments that I shall be subsequently making. Present value—see note 45—is the expected sum of a company's discounted future earnings. If you believe that the profits of Xyzco—an imaginary maker of multilayered microchips—will come to $1.5 million at the end of this year and that earnings will then grow at 20 percent over the next five years, the present value of the company, discounted at 12 percent, is about $23.9 million.[51] But maximizing present value means that Xyzco's management is running the company with an eye to maximizing profits—attaining the highest possible net earnings year in and year out—and that implies a lean, mean company from the top down. It assumes, first, that there are no executive perks and that manufacturing costs are tightly controlled through the use of state-of-the-art equipment and well-trained people; and second, that relentless efforts are made to develop new and better products with an eye to gaining a decisive edge on the competition. No one in a world of uncertainty can be very precise about what the maximized present value of Xyzco could be or should be. But ambitious earnings goals can be set, penalties for failing to achieve them can be exacted from managers, and progress can be constantly measured against the performance of close competitors.

Practical investors, as distinct from economists and securities analysts, don't think in terms of present values, but rather earnings per share, or EPS. If Xyzco's profits for this year are $1.5 million and there are 300,000 shares of stock outstanding, its EPS is $5.00. The market price per share will be some multiple of those earnings as indicated by the price-earnings ratio, or P/E. If investors in the market are willing to pay $79.70 for Xyzco—a per share price that would make its total market value equal to the estimated present value of $23.9 million—the P/E would be a little more than 15.9.[52] A company's P/E—when related to those of close competitors and the market as a whole—is a measure of how investors, at any moment, evaluate its prospects.

Donaldson's strategy of maximizing corporate wealth, or management's command over goods and services, is very different from maximizing profits or present value. It's a policy that's perfectly consistent with gaining the largest share of a market irrespective of profitability. Citibank has big market shares, as reflected by its total assets, which are the country's highest, but its normalized return on those assets, 0.63 percent in 1988—after eliminating one-time payments and unusual items—is decidedly mediocre, since the most profitable banks earn over 1 percent on assets. Striving for the largest market share means that a company is maximizing its sales revenues which, in turn, implies maximizing employment or "corporate command" over services. Although revenue maximization serves the interests of managers—especially when their salaries and promotions are tied to the numbers of people they supervise—it hurts shareholders since earnings, dividends, and the present value of shares are lower than they otherwise might be. Nor is that the end of the harm.

What are identifiable as the "agency costs" of the separation of ownership from corporate control annually run to hundreds of billions of dollars for the U.S. economy as a whole. The largest component consists of the gains forgone—unrealized additions to the national output of goods and services—because of the failure to maximize profits and present values. Then there are the costs of the elaborate perquisites that managers provide themselves. And finally, there is the burden of constantly monitoring the performance of corporate managers, not only by outside auditors and the prompt public disclosure of quarterly earnings, but by the stock markets, which quickly change a company's P/E in reaction to good or bad news.

Now it's true, as the new theorists argue, that the separation of risk bearing—a function that common shareholders perform by virtue of the unrestricted alienability of their claims on corporate income—from managerial decision making is an inherently efficient arrangement.[53] Outside investors can't make any more critical corporate decisions than passengers can pilot the planes they fly. But the inherent efficiency of an organizing principle is not sufficient to confer legitimacy or assure the survival of an economic institution.

Several economists have advanced models of corporate behavior in which sales revenues rather than profits are maximized.[54] I agree with the fundamental premise of their thinking: most corporate managers don't, in fact, strive to maximize profits because they don't view such behavior to be in their interests. Where I differ—because I believe it best serves both individual companies and the society—is in insisting that corporate managers can and *should* be striving to maximize profits and present values.

Profit and value maximization transcends the well-being of managers and shareholders. Companies operate at peak efficiency and confer the greatest benefits on consumers by setting prices, controlling costs, and designing innovative products with an eye to realizing the highest profits and/or present values in their struggle with competitors. A company—and the argument holds for the entire economy as well—achieves peak efficiency when, by employing the best available technology, its every hour worked and every dollar of capital invested produces the largest possible output of goods and services. Profit and value maximization serves the interests of consumers—whose satisfaction is, after all, the ultimate end of all economic activity—by showering them with the largest supplies of goods and services at the lowest possible prices. Those benefits—which flow from what economists call an "efficient allocation of economic resources"—are the nub of the conflict over *perestroika*, or the economic restructuring of the Soviet Union, and they are a fundamental, though generally unspoken, issue in the current confrontation between autonomous corporate managers and owner-shareholders in the United States.

For reasons that I haven't yet touched upon, the control of corporations by autonomous professional managers—or what the British economist Robin Marris and the Harvard Business School historian Alfred D. Chandler, Jr., call "managerial capitalism"[55]—is clearly breaking down. The makeover of corporate America through hostile takeovers, leveraged buyouts, and the preemptive recapitalization of threatened companies puts all incumbent managers at risk. There was a time when corporate chief executives were almost as secure in their tenure as university professors. Today their status is much closer to that of managers in big-league professional sports.

# 2

# ON DINOSAURS AND HARES:

## Corporate Size, Profitability, and Survival

**P**reeminent among our voluntary associations, business corporations account for the bulk of our goods and services, and if they fail to pursue value-maximizing strategies, if their earnings and capital investments fall short of what's needed for the achievement of higher levels of income and wealth, we cannot maintain our high standard of living. And so there can be no arguing with the necessity for organizing economic activity and no denying that organizational success hinges on effective authority.

But the wisest of authority is ineffective when exercised within the framework of an essentially flawed structure. Businesses that have grown too large or too diverse to function efficiently are flawed. They fail to achieve their goals; and largely as a consequence of the tensions that failure generates, they become disagreeable places in which to work.

Having worked in five large universities, two large newspapers, a large book publisher, and this country's largest commercial bank, I must confess that familiarity with bigness breeds a certain contempt. If pressed to generalize, I would say that beyond ten people, inter- and intra-group tensions and incivilities increase faster than the size of the staff.[1] That doesn't mean that I endorse the limit of eleven on any human endeavor playfully recommended by Norman Macrae, formerly an editor of *The Economist,* who cited the unfortunate experience of Christ with his twelfth disciple. I don't think that "small is beautiful" because in point of fact small organizations are often too small to reach their goals. What I do believe is that giantism—whether in business corporations or in nation states—is perforce disadvantageous, that it imposes heavy psychic and pecuniary costs which can only be justified by clearly compensating benefits.

## Why Business Organizations Emerge and Persist

What accounts for the prevalence of business organizations, especially large establishments—offices, shops, or factories—where all sorts of goods and services are produced within the organization rather than purchased from outside suppliers?[2]

Perhaps the best way of approaching that question is by way of one of my grandfathers. He was a Philadelphia coffee and tea jobber who for nearly sixty-five years earned an adequate living without a single employee or assistance of any sort and with no more equipment than a hand-powered coffee grinder, a badly chipped enamel percolator, a desk in the corner of his parlor, a set of buckram-bound ledgers, ancient stationery, and a telephone. He purchased his teas and coffees—after brewing and savoring samples—from New York commodity houses, which shipped them to a warehouse-bank in Philadelphia. That venerable institution not only weighed the incoming shipments but extended credit that was prudently collateralized by his stored inventories. When grandfather sold coffee to grocers or restaurateurs, he called his roaster, who picked up the green beans at the warehouse bank, roasted them, packed them, and arranged for a carter to deliver them to his customers. The secrets of my grandfather's small success were all in his head—what economists now call "human capital." His taste in coffees, after years of savoring, was so impeccable that he was able to spot quality and sell blends loaded with cheaper African beans at all-Brazilian prices, a strategy that fattened his profit margins. He was an avid analyst of the international coffee market who reaped windfall profits and avoided losses on large inventories after both world wars, strokes of good fortune since he lived into his ninety-fifth year. And he really did know his customers.

I never gave much thought to the significance of my grandfather's operation, and others like it, when I was a student and later a teacher, because economics was then largely concerned with the functioning of open markets for goods and services, not with what was produced within organizations. In the early 1920s, Dennis Robertson, a witty and wise British economist, expressed what was to be the conventional view of the role of the business organization for decades. After noting that the "normal economic system" works by itself, since supply is adjusted to demand and production to consumption by a process that is automatic, elastic, and responsive, he noted that:

> Here and there, it is true we have found islands of conscious power in this ocean of unconscious co-operation, like lumps of butter coagulating in a pail of butter-milk. The factory system itself, while it involves endless specialization of the work of ordinary men, involves also deliberate co-ordination of their diverse activities by the capitalist employer; and the head of a single big business today exercises a width and intensity of industrial rule which a Tudor monarch might have sighed for in vain. Further . . . the integration of raw materials and marketing processes, the financial penetration of industry, all in their way and their degree increase the number and size of the patches of ground which are brought within the vision and to some extent within the control of a single intelligence. But even those patches are still small in comparison with the whole field of economic life.[3]

As I noted in the first chapter, it wasn't until 1937 that those "lumps of butter" and "patches of ground" were accorded the attention by Ronald Coase that is their due, but Coase's insights were largely ignored for about thirty years.[4] What Coase in essence said is that there are costs—he calls them transactions costs—of buying goods and services from outside suppliers rather than producing them inside the organization. Such transactions costs encompass the acquisition of information about the competence of suppliers, losses occasioned by delays in delivery or shipments of poor quality, and uncertainty about price hikes. So the higher the transactions costs, the more the work that is done in house and, hence, the larger the business organization.

My grandfather was able to function as a one-man organization because his transactions costs were negligible compared with the costs of doing everything on his own. Although profitable, his business was too small to sustain his own warehouse space or roasting-and-packaging facility or delivery truck. To put it in another way, my grandfather thrived because he realized the economies of relatively large, highly specialized, and efficient vendors of services—the warehouse bank, the roaster, and the carter. Economists call them external economies of scale because they are conferred by one independent organization upon another. A U.S. company that assembles ten thousand personal computers annually realizes an external economy of scale when it buys monitors from an efficient cathode-ray-tube manufacturer with an output of perhaps a million units—at prices far below costs of production it could ever even dream of achieving in house. Such external economies drastically lower transactions costs and thus increase the viability of smaller business enterprises.

If external economies of scale were ubiquitous, no business organization would ever have to become very big, but clearly they are not ubiquitous and may in fact hardly exist in the early development of a new industry. Let's look at automobiles, where there is a wealth of historical information.

In 1885 a twenty-four-year-old insurance salesman in Flint, Michigan, William C. Durant—the man who in 1908 formed the General Motors Company—joined with a partner, a hardware salesman named J. Dallas Dort, to manufacture a patented two-wheeled horse cart.[5] Because they succeeded in selling into a national market through dealerships and distributorships, Durant-Dort Carriage prospered mightily—Durant became a millionaire before he was forty—and was soon producing a variety of carriages, buggies, and spring wagons, all under the Blue Ribbon trademark. Even though Flint was already one of the country's larger vehicle-manufacturing centers by 1885, Durant was obliged to integrate backward—to set up his own Flint assembling factory and participate in the establishment of independent producers of bodies, paints, wheels, and even whip sockets—so that he could meet the rising demand by production that exceeded two hundred carriages a day in the mid-1890s. Durant had no choice but to integrate since there were then no carriage-making counterparts of our big producer of computer monitors from whom he could realize external economies of scale.

After Durant entered the automobile business—by taking over the defunct Buick Motor Company in 1904—and was again successful, his problem was not only finding suppliers but those who could measure up to the more exacting technical demands of the new product, such as truly interchangeable, mass-produced engine parts and functional electrical systems. His solution was to induce well-established specialty producers—among others, Charles Stewart Mott's Weston-Mott wheel and axle company of Utica and Alfred Champion's spark plug company of Boston—to locate in Flint. Eventually, as recounted in chapter 1, all of Durant's independent suppliers, including Alfred P. Sloan's Hyatt Roller Bearing Company and Charles F. Kettering's Dayton Engineering Laboratory, became GM operating divisions.

There are several answers to the question of why GM absorbed its suppliers and grew very large, or, conversely, why the suppliers didn't opt to remain independent. First, Durant, who initially exchanged GM stock for stakes in their companies, made the suppliers offers they couldn't refuse. Unlike J. P. Morgan's formation of U.S. Steel in 1902—the purpose of which was to eliminate competition from Andrew Carnegie's more efficient mills, reduce production, and thus raise prices and profits in an old industry—Durant's formation of GM was the first consolidation in what was clearly the wave of the future. Unlike Morgan, Durant did not have to water his stock by paying prices that were far in excess of reasonable market values. Alfred Sloan doesn't say so in so many words, but when he sold his Hyatt Roller Bearing Company to GM for $13.5 million of its stock in 1916, he clearly thought that he would be much better off inside the big tent than out. So did the other component suppliers and independent auto makers. They also must have taken into account Durant's loose managerial style, which would allow them a good bit of autonomy once they came into GM.

The second answer is that, as in the carriage case, none of the auto-parts suppliers were sufficiently large, in relation to the growing auto market, to generate external economies. Reverting to the example of the personal computer in the 1980s, the early auto manufacturers could not draw on counterparts of today's producers of cathode-ray tubes, whose unit costs are low because of experience with mass production that began with the development of television receivers in the 1940s. In the absence of an early industry consolidation, the auto-parts suppliers would doubtless have grown large enough to provide those economies, as the presence of Warner-Swazey, now a major outside supplier of automatic transmissions, and other parts makers suggests.

A third reason for large organizations in the auto industry has to do with the very specific design of the capital equipment—body dies and stamping machines that could be used only by one company or for one line of models. According to Sloan, GM purchased the remaining 40 percent of the stock in the Fisher Body Corporation in 1926 because Chevrolet sales were then limited by its ability to produce "closed bodies," there "were operating economies to be obtained by co-ordinating body and chassis assemblies," and it was "desirable also to bring the Fisher Brothers into closer relationship with our organization."[6] Contemporary economists who analyzed the GM–Fisher Body relationship provide a more convincing supplement to Sloan's account. According to extensive testimony and other documents that are part of an antitrust case, GM was very unhappy about the prices that the Fisher brothers were charging for closed bodies, which in the mid-1920s were growing in popularity, and the Fishers, for their part, feared that a move adjacent to the GM assembly plants would lock them into a big investment in highly specific equipment that could be useful only to GM. The solution to that impasse was an outright merger.[7]

A reading of GM's history—particularly after 1920 when Pierre S. Du Pont replaced Durant as president and made Sloan the operating chief—suggests that at the time most of the integrative acquisitions, vertically into components and horizontally through the merger of such independent auto makers as Chevrolet, made good economic sense. The Du Pont people replaced Durant's ebullient intuition with an effective system of cost accounting, and Sloan recognized the limits of integration. Here is his perceptive explanation of why auto makers never got into the business of distributing their own products:

> When the used car came into the picture in a big way in the 1920s as a trade-in on a new car, the merchandising of automobiles became more a trading proposition than an ordinary selling proposition. Organizing and supervising the necessary thousands of complex trading institutions would have been difficult for the manufacturers; trading is a knack not easy to fit into the conventional type of a managerially controlled scheme of organization.[8]

The first Henry Ford never integrated forward into retail distribution. He used his independent dealers as a source of free working capital, as in the deep postwar recession of 1920–21, when he forced them to buy more inventory than they could sell. But resisting the temptation to take over the dealerships is probably the only integrative error that Ford avoided.

For Henry Ford, backward integration into parts and raw materials became something of an obsession. And unlike GM, which acquired going concerns, Ford liked to build from scratch. It began in 1905 with the smash-up of a French machine in an auto race. Ford picked a vanadium steel valve stem out of the wreckage and noted how light and tough it was. He then prevailed upon a small Canton, Ohio, company to experiment until it came up with the first vanadium alloys produced in this country.[9] But he was not for long disposed to rely on outside suppliers. Once Ford achieved his stunning success with the Model T and then in 1919 froze the other shareholders out of the company, he went on an integration binge. A huge steel mill was built in the River Rouge complex, and Ford integrated backward with the acquisition of 313,400 acres of iron-ore and timber lands in northern Michigan, coal fields in Kentucky and West Virginia, freighters to haul iron ore on the River Rouge, and finally control of the Detroit, Toledo and Ironton Railroad. Later moves included the purchase and construction of glass plants and the organization of a company to grow rubber trees in Brazil. It's doubtful that any of those projects—which were eventually abandoned—would have survived the scrutiny of rational cost accounting and financial controls. But Ford was implacably hostile to the sort of system that General Motors had in place by the beginning of the 1920s, and there were no outside shareholders to whom he had to account. In 1920, he sacked his chief auditor, and a few years later he abolished the entire accounting department.[10]

The objection to Ford's policies is that they lock the integrator into costs that may be far higher than those on the open market. In other words, once he owned coal and ore mines, Ford was obliged to use them even though he could have gotten better deals in the marketplace. It's significant that when he sold the Ironton for $35 million—hardly at a profit—to the Pennsylvania Railroad in 1929, it was on the condition that the road would continue to enjoy Ford tonnage.[11]

One of the most famous theorems in Adam Smith's *The Wealth of Nations* is: "That the Division of Labour is Limited by the Extent of the Market."[12] What it says is that there is no incentive to develop specialized labor skills or specialized capital equipment when the market is very small. Specialization and market growth go hand in hand, and so we should expect much less vertical integration in mature industries with large markets or in nascent industries that draw upon a well-developed technology for which there is already an extended market.

Let's look at the two ends of the industrial age spectrum, steel and personal computers.

Twenty-five years ago the domestic steel industry was dominated by large, vertically integrated companies. U.S. Steel, the leader, mined its ores, operated its own ore-hauling railroads and ships, and on the other end went beyond basic steel to fabricate barrels, oil field equipment, and industrial structures. The extent of that vertical integration was, I think, incompatible with profit maximization, but that was not a matter of great moment in view of U.S. Steel's great market power. George J. Stigler, a Nobel Prize–winning economist of the University of Chicago, analyzed the very high rates of return to U.S. Steel shareholders from 1901 through 1924 and concluded that the consolidation—viewed by contemporary critics as J.P. Morgan's exploitation of investors through stock watering—was in fact "a master stroke of monopoly promotion."[13]

But the competitive position of our big integrated steel producers was quickly eroded by the revival of Europe and Japan after the Second World War, the growth of steel-making capacity in newly industrializing countries, the development of such substitutes as aluminum, plastics, and reinforced concrete, and the reluctance of the domestic producers to adopt new technologies. The result was a decline and fall. USX—alias U.S. Steel—is now not very profitably diversified into oil and gas, and in 1988 announced its intention of selling all its rail and ocean shipping facilities. LTV—a 1960s conglomerate that took over Jones & Laughlin among other integrated producers—is bankrupt, and Bethlehem Steel, number two in the industry, is shaky. After more than a decade of protection from foreign competition by "voluntary" import quotas, the fortunes of the old-line steelmakers have improved a bit.[14] High profits are still being earned in domestic steel production, but the name of the new game is *disintegration*. Mini-mills, such as the big Chaparral Steel Company in Midlothian, Texas, which boast state-of-the art technology and rely not on their own supplies of ores but on abundant supplies of scrap and imported steel slab, are highly profitable.[15] Their success underscores the validity of Smith's theorem, though bear in mind that monopoly power—prolonged by the ravages of war—sustained vertical integration in the steel industry for more than half a century.

The personal computer industry is new, dating back only to the mid-1970s, and yet, unlike the early development of automobiles, there is little if any evidence of vertical integration in the development of PCs. IBM has the largest, though a shrinking, share of a growing market. But aside from its role as a large producer of microchips, it is essentially a designer, assembler, promoter, and distributor of PCs, surely not a manufacturer in the same sense in which Ford was the manufacturer of the Model T. Until recently its monitors, keyboards, circuit boards, disk drives, modems, and other elements were produced by other, independent firms.[16] The same is true of the numerous IBM "clones," computers that run on the disk operating system (DOS) developed by Microsoft.

Technology made the crucial difference between the launching of the automobile and that of the PC. In the case of the PC, the essential component—the integrated circuit chip or microchip—not only had been developed for other purposes but was being mass produced, first in the United States and then in Japan and South Korea. It was almost as if Henry Ford had been able to assemble his first Model T from commonplace, on-the-shelf parts. The impediment to an even more rapid growth of the PC industry has never been hardware, but rather better software.

What is striking, not only in PCs but in the computer industry as a whole, is that the frantic pace of technological progress has created a degree of fluidity that not only mocks dominance by any single company but serves as a general check on relative size. IBM, still the king as I write, is everywhere under siege: by the clones and Apple as well as Japanese, Korean, and Taiwanese manufacturers in the PC market; by Digital Equipment Corporation (DEC) in mini-computers and networks; by Sun Microsystems in engineering work stations; and by Cray and Amdahl on the supercomputer end.

To return to the general issue of size and vertical integration, there is much evidence that points to the disintegration and downsizing of what are now highly integrated companies. In automobiles, increasing competition for the domestic market and the steady erosion of General Motors' dominance—there are now twice as many sellers in the North American market than there were in the late 1940s—mandates cost cutting, which in turn is leading to a greater reliance on outside suppliers, particularly for modules or sections of automobiles, such as seats, instrument panels, and soon doors. But the process of vertical disintegration in the U.S. auto industry has just begun and has a very long way to go. GM—which in 1988 planned to lay off 100,000 workers over a five-year period—manufactures 70 percent or $30 billion worth of the parts, such as batteries, electrical systems, and spark plugs that go into its cars. Since GM salaries are higher than those of independent suppliers, its high degree of vertical integration is a drag on earnings. Ford—no thanks to Henry I—is only 40 percent vertically integrated, and Chrysler is at 30 percent.[17] The degree of vertical integration in the spectacularly successful Japanese auto industry, which became the world's leading producer in 1980, is considerably lower than in the United States.

Gyrating crude oil prices—the sharp run-ups to a peak of $37 a barrel in 1979 orchestrated by the OPEC cartel and the plummet to $8 in 1986—had a profound impact on the U.S. petroleum industry. Until recently, such leaders as Exxon, Mobil, Chevron, Atlantic Richfield, Amoco, Sun, and Texaco were involved in every step from oil exploration through retail service stations, even though such vertical integration contributes little to higher profits or greater market shares.[18] But in the 1980s they were confronted by a vexing problem that could only be solved by divestitures and disintegration. Their earnings were poor, and as a consequence of low share prices their crude oil reserves—reserves in the ground and proven—were undervalued. In 1984, the industry's asset value exceeded the market value of its share by $191 billion. So it was cheaper to acquire crude oil by purchasing the stocks of companies with reserves than it was to develop new sources, especially in the United States, where it became clear that—because of low oil prices—every dollar invested in a drilling program was going to be worth about 60 cents.

The imbalance led to a general restructuring of the U.S. petroleum industry. Gulf, one of the fabled "Seven Sisters," lost its independent identity when it was acquired by Socal, now Chevron. Phillips, Atlantic Richfield, Unocal, and Texaco were compelled to disintegrate, to sell off businesses—chains of filling stations, refineries, and oil fields—in order to enhance their profitability and fend off corporate raiders. And I look to the further, salutary disintegration of the industry as competition intensifies and world oil prices remain well below $25 a barrel, mocking the impotence of the OPEC cartel.

## The Crucial Triad: Innovation, Efficiency, and Profit

Why are some businesses so much more profitable than others?

As a thought experiment, try to imagine a world without change: no new knowledge, no new technology, literally nothing new. Suppose that we could put an indefinite freeze on all change in much the same way that we stop at a frame by pressing "pause" on the remote control of our VCR. What would business be like in that changeless world?

Assuming a level playing field—no governmental intervention or regulations that favor one industry or company over another, and no private monopolies or cartels—differences in profit rates, the returns on the capital invested, would be very small and tend toward uniformity across industries and among companies. The reasoning, as once suggested by the great Victorian economist Alfred Marshall, is analogous to what happens to the trees of a forest. Like the mighty trees, the strongest, most efficient companies in an industry—those with lower costs and therefore higher profits—gradually lose their competitive edge over time as the managers grow tired and smaller organizations become stronger, more efficient, and more profitable. The process of growth and decay continues in an endless cycle, the only change in a technologically static world.

Now let's end the thought experiment and answer the question of why profit rates in the real world of change differ widely, not only between industries but among companies in the same industry. Efficiency—operating at the lowest possible costs—as I have already suggested is important, but it leaves much of the variation in profits unexplained. The other element is innovation, a concept introduced by the Austro-American economist Joseph A. Schumpeter, celebrated for his analysis of entrepreneurship and technology in the process of economic change.[19]

An innovation is any change that alters the relationships between inputs of labor and capital and outputs of goods or services—what economists call production functions. The PC on which I wrote this book is innovative because it enabled me—and my editors—to turn out a finished product in a significantly shorter time than it would have taken with typewriters. Another example: my $25 pocket calculator, which with its microchip circuitry performs a variety of mathematical functions, is many times more powerful and faster than mechanical, desktop calculators that sold for an inflation-adjusted equivalent of $6,000 in the early 1950s. The drastic reduction of computational costs facilitates basic research in the sciences and enhances the efficiency of all businesss operations.

Some innovations stem from fundamental contributions to human knowledge—flight, atomic energy, semiconductors, and perhaps superconductors, should they have an impact on economic life. Others, such as flavored corn for popping in microwave ovens—a $300 million-a-year business—are technologically insignificant and ephemeral but not economically trivial. Canals, railroads, and steamships were among the most far-reaching innovations of the eighteenth and nineteenth centuries and, for that matter, in all modern history. By radically reducing the costs of overland and ocean transportation, the time and effort expended to move goods, they opened up whole continents to new settlement, or—in terms of Adam Smith's great theorem—they accelerated and intensified the division of labor by greatly extending markets.

Innovations generate profits far in excess of those that would prevail in a changeless or static environment. In Schumpeter's model, innovations generate business cycles, which he views as inherent to capitalism. His entrepreneurs—who rarely are original inventors—reap large profits by building the first successful power looms, railroads, or petroleum refineries, new industries that replace old ones in a process that he calls "creative destruction." For example, most of the big American canals built in the first half of the nineteenth century were destroyed by railroad competition. The initial success of the innovator attracts a horde of imitators whose efforts, usually financed by a sharp expansion of credit, lead to a business boom and bust.

But it is Schumpeter's innovations and the profits they generate, not his business cycle model, that are relevant here. The crucial link between innovation and profit is underscored by the story of Henry Ford, a great innovator who later almost came a cropper when he refused to go on innovating. By designing his Model T, perfecting the processes of assembly-line production, and fearlessly slashing prices to increase demand, Henry Ford captured more than two-thirds of the rapidly growing domestic auto market in the years before the First World War. But in the 1920s he threw away his lead because of what can only be characterized as stubborn arrogance in clinging to the Model T long after it was obsolete. The Model T's transmission, operated by three foot pedals, wasn't—as we might now say—very driver friendly, and style-wise Ford didn't help matters by declaring that buyers could have any color they wanted so long as it was black! Alfred Sloan, Ford's General Motors rival, explains what happened and why:

> From 1925 to 1927 the Chevrolet, as its cost position justified a lower price, became more competitive with Ford. . . . The old master had failed to master change. Don't ask me why. There is legend cultivated by sentimentalists that Mr. Ford left behind a great car [the Model T] expressive of the pure concept of cheap, basic transportation. The fact is that he left behind a car that no longer offered the best buy, even as raw, basic transportation.
>
> It was not difficult to see in 1925 and 1926 that Chevrolet was closing in on Ford. . . . His precious volume, which was the foundation of position, was fast disappearing. He could not continue losing sales and maintain his profits. And so for engineering and marketing reasons, the Model T fell. And yet not many observers expected so catastrophic and almost whimsical a fall as Mr. Ford chose to take in May 1927 when he shut down his great River Rouge plant completely and kept it shut for nearly a year to retool, leaving the field to Chevrolet unopposed and opening it up for Mr. Chrysler's Plymouth. Mr. Ford again gained sales leadership in 1929, 1930 and 1935 but speaking in terms of generalities, he had lost his lead to General Motors. . . .
>
> Mr. Ford failed to realize that it was not necessary for new cars to meet the need for basic transportation. . . . The basic transportation market in the United States (unlike Europe) . . . has been met mainly by the used car.[20]

Sears, Roebuck's story is of a company that innovated twice with enormous success and then fell on hard times.[21]

In 1886 Richard Warren Sears, a strikingly handsome, flamboyant twenty-three-year-old, left a railroad stationmastership in rural Minnesota to move to Minneapolis and establish the R. W. Sears Watch Company, a direct-mail operation that sold gold-filled watches to farmers at prices—about $12—far below those of local jewelers. Sears prospered, and about two years later, in need of someone to make repairs, he hired Alvah Curtis Roebuck, a mild-mannered watchmaker from Indiana who was his partner in several ventures before the name Sears, Roebuck and Company was adopted in 1893. Minneapolis was a disadvantageous point from which to ship, and at the end of the year they set up an operation in Chicago. Their 1894 catalog, a 322-page book, offered not only watches but silverware, firearms, bicycles, boys' and men's clothing, pianos, and organs. At the beginning of 1895, with the business growing but short of working capital, they abandoned Minneapolis, and at the end of the year Roebuck sold his stock to Sears for $25,000. New partners were found who invested $150,000 in the recapitalized company: Julius Rosenwald, a men's cloak and suit manufacturer from whom Sears had already been buying in large lots, and his brother-in-law, Aaron E. Nusbaum, part-owner of a company that made pneumatic tube systems for quickly moving cash and vouchers through department stores. From the beginning there was a clash of temperaments, and in 1901 Sears and Rosenwald bought out Nusbaum's 23.3 percent share for $1.25 million, a bitterly haggled-over price that reflected the company's impressive growth.

By the spring of 1904, the circulation of the Sears, Roebuck catalog exceeded 1.1 million, and the offerings were expanded to cover everything that farm and small-town families might wish to buy, especially such big-ticket items as cream separators, washing machines, sewing machines, and plumbing fixtures. Sears, Roebuck didn't invent direct-mail marketing—Aaron Montgomery Ward was issuing direct-mail catalogs before Richard Sears got into the watch business—but it was an innovator which not only took advantage of the increasingly dense rail network to expand the market for retail goods but devised new and more efficient ways of selling at lower prices than local merchants charged. By 1913, Sears's sales were more than double those of Montgomery Ward, its closest competitor. Sears was the country's largest advertiser and built an enviable reputation for standing behind the quality of whatever it sold. The mechanized mail-order assembly line of their huge Chicago operation, a plant on a forty-acre site, influenced Henry Ford's decisions in producing the Model T. But unlike Ford, they were cautiously rational about backward integration, investing in suppliers of goods only when there was no other source at a comparable price and—at least in the beginning—following Richard Sears's rule of restricting its interests to a limit of 50 percent.

By 1906, with sales at about $50 million annually, Sears, Roebuck went public. Henry Goldman of Goldman, Sachs—Rosenwald's childhood friend, who once said of Richard Sears, "I think he could sell a breath of air"—arranged for the stock offering after the company was reorganized and capitalized at $40 million. But during the sharp recession of 1907, the ever ebullient Sears, who fervently believed that the slump in demand could be quickly countered by expanded advertising, was overruled by Rosenwald and some of his own protégés. He gave up the presidency in 1908 and his seat on the board before his death in 1914.

At the end of the First World War Rosenwald, by then one of the world's richest men, wished to devote his time to philanthropy on behalf of black people. He recruited new managers, and one who came on in 1925 was General Robert E. Wood, a West Point graduate who was the quartermaster general during the war and afterward joined Montgomery Ward. An avid student of demographic data, Wood was convinced that the country was becoming increasingly urbanized, a trend that would check the growth of the mail-order catalog business, but his argument fell on deaf ears at Montgomery Ward. Sears, Roebuck permitted him to pursue an innovative strategy of opening a great chain of retail stores that would be accessible by automobile and serviced by the existing buying organization. There were eight Sears stores in 1925 and 378 by 1931, the year in which they validated Wood's hypothesis by forging ahead of catalog sales.[22] "The General," as he was known to a generation of employees, succeeded to the chairmanship of Sears in 1928, and even after his "retirement" in 1954 he exerted great influence over the company until his death in 1969.

After 1945, the Sears stores—which featured their brand names such as Kenmore washers, Craftsman tools, and Allstate (later Die-hard) batteries—followed the population into the suburbs and were highly profitable. In 1955, a banner year, Sears's return on equity was over 16 percent. But the fat years were numbered.

Trouble came in the late 1970s when the huge Sears organization with a work force of more than 400,000 fell on hard times. It was plagued by inflation, increasing competition from discount-store chains, dismal profits, the depressed price of its once solid common stock, a bureaucratic war between the big Chicago skyscraper head-quarters—*Fortune* called the world's tallest building, "The Leaning Tower of Sears"—and the store managers in the field, who bitterly resisted any effort to limit their autonomy.

There was also a scandalously bad system of purchasing and in-voicing. The prices that Sears's buyers paid suppliers for merchandise were much lower—as much as two-thirds lower—than those they charged the retail stores. The difference, which amounted to billions of dollars, went into a "slush fund" that the buyers used for special advertising promotions or, after bargaining, to make price conces-sions to managers of troubled stores. It was a practice that hindered Sears in meeting discounters' competition; it hopelessly confused product cost and profit calculation; and it was an invitation to kick-backs and other corruption.

Edward R. Telling, a reflective, much-maligned Sears veteran who served as chief executive from 1977 to 1986, faced up to the unen-viable task of restructuring America's largest retailer: abolishing the slush fund system, asserting Chicago's authority over the store man-agers in the field, reducing the work force by massive layoffs and early retirements, closing down hundreds of unprofitable stores, and scaling back investments in suppliers. Simultaneously, he initiated a strategy of shifting Sears into the financial services business by adding Dean Witter Reynolds, a big retail securities house, and Coldwell Banker Group, said to be the world's largest real estate broker, to the existing Allstate Insurance business, which had been founded in 1931.

But those efforts failed, and Sears's earnings continued to be dis-mal. Telling's successor, Edward R. Brennan, made headlines in October 1988 with decisions to sell off the Chicago headquarters tower, for a price he hoped would exceed $1 billion, along with Coldwell's commercial real-estate business and to replace promotional sales with continuous price discounting in the stores. But those moves—whose objective was to permit the Sears treasury to buy up 10 percent of its outstanding stock as protection against raiders—touched off speculators' anticipations of a takeover,[23] and it's doubtful that the company will long endure as a giant among retailers.

Most innovations don't involve decisions on which the life or death of a company hinges, but that doesn't diminish their importance. When Citibank combined an encoded customer's card with an automatic teller machine to produce the Citicard technology in 1974, it gained a clear edge over other retail banks in the greater New York City market. Such advantages are likely to be eroded as others imitate, but other things being equal, the original innovator will enjoy the largest profits gain and end up with a bigger share of the market.

It is important to understand that a successful innovation—especially when it's very costly, and most of them are—requires an imaginative, or at least indulgent top management, one willing to squelch parochial or bureaucratic objections, and a team, technicians as well as line people, that is truly dedicated to making things happen. In addition to the excellence of the technology—its flexibility, reliability, and expandibility—the Citicard system went off well because John S. Reed, the man then responsible for it and now chairman of Citicorp, commanded great confidence and authority.

## Mergers, Size, and Profits—Pitfalls and Fallacies

A distinction has to be made—even though fine lines can't be drawn—between mergers in which the acquired company becomes an integral part of an operating business organization and those acquisitions that are made with an eye to quick resale.

The difference is illustrated by the story of the proprietor of a Far North Canadian trading post who came to town every summer to stock up from his wholesaler. On one of those visits, the wholesaler, a wily old Scot, urged him to buy a large wooden crate of canned kippers at a bargain price. While the wholesaler was attending another buyer, the trading-post proprietor opened one of the cans with his pocket knife and was repelled by the awful stench.

"These kippers you want to fob off on me are foul," said the angry proprietor to the returning wholesaler.

"Ah, laddie," shot back the wholesaler, "yuh dunnah understan'. These kippers are nah for eatin'. They're for buyin' and sellin'."

Avis, the car renter, by last count has had five owners since the end of the Second World War. A lawyer with W. R. Grace told me that he was involved in buying and selling the same company three times. For reasons that will become apparent in the next chapter, the current economic environment is conducive to a commerce in companies—by wholes or in pieces delineated by lines of business. But we can make distinctions, at least when considering initial intentions, between speculators, who would profit from quick turnovers, those wishing to function as passive or portfolio investors with blocks of equity in several companies, and people seriously interested in the hands-on management of a business.

One of the arguments made for horizontal mergers is that they capture economies of scale. The proposition that larger companies can achieve lower unit costs than very small ones is valid, but within limits. If it were true, for example, that costs decreased faster than the capacity to produce over an indefinite range of output—that you could produce two million trucks at a cost per truck of less than half that of producing one million, four million at less than half the unit cost of two million, and so forth—there could be no competition, because the firm that got big first could profitably undersell all the smaller ones and drive them out of business. But the survival of small companies and the absence of true monopolies—literally, cases of a single seller—invalidates the notion of limitless economies of scale and suggests that there must be *dis*economies of size as well. Diseconomies occur, first, because of difficulties of communication and coordination as companies grow larger. Alfred Sloan sought to solve those problems at General Motors through decentralization and a measure of divisional autonomy, an eventually counterproductive policy emulated by other large corporations. The other source of diseconomies in large organizations, both centralized and decentralized, is bureaucracy: layers of parochial and often antagonistic authority, as in the case of Sears, Roebuck, which delay crucial decisions unless they are overridden.

The direct measurement of economies of scale and the determination of an optimal or lowest cost size is fraught with all sorts of difficulties. But George Stigler circumvented them by a simple yet powerful survival test: "Classify the firms in an industry by size, and calculate the share of industry output coming from each class over time. If the share of a given class falls, it is relatively inefficient, and in general the more inefficient the more rapidly the share falls."[24]

For firms in the steel industry—over the years 1930–55, before the onset of strong foreign competition mentioned above—the constancy of output shares led Stigler to conclude that there were neither economies nor diseconomies of scale over a wide range of company sizes. He attributes the share losses of the very smallest firms to the diseconomies of their small plants and the losses of the largest firm, U.S. Steel, "to diseconomies of multiplant operation beyond a certain scale."[25] In other words, even if all of the plants are of an efficient size, difficulties of coordination and other purely managerial (as opposed to engineering) problems can result in diseconomies of size.

The same tendency for the dominant firm to lag behind shows up in the mail-order industry in the golden years of 1913–25, a period when it grew at an annual rate of more than 9 percent. In 1913 Sears, Roebuck had a more than 63 percent share of the combined sales of the top three—Montgomery Ward was second, and National Bellas Hess, which tended to specialize in clothing, was a poor third. By 1925, Sears's share was down to under 53 percent, and the second-place Ward was up substantially.[26] Since both firms were exploiting the same technology of marketing, it's a fair surmise that Sears's huge size, the diseconomies of large scale, had something to do with its loss of market share, even though its profit margins on sales were better than Ward's in almost every year.

General Motors, the largest U.S. corporation since the breakup of AT&T and the only one with sales of more than $100 billion, had a more than 50 percent share of the domestic auto market through the 1960s; but in 1987—plagued by poor-quality styling, inferior to

Ford's and its Japanese and European competitors'—it had only 36 percent. For the third year in a row Ford, which is only two-thirds the size of GM, had higher earnings, and the thought of its becoming number one, especially in view of GM's 1988 plans for a radical reduction of product offerings, isn't "a laugher anymore" in Detroit.[27]

What the foregoing suggests is that in each industry and/or product market there is an optimal company size—it varies with changing technology and market structure—that balances off the economies and diseconomies of scale. When that optimal size is exceeded, as often happens in managerially controlled companies, losses are incurred that eventually result in downsizing.

Bigness—whether by horizontal merger or internal growth—is a guarantee neither of high profitability nor survivability. But what of conglomerate corporations that grow large by moving into several unrelated markets? It began in the early 1950s when Royal Little began bringing all sorts of disparate businesses—ball bearings, gas meters, helicopters, and golf carts—into the corporate tent of a New England textile company called Textron. There was a groundswell of conglomerate mergers in the later 1960s, in part because the Cellar-Kefauver amendments of 1950 strengthened the antimerger provisions of the Clayton Act, thus rendering vertical and horizontal mergers difficult in that era of strict antitrust law enforcement.

Let's begin with Harold Sydney Geneen,[28] who became chief executive officer of the International Telephone and Telegraph Corporation (ITT) in 1959. ITT was then moribund, in the words of one insider, "a real dog" with revenues of less than $766 million and earnings of only $29 million for a profit margin of 3.8 percent. When Geneen was finally pushed out in 1980, ITT was a conglomerate with divisions in a dozen industries and $22 billion of revenues—a more than ten-fold increase over 1959 after the effects of price inflation are factored out. But earnings were quite another matter—there was a quarterly loss in 1980—and they're the nub of the ITT story.

Geneen, the British-born son of middle-class immigrants, came of age during the Depression and worked days while attending evening classes at New York University where he earned a degree in accounting. In 1942—after nearly eight years at the predecessor of what is now Coopers & Lybrand, a major accounting firm, where he was regarded as able but tactlessly impatient—Geneen joined Amertorp, a St. Louis subsidiary of the American Can Company that manufactured torpedoes for the Navy. He gained valuable experience in handling both cost-accounting and general managerial problems, and after the war moved up the ladder a rung when he was appointed comptroller of Bell & Howell, a Chicago manufacturer of motion picture cameras and projectors which had appointed Charles H. Percy, later U.S. Senator from Illinois, president when he was only twenty-nine.

Geneen succeeded in tightening up B&H's cost and inventory controls before leaving in 1950 for a much higher-paying comptroller's post at Jones & Laughlin, one of the larger and less efficient of the Pittsburgh steel companies. His six years at Jones & Laughlin were marked by bitter clashes as he struggled, with mixed success, to impose managerial discipline in an old-line company which in the easy 1950s didn't have to try at all hard to turn a profit. The next stop was Raytheon, which made vacuum tubes and other electronic products in Waltham, Massachusetts, where Geneen—although number two—was the de facto chief. He made a number of far-reaching reforms at Raytheon and began to compile a list of potential acquisitions when ITT offered him the top spot which he couldn't refuse.

There can be no denying that Geneen, who could be about as gentle with his minions as a junk-yard dog, was a strong leader. Unlike some of the other conglomerators of the 1960s—Charles B. Thornton of Litton Industries, James J. Ling of Ling-Temco-Vought (later LTV), G. William Miller of Textron—he was the quintessential hands-on manager, a man driven by a desire to enhance efficiency in a decade not noted for executive zeal. His widely emulated budgeting system—with its interminable meetings, frequent reports on current earnings, and projections into the future—forces line managers to measure up, to achieve their goals or come up with reasonable excuses for their failures. But Geneen's performance has to be viewed in perspective. His great success came in 1963–73, a period of virtually unbroken expansion for both the U.S. and the world economy. From 1973 onward, it was downhill for ITT. And its halcyon growth—as we shall see—was achieved by playing a merger game that was not without its deceptions.

Geneen's first accomplishment was in doing what he really did best, bringing rationality to an organization of incongruous parts presided over by managers bent more on maintaining their turf than on achieving common goals. The problem was particularly difficult because of the European and Latin American holdings which accounted for the bulk of ITT's earnings. Geneen brought the company together with a minimum of bureaucratic bloodshed, but in his haste he made several early mistakes. He sold ITT's 22 percent shares in both L. M. Ericsson, Sweden's big telephone company, and Nippon Electric Corporation (NEC), as well as a 13 percent stake in Sumitomo Electric Industries, all at mere fractions of what they would soon be worth.

In 1963, Geneen began what was to be a veritable binge of acquisitions with Bell & Gossett, an Illinois pump maker with $45 million of annual revenues. He continued with Avis; Sheraton Hotels; Continental Baking Company; Rayonier Inc., a large rayon-fiber producer; and Bobbs Merrill, the book publisher, to name only a few of some one hundred mergers.

But the pace began to falter when a proposed ITT–American Broadcasting Company merger was delayed and finally abandoned in 1967. Opponents of that union pointed to possible conflicts between the objective reporting of the news and ITT's other international interests.[29] And Geneen's aggressive Washington public relations team embarrassed his cause when they attempted to intimidate a *New York Times* reporter. Then there was a major scandal in 1971–72 when Geneen, with the active assistance of his investment banker, Felix Rohatyn of Lazard Frères & Co., sought to acquire his crown jewel, the Hartford Fire Insurance Company, the nation's sixth largest property and casualty insurer with assets of more than $1.8 billion. To derail the Justice Department's antitrust action against the merger, Geneen's high-powered lobbyists took their case directly to the White House. President Nixon—as his infamous tapes later revealed—ordered Attorney General Richard G. Kleindienst, later convicted for his role in the Watergate scandal, to kill the suit. But news of that deal—and a large ITT contribution to the Republican campaign chest for 1972—was leaked to the press and there was a full-scale Congressional investigation which blackened ITT's already tarnished image.

But it wasn't overreaching in Washington that did Geneen in. It was his own poor business judgment. The Hartford Fire merger was approved by the Justice Department after ITT agreed to divest Avis and other properties. Yet contrary to Geneen's rosy expectations, it became a money-losing albatross in the mid-1970s when, because of inflation, the costs of settling claims were rising much faster than insurance rates. On the whole Geneen tended to do well with acquisitions in manufacturing businesses—where his mechanical, by-the-numbers approach worked reasonably well, at least for a while— and poorly in industries where success hinged on intimate knowledge, intuition, and judgment in grappling with uncertainty. Only the advice of a seasoned professional—and his willingness to abandon grandiose plans—saved Geneen from costly errors in the hotel business. But no one saved him from disaster in his mergers with Levitt and other tract home builders. In the late 1960s and early 1970s Geneen's famous system led to about every mistake in the book; and when ITT's housing industry assets were finally sold off in 1975, the losses surely exceeded the admitted $260 million. Finally, there was a $320 million Rayonier write-off in 1979 because Geneen—who wrongly believed that ever-rising oil prices would touch off a boom in the demand for rayon—built the world's biggest sulphite plant in Port Cartier, Quebec. These were the sorts of fiascos that underscore the wisdom of the old proverb "Shoemaker, stick to thy last."

Geneen did not lack company. For sophisticated investors, the later 1960s and early 1970s were the years of the conglomerates. And even though the hype and excitement of that boom faded long ago, it would be well to understand just how the game was played.[30]

Most conglomerate merger deals were done by the exchange of stocks and were, almost without exception, friendly. Geneen, as already noted, accumulated some stock and at one stage threatened a hostile takeover of Hartford, but in the end its board agreed to the merger.[31] Because of the rising influence of securities analysts in the 1960s, companies with high growth of earnings per share attracted favorable attention. But the market—which is my shorthand for the people in it—wasn't very critical or curious about how those high per share earnings rates were achieved.

Other things being equal, the higher the growth of a company's earnings per share (EPS), the higher the price of its stock and the higher the ratio of that price to its earnings, or its P/E. Suppose Alpha and Beta both have a million shares outstanding but that Alpha sells into a fast-growing, high-technology market while Beta's product market is mature and slower growing. If the market expects Alpha's net profits or earnings to grow half again as fast as Beta's and those expectations are fulfilled, then it's axiomatic that Alpha's EPS will be half again as high as Beta's. And it is also reasonable to infer—though it's far from axiomatic—that Alpha's P/E will be half again as high as Beta's. Here's how the numbers might look:

|  | GROWTH | EPS | SHARE PRICE | P/E |
|---|---|---|---|---|
| *Alpha* | 9% | $1.50 | $27 | 18 |
| *Beta* | 6% | $1.00 | $12 | 12 |

Now let's consider the advantages that a higher P/E confers on a merger-minded Alpha. In a merger by a tax-free exchange of shares,[32] Alpha could get a full share of Beta for only .444 of a share of its own stock—12/27. That means, in effect, that Alpha is buying Beta for 44.4 cents on the dollar. It acquires a company with a total market value of $12 million—a million shares at $12 each—by issuing 444,444 shares of new stock at $27 a share. Assuming that postmerger plans for increasing Beta's earnings pay off, Alpha's stock will not suffer any earnings dilution—that is, its EPS won't drop.

Because of the stock swapping, conglomerate mergers were said to have been financed with "funny money," with the stock of the company with the higher P/E. For the acquirer, the trick was to boost its P/E and keep it well above that of any company it contemplated buying. In that way everyone was happy. Shareholders of the slower-growing acquired companies exchanged their lackluster stock for that of a hot conglomerate. Once the game was really under way in the later 1960s, a Geneen or a Ling or a Thornton didn't have to beat the bushes for likely merger candidates. Instead, the candidates came to them, hats in hand, and the deals usually included generous provisions for employing the managers of the acquired companies.

The original and more successful of the acquirers—ITT, Ling-Temco-Vought, Litton, and Textron—enjoyed higher-than-average P/Es by virtue of being in high technology markets, in defense work, or both. To keep their P/Es high, they invoked "synergy," the emptiest buzzword in the conglomerate lexicon. In biology the term is clear and testable: the interaction of two or more substances or organs to achieve an effect of which each is individually incapable. But in business mergers the benefits of synergy are only promises—and almost always empty ones at that. One of the notorious facts about the disastrous merger of the Pennsylvania and the New York Central railroads in the 1960s was that Penn-Central produced no synergy, not even any operating economies. And if that was the case with two railroads, claims that the Jones & Laughlin merger would somehow work wonders for LTV or that the Continental Baking merger would spare ITT from the exigencies of the business cycle should have been regarded with incredulity. They weren't.

In addition to synergy, the conglomerators resorted to deceptive accounting practices in their desperation to keep their P/Es high and rising.[33] One ploy was the lumping of earnings. Reverting back to our example, suppose that Alpha's managerial plan doesn't work and that a year after the merger Beta's earnings—now concealed in the consolidated income statement—fall from $1 million to $900,000, a 10 percent drop. But Alpha doesn't reveal that embarrassing fact. It reports total earnings of $2.25 million—its own total earnings having increased by 35 percent—and an EPS of nearly $1.56 a share, up nearly 4 percent.

Another dubious practice was the pooling of merged assets or what Abraham J. Briloff, a distinguished accountant, called "dirty pooling." Suppose that Alpha bought Beta for $12 million in cash but enters its assets on the consolidated balance sheet at $8 million, the historical, or book, value. The suppression of the $4 million raises Alpha's returns on assets—since the base is lower than it should be—and it boosts earnings because of a comparable reduction of depreciation charges. And there is yet another distortion if a disappointed Alpha sells Beta for $10 million and records a $2 million "profit."

In retrospect, conglomerates were swollen monuments to the misperceptions of supposedly sophisticated investors; yet the game didn't end because the public suddenly got wise. Instead, two things happened. The merger deals became riskier as weak, third-rate conglomerates pursued even weaker fourth- and fifth-rate merger partners. A number of conglomerates couldn't keep their EPS rising, not with accounting tricks, not even with mirrors, and they soon gave all the others a bad name and sharply lower P/Es. Equally important, the 1970s, far from being another decade of rapid growth, were plagued by bursts of inflation, uncertainty about oil, and the deep, worldwide recession of 1973–75. It was a time when you didn't have to be running a conglomerate to suffer big losses of earnings.[34]

Since 1975 the chief executives of conglomerates have had their work cut out for them—to undo by divestiture and leveraged buyouts the mergers consummated by their predecessors. Their task is lightened when, as often happens, the break-apart value of conglomerates—the combined proceeds from selling off the businesses piece by piece—exceeds their current value. The reason is that one or two losing divisions can be a drag on a conglomerate's earnings and share price. Selling off losers—presumably to buyers with strategies for turning them around—strengthens the conglomerate's balance sheet and raises its share price.

ITT's chairman, Rand V. Araskog—a Geneen protégé who in despair banished his mentor from the boardroom—sold off one hundred businesses, thereby cutting revenues by more than 20 percent in an as yet unsuccessful effort to check the erosion of profits. In 1986, something of a record for the failure of a telecommunications product was set when ITT wrote off $100 million of losses on a digital switching system designed for the U.S. market. Textron is now smaller and leaner, despite some recent major acquisitions. Tenneco sold its oil and gas properties for more than $7 billion in 1988 in order to retire debt. Household International plans to sell off all of its manufacturing operations and concentrate on financial services. Beatrice was broken up. LTV—the brainchild of James J. Ling, a high-school dropout with a gift for mixing business with Texas-style politicking—is bankrupt and its Jones & Laughlin division is unable to meet its pension obligations. General Electric, the largest of the still expanding conglomerates—it embraces Kidder, Peabody, the investment banking house, the Employers Reinsurance Corporation, and RCA as well as chemical and medical equipment businesses— draws as many brickbats as rounds of applause. Michael Porter of the Harvard Business School points out that Chairman John F. Welch, Jr.'s, strategy of being number one or number two in any market he enters focuses on size rather than competitive advantage; and Thomas Peters, author of *In Search of Excellence,* laments that once "the most glorious technology company of the century, GE has become a hodgepodge."[35]

## Size and Internal Financing— or Whose Money Is It, Anyhow?

Aside from a reference to the exchanging of stocks by conglomerates, I've said nothing about how mergers are financed and the role played by undistributed corporate profits—the earnings that are retained by the company. They are part of what Gordon Donaldson of Harvard's business school, cited at the end of the first chapter, calls the "wealth over which management has effective control."

In 1988, the total after-tax profits of U.S. corporations came to around $183 billion, of which some $104 billion or about 57 percent was paid out in dividends to the shareholders and about $78 billion were undistributed, retained by the companies. For the years 1945 through 1988, the average dividend payout was around 48 percent of earnings. It was under 50 percent in thirty of those forty-four years, and it rose very sharply in recession years—such as 1982 when it was at a record 76 percent—because corporations tend to maintain dividends despite sharp declines of earnings. Since 1945, more than $1.35 trillion of corporate earnings was retained; and if allowance is made for inflation—that is, if the retained earnings are valued at 1982 prices—the total comes to more than $2.50 trillion.[36] Neither is a paltry sum.

Retaining a large share of annual earnings isn't a universal corporate practice. In Britain and on the Continent, where shareholders vote on dividends, income retentions are modest, and in instances where they have recently grown larger, British newspapers make derisive references to "free capital." It is free because in the absence of undistributed earnings companies would have to go to the market and sell stock or bonds to obtain that capital.

Benjamin Graham and David L. Dodd in the first edition of their classic treatise *Security Analysis*[37] explain that the practice of retaining earnings began at the beginning of this century, when many of the large corporations—U. S. Steel, Sears, Roebuck, F. W. Woolworth, Cluett Peabody, National Cloak and Suit, and others—were overcapitalized. The face value of securities issued at the time of corporate organization or reorganization, stocks and bonds, exceeded the fair market value of the company's assets. The excess value—if it wasn't concealed as it was by U.S. Steel—was carried as an item of "goodwill" among the assets on the balance sheet. And since the purpose of accounting is to arrive at the most accurate possible estimate of a company's value, such goodwill must be amortized, or written down over the years, by charges made against its annual earnings. The cumulative total of those charges appears as a "surplus" item on the corporate balance sheet, a part of "net worth," or shareholders' equity, which is essentially the difference—positive if the company's solvent—between assets and liabilities. In such highly successful companies as U.S. Steel, Woolworth, and Sears, the appreciation of the outstanding shares of stock soon dwarfed the goodwill, which implies that the surpluses were very profitably reinvested in the businesses.

Other companies with no goodwill to write off defended large income retentions as a part of a policy of "conservative" corporate finance. Writing fifty-five years ago, Graham and Dodd sharply challenged that view, something that is almost never done today:

> The customary reasoning on this point may be stated in the form of a syllogism, as follows:
> Major premise—Whatever benefits the company benefits the shareholders.
> Minor premise—A company is benefited if its earnings are retained rather than paid out in dividends.
> Conclusion—Stockholders are benefited by the withholding of corporate earnings.
> The weakness of the above reasoning rests of course in the major premise. Whatever benefits a business benefits its owners *provided* the benefit is not conferred upon the corporation at the *expense* of the stockholders.[38]

They then cite chapter and verse where shareholders suffered as the result of income retentions, notably in the later 1920s when share prices, along with surpluses and book values, or the net worth per share, rose sharply, only to collapse in the 1930s when losses wiped out the surpluses.

But there is a more fundamental and principled objection to internal financing: it is inherently antithetical to the maximization of the present value of a company. If managers are not compelled to earn a competitive return on capital, what assurance is there that they will strive to invest it wisely? Suppose that the cost of raising capital externally—by issuing stock or bonds—is 10 per cent. That means that the interest and underwriting fees on the bonds come to 10 percent on the capital raised and that the costs are the same for a new issue of common stock after taking into account its offering price, underwriting fees, dividend payout, and the dilution of the shareholders' equity that results from more shares outstanding. But the company that relies on internal financing is not directly pressured to meet that 10 percent cost of capital. It pays no direct or immediate penalty for the failure of a new undertaking in which internally generated capital is invested, and hence its managers aren't going to be as careful or try as hard as they would if they were compelled to finance externally. Fiascos in the investment of free or internally generated capital may eventually depress the price of a company's stock and perhaps put its managers in jeopardy. That, however, is at best a slow and very uncertain process of retribution. If all new investment were externally financed, the cost of capital to companies with poor earnings records—for whatever reason—would be higher, reflecting a risk premium, and the higher costs would tend to discourage the weaker companies. In other words, many of the acquisitions that proved to be lemons—especially mergers for diversification—and that were effortlessly financed from retained earnings would never have passed the test of the marketplace. The stocks or bonds required for their external financing could have been issued only at prohibitively high costs.

Michael C. Jensen makes a related point in his "free cash flow" theory of mergers and acquisitions.[39] Cash flow is the sum of a company's earnings and depreciation allowances, and the free cash flow is in excess of what can be profitably invested.[40] What Jensen's theory correctly predicts is that companies in slow growing or mature industries—retailing, food, automobiles, and petroleum—tend to invest their free cash in mergers and acquisitions that frequently go sour.

Now let's look at the record. I've already suggested that the results of Sears's shift into financial services are less than spectacular. Sears, as is common practice, provides information on the earnings of its separate divisions but doesn't, in its public disclosures, relate those earnings to divisional investment—that is, the acquisition price plus capital subsequently poured in. Dean Witter Reynolds was acquired in October 1981 at a cost of more than $607 million, and despite high hopes of exploiting Sears's big presence in the national retail marketplace, the investment hasn't paid off. From 1983 through 1986, Dean Witter—which lost money in two of those years—earned a total of only $33 million, or an average annual return of less than 1.4 percent on $607 million, which understates Sears's actual investment since it takes no account of investment outlays made after the acquisition. That same $607 million invested in U.S. government bonds—yielding about 12 percent from interest and appreciation—would have grown to more than $1 billion over the same period.

By contrast, the returns from Coldwell Banker, purchased for $179 million in the same month as Dean Witter, are much better. But Coldwell's success is counterbalanced by the fiasco of the Sears World Trade Company, a 1982 startup effort at "merchant banking"—a nineteenth-century practice in which investment bankers, in addition to serving as financial intermediaries by underwriting and brokering new issues of stocks and bonds, also make substantial purchases for their own account. The WTC was the vaguely conceived brainchild of Roderick M. Hills, a Washington lobbyist-lawyer who charmed Edward Telling when he served as Sears's outside counsel on the Coldwell and Dean Witter deals. Even if the worldwide inflation had continued unabated, the WTC would have failed. As it turned out, Hills succeeded only in papering Asia with his elegant business cards and providing highly paid jobs for equally inept former Washington bureaucrats—among them Frank Carlucci, the WTC's president, later secretary of defense and more recently associated with a Washington-based merchant banking house. To the relief of Sears's senior managers, Telling sacked Hills in 1985, and before the WTC was finally liquidated Sears lost at least $87 million and perhaps as much as $100 million. Not large by the grand scale of recent managerial errors, but to paraphrase Everett McKinley Dirksen, the late senator from Illinois, a hundred million here, a hundred million there, and soon you're talking about real money.

Speaking of real money, there's Sears's cash-back Discover credit card, which lost more than $400 million in 1986–87. As *The Wall Street Journal* put it in a lead page-one story: "The Discover card, Sears, Roebuck & Co.'s brash effort to take on Visa and MasterCard, is in danger of joining the Edsel and New Coke in the lineup of great product disasters." Because Sears management didn't understand the business, Discover, according to the publisher of a credit-card industry newsletter, "does a land office business selling dollar bills for 98 cents."[41] Sears, in short, was offering credit at below its cost.

Mobil Oil, with billions more in the till, eclipsed Sears's record of dismal diversification. For sheer frivolity its pin-money purchase and subsequent sale of the Ringling Brothers and Barnum & Bailey Circus speaks for itself. In 1976 Mobil paid $1.86 billion for Marcor—a combination of Montgomery Ward and the Container Corporation—and had little save red ink to show for it. It sold Container in 1986 and in March 1988 finally disposed of Montgomery Ward in a leveraged buyout for $1.5 billion in cash. Mobil said that since the cash price covered the book value of Montgomery Ward, it would not record a profit or loss on the sale. But since no return was realized on the Montgomery Ward investment between 1979 and 1987, Mobil's shareholders surely suffered a loss.[42]

Exxon got burned on its $1.24 billion investment in Reliance Electric as well as on a smaller investment in the long-since abandoned Quix lines of typewriters and word processors. Citicorp poured about $1 billion into Quotron, a mature network of stock quotation terminals. The first $680 million was for the initial 1986 purchase of what some insiders called a competitively vulnerable "sick elephant." Since then operating losses and enhancements to the system are running in the hundreds of millions. Yet Citicorp is as far from realizing its goal of a viable financial information business as when it started. Finally, there is General Motors' truly humiliating experience in attempting to diversify through its 1984 purchase of H. Ross Perot's Electronic Data Systems Corporation (EDS). After a noisy controversy in 1986 over a failure to trim bloated costs and produce better autos, GM paid Perot nearly $743 million—or nearly twice what it originally paid for his company—to depart from both its board and from EDS. Since then EDS revenues have been flat, and it's heavily dependent on GM for business and under competitive pressure from a rival formed by the irrepressible Perot. GM's 1985 purchase of Hughes Aircraft, at $5.1 billion, nearly $800 million more than its book value, is also difficult to defend, either as an investment or as a source of technology. Earnings were disappointing, and in the late autumn of 1988 GM, standing on provisions of the sales agreement, asked the seller, the Howard Hughes Medical Institute, for a rebate. As John P. Kotter of the Harvard Business School ruefully comments, GM "didn't used to have to buy technology and growth opportunities."[43]

In 1984, IBM paid $1.5 billion for Rolm—a producer of computerized telephonic switching equipment—as part of a much-heralded move into the telecommunications business. But at the end of 1988, the Big Blue acknowledged its failure by selling most of its Rolm facilities to Siemens A.G. of West Germany. Neither the price nor the probable loss was disclosed. Earlier in the year, MCI Communications Corporation, the long-distance telephone company, bought back IBM's 16 percent ownership of its stock, acquired in 1985 when the computer maker abandoned an effort to transmit data by satellite. An official, while refusing to say whether assets would be written off as losses, assured the public that Rolm's sale to Siemens would have little effect on IBM's bottom line. All of which demonstrates the ease with which giant corporations bury their mistakes.[44]

What those acquisitions have in common—except Citicorp's purchase of Quotron, for which there was a new stock issue which elicited little investor enthusiasm—is that all were internally financed and thus not subjected to any direct external scrutiny, either by the shareholders, in whose interest the directors are supposed to act, or by the financial markets. The upshot is that big mistakes are made, bigger than they would be if directors didn't have carte blanche. And companies continue to be larger and less profitable than they would otherwise be.

By dint of three years of strong sales Ford, even after raising its dividend and buying back stock, had more than $10 billion in cash by the autumn of 1988. And the money seemed to be burning a hole in the corporate pocket. Ford's subsidiary, First Nationwide Bank, arranged to acquire a total of 159 insolvent savings and loan associations (S&Ls) during 1988 in a drive to become a major player in the thrift industry.

At the end of 1987, *Business Week* commented that Bruce L. Blythe, the 43-year-old chief strategist of Ford's European subsidiary, was "getting frustrated" because he couldn't pull off anything larger than a $27 million, 75 percent stake in Britain's Aston Martin Lagonda Group. But then the author, almost as if to reassure readers, added that Ford Chairman Donald E. Petersen called Blythe back from Europe and issued him a license to stalk U.S. companies in electronics, financial services, and defense—"the bigger the target the better."[45]

There's not a word about the sad record of recent diversifications, the high risks of resuscitating bankrupted S&Ls, or even a hint that the money could be put to much better use by paying it out as an extraordinary dividend so that Ford's shareholders, not Donald Petersen, would decide how to invest *their money*. Quantum Chemical Corporation—once called National Distillers and the country's largest producer of polyethylene, a principal building block for plastics—did just that. Concerned about the undervaluation of its shares at the end of 1988, Quantum declared a special $50 dividend. The market's initial response was a more than 21 percent jump in the price of the stock.[46]

With greater reliance on debt financing—a trend which is explained in the next chapter—internally generated capital and its flagrant misuse by corporate managers will diminish. But Congress can enhance the returns on capital investments by enacting a corporate income-tax credit for dividends paid shareholders. With a 20 percent dividend tax credit—20 cents of credit for every dollar of dividends paid—there would be a strong incentive to raise dividend payouts since a company with a 45 percent corporate income-tax rate would incur an after-tax cost of only $36 on every $100 of dividends.[47] In addition to raising the efficiency of investment, a dividend credit would eliminate at least some of the double taxation of dividends. Corporate earnings are now taxed once under the corporate income levy and a second time as personal income when they're paid out as dividends.

## Size, Profit, and Survivability

Alfred Marshall—who, among his many contributions to economic theory, developed the concepts of internal and external economies—took a Darwinian view of business enterprises. He compared their life cycles to those of

> the young trees of the forest as they struggle upwards through the benumbing shade of their older rivals. Many succumb on the way,

and only a few survive; those few become stronger with every year, they get a larger share of light and air with every increase of their height, and at last in their turn they tower above their neighbours, and it seems as though they would grow on forever, and forever grow stronger as they grow. But they do not. . . .

And as with the growth of trees, so it was with the growth of businesses as a general rule *before the great recent development of vast joint-stock companies, which often stagnate, but do not readily die*. . . . Nature still presses on the private business by limiting the length of the life of its original founders, and by limiting even more narrowly that part of their lives in which their faculties retain full vigour. And so after a while, the guidance of the business falls into the hands of people with less energy and less creative genius, if not with less active interest in its prosperity. If it is turned into a joint-stock company, it may retain the advantages of the division of labour, of specialized skill and machinery: it may even increase them by a further increase of its capital; and under favourable conditions it may secure a permanent and prominent place in the work of production. *But it is likely to have lost so much of its elasticity and progressive force, that the advantages are no longer exclusively on its side in competition with younger and smaller rivals.*[48]

When account is taken of the imperatives of technology and innovation in an ever more rapidly changing world, Marshall's observations are even more apposite. Scarcely sixty years ago, in *The Modern Corporation and Private Property*, Adolf A. Berle, Jr., and Gardiner C. Means looked upon U.S. Steel and the Pennsylvania Railroad as the most awesome of managerially controlled behemoths. Now only corporate archaeologists are fascinated by their transmogrified remnants.

The evolution of corporate enterprise, like that of animal species, is fraught with uncertainty and surprise, elements on which the most careful of predictions founder. Nonetheless, much has been learned about the process of industrial change since the heyday of Berle and Means.

A first insight is that business organizations are formed and grow because it is cheaper to produce many goods and services in house than to bear the transactions costs of buying them from suppliers in the open market. Other things being equal—which they seldom are— the higher the transactions costs, the bigger the organization and vice versa.

Second, the economic or efficiency-based justification for large, vertically integrated businesses—as opposed to the bureaucratic or managerial rationale—diminishes as markets are extended, technology is diffused, and specialization, which gives rise to external economies of scale, is intensified. Technological diffusion portends smaller business organizations—not absolutely smaller but in relation to the size of the market.

For each industry or product market, there is an optimal company size which is determined by the balancing of internal economies of scale against the diseconomies in large organizations. Optimal size, which is heavily affected by technology and the structure of markets, changes over time. When it is exceeded, as frequently happens in managerially controlled companies, profitability suffers and large organizations may be split up.

The current move toward the "downsizing" of companies by spinning off incongruous businesses and reducing employment is prompted in large part by a postinflation profit squeeze and the persistent failure to maximize present values under the now collapsing regime of corporate control by managers who are not owners. But it is also consistent with longer-term technological trends.

Third, efficiency and innovation are essential to corporate survival; but the larger and more bureaucratic the organization the more difficult it is to achieve either. Making changes in a General Motors, a Sears, Roebuck, or a Bank of America is analogous to changing the course of a river, possible but very difficult and slow. Such companies are afflicted by diseconomies of size—difficulties in coordinating operations and making timely managerial decisions—that result in diminished profitability. The larger and the older the company, the more likely it is to stagnate—or perhaps disappear—over the long haul.

Fourth, there is new light on corporate mergers. The conventional objection to mergers among large companies—one that grew out of the U.S. antitrust tradition—is that they result in a concentration of economic power that permits a few sellers of a product or service to raise their prices with impunity at the expense of hapless consumers. But there is scant evidence that consumers in fact suffer much as a consequence of corporate mergers, especially in increasingly interrelated and intensively competitive world markets such as those for automobiles and electronics. Only actions of governments, usually in response to political pressure from producers, can for long hold prices far above their competitive levels. Among the important examples are the OPEC cartel during its years of effectiveness in the 1970s as well as the current limitations on imports imposed by the United States and Japan. In the United States, import barriers affect automobiles, steel ingots, textiles, food products, and computer chips, and in Japan, beef, rice, and, among many other industrial products, telecommunications equipment.

A more compelling objection to big mergers is that most are undertaken to further the interests of autonomous managers rather than those of shareholders, that they increase corporate work forces and salaries at the expense of profitability and the present value of companies, that they, in short, diminish overall economic efficiency and welfare. Many ill-fated mergers or acquisitions were consummated only because of the availability of retained earnings and wouldn't have passed muster had their managers been forced to rely solely on the bond or the stock market for financing. The larger the company, the easier it is to deflect investors' attention from failed acquisitions.

Conglomerate mergers were thoroughly discredited by the experiences of the 1960s and 1970s, and conglomerate enterprises are on the whole shrinking. They demonstrate both the perils of managing highly incongruous businesses and the virtues of concentrating in one or a few closely related product markets.

Horizontal merger—expanding in the same or closely related markets—is a viable corporate growth strategy so long as it stops before the diseconomies of large size outweigh the economies of scale and depress profits. That critical point, I believe, was crossed by Philip Morris in 1988, when it paid a very stiff $13 billion for Kraft, Inc., to become the world's biggest food and tobacco products producer.

At the same time that the Philip Morris–Kraft megamerger was consummated, bidding was under way for the $25 billion buyout of all publicly held shares of the other big food-and-tobacco combination, RJR Nabisco. After taking the company private, the buyout partnership planned to maximize RJR Nabisco's present value by splitting off the highly profitable R. J. Reynolds tobacco businesses— Camel, Salem, and Winston—from the less attractive Nabisco and Del Monte food operations. I believe that the RJR Nabisco downsizing course was the correct one and that the Philip Morris–Kraft merger, like many before it, will unravel in the not-too-distant future. Dinosaurs endured for some 160 million years in the Mesozoic era, a standard against which the life span of their corporate counterparts will be trivially brief.

I closed the first chapter by lamenting the failure of autonomous managers to maximize the present values of their companies and then showed that one of its consequences is a tendency for companies to become too large to survive. What I haven't yet touched on are the forces that threaten the lives of the managerially controlled corporate giants. Happily, they are much less of a mystery than the cataclysmic changes that doomed the dinosaurs.

James E. Meade, the British economist and Nobel laureate, wrote in 1968 that "a company which sacrifices profit either to an easy life or unprofitable growth makes itself liable to a takeover bid."[49] Meade's warning was based on current British experience, but nearly a decade passed before its validity was dramatically confirmed in the United States. That story is the subject of the next chapter.

# 3

---

# THEY'RE SYMPTOMS,
# NOT THE DISEASE:

## Hostile Takeovers, Leveraged Buyouts, and Recaps

The wave of hostile takeovers is the result of profound structural changes in the American economy. But it is in itself a serious disorder.

By now it has become accepted widely—except on Wall Street and among Wall Street lawyers—that the hostile takeover is deleterious and in fact one of the major causes of the loss of America's competitive position in the world economy. One way or another the hostile takeover will be stopped.

—Peter F. Drucker (1986)[1]

**N**either Peter Drucker nor the beleaguered corporate chieftains who level the same charge buttress it with even a shred of evidence. It's not true that the hostile takeovers of the 1980s were a major cause of the loss of American competitiveness. On the contrary, the ousting of incompetents and the threat to incumbent managers posed by takeovers and buyouts enhances corporate efficiency and competitiveness.

The wave of hostile takeovers and leveraged buyouts is a symptom of the failure of the control of corporations by autonomous managers—very much as atypical pneumonias, leukemias, and cancers are symptoms of the acquired immune deficiency syndrome, AIDS, not the syndrome itself.

Profits and the present values of companies are not for the most part maximized because doing so runs counter to the interests of the autonomous managers who control most large corporations. They behave not out of perversity or antipathy toward the shareholder-owners, but as people acting in rational conformance to the well-established rules of the managerial game. Bureaucratized corporate convention mandates that the real income of top managers—cash, stock options, and generous pensions as well as such perquisites as elegant offices, jet planes, limousines, club dues, and company-owned vacation homes—be tied to the number of one's minions, the head count, and to gross sales rather than to profits or the value of the company's stock in the marketplace. Maximizing company values would compel managers to opt for profitability over sheer size and mandates, among other things, tight reins on the expansion of work forces, tying executive compensation to profitability, and eliminating perquisites—all measures utterly antithetical to current corporate lifestyles.

As a consequence of the failure to pursue value-maximizing policies—as well as of inflation and other external economic forces that impinge on business—corporate stocks are "undervalued," priced lower in the markets than they would be under effective management. Undervaluation creates opportunities for "raiders," people with effective plans for enhancing profitability, who appeal—over the heads and the vehement opposition of incumbent manager-directors whose jobs are threatened (hence the term "hostile takeover")—to the interests of shareholders by offering to pay them premiums over the current market price of their shares in return for control of the company.

After the October 1987 stock market crash Lee A. Iacocca of Chrysler expressed relief that "the raiders are dead, thank God." But his premature epitaph overlooked two factors: the role of lower share prices in creating new takeover opportunities once the market stabilized; and uncertainty about antitrust policy after the 1988 presidential election. By January, with takeover activity still strong and the total market value of Chrysler stock at only $5.7 billion, Iacocca and his fellow board members—brave souls who extol the virtues of competition save when it strikes close to home—armed themselves against corporate raiders with takeover repellents.[2]

The first great battle for the control of a private business corporation was fought in 1868 when Jay Gould, Daniel Drew, and James Fisk of the Erie Railroad defeated the raider, Cornelius Vanderbilt of the New York Central, by manufacturing the favorable votes needed to preserve their control. In what was then regarded as a scandalous tactic—legally sanctioned, ex post facto, by bribed judges—the Gould gang issued themselves a huge number of new shares of stock from the Erie treasury which they voted to elect their directors and thus defeat Vanderbilt. Playing by prescribed and very different rules in 1932, Amadeo P. Giannini, a San Franciscan who founded what we now know as the Bank of America, recaptured his Transamerica holding company from eastern interests in a fair proxy fight—by publicly soliciting and winning the votes of thousands of small shareholders. Robert R. Young, the railroad tycoon, made brilliant use of the same strategy to take over the New York Central in 1954.[3] And there were some failed proxy campaigns: among others, Louis Wolfson's for control of Montgomery Ward and the struggles of Spyros Skouras and Charles Green over Twentieth Century-Fox, the film studio. But they were exceptions in an era of quietly negotiated and for the most part friendly transactions which, as in most of the conglomerate mergers of the 1960s, protected the jobs of the incumbent managers.

A hostile takeover, by contrast, means precisely what those words imply: the raider strikes by making a direct, public offer to buy the stock from any holders willing to tender their shares for the purpose of ousting the incumbent management and securing control.[4] Hostile takeovers were for long part of the corporate scene in Great Britain and were elegantly analyzed by the economist Robin Marris in the early 1960s.[5] But they weren't common in this country until the mid-1970s, when proxy fights were eschewed as too slow and costly, especially in view of the increasing concentration of share ownership in such institutions as pension and mutual funds. But by the spring of 1988 the number of proxy fights increased sharply because of efforts by state legislatures to prohibit hostile tenders and the stiff tax penalty on greenmail payments.[6]

It's generally agreed that an unspoken taboo against hostile takeovers was broken in 1974 when the then cash-rich International

Nickel Company of Canada (Inco) took over ESB, Inc. ESB, formerly the Electric Storage Battery Company, founded in 1888, was once the world's largest manufacturer of batteries and a major player on the Philadelphia industrial scene.[7] Its once-familiar auto batteries were marketed under the Exide and Willard trademarks, and it also produced Ray-O-Vac dry cells. But by the 1970s, ESB—one of whose huge and bustling plants I passed on my way to high school in the 1930s—was a burnt-out corporate case. It had lost much of its auto-market share when Delco and Allstate got the jump in developing long-life, nickel-cadmium batteries, and a parallel failure to innovate caused Ray-O-Vac to fall far behind Duracell and Eveready in the dry-cell market. By mid-1974, ESB's stock was selling at only six times earnings and falling faster than the market as a whole. Inco's chief, Charles Baird—coached by Robert F. Greenhill of Morgan Stanley and Joseph H. Flom, managing partner of Skadden, Arps, Slate, Meagher & Flom, who would become the doyen of takeover lawyers—believed that he could turn ESB around in a successful vertical merger. Their tactic was one of taking no prisoners in dealing with the introspective Frederick Port, ESB's president and chief executive officer. There was a deadlined ultimatum: approve a take-over or Inco, which already had a block of ESB stock, would turn directly to the shareholders with a tender offer. Although ESB resisted and tried to find a friendly suitor, a "white knight," Inco, after raising its tender offer, easily prevailed. But as a business venture, that precedent-shattering hostile takeover was a failure. After losing a good deal of money on ESB—and troubled by vanishing profits on its nickel mining business in the later 1970s—Inco sold it off, piece by piece.

## More Than Greed—or What's Driving the Takeover Wave

As a chronicler of corporate America's vagaries, on both Wall and Main streets, John Brooks is without peer. His books over the last thirty-five years are limpid, wry, and critical. His latest, *The Takeover Game,* offers one explanation of why it's happening. After rejecting theories that were advanced to account for earlier bursts of mergers, Brooks writes that this latest one is fee driven, "that the executives who made *such deals* were sold on them by investment bankers (and lawyers) motivated by the prospect of high fees. . . ."[8]

Brooks points specifically to the highly litigious takeover of Revlon by Ronald Perelman's Pantry Pride in 1985. He quotes Simon H. Rifkind, once a federal judge and a long-time Revlon director, who told him that the acquisition was "devoid of any redeeming virtue," an opinion Brooks reverently accepts. But there is the question of Rifkind's objectivity; defeat in a merger fight can surely pique even the most distinguished of former jurists.[9]

Brooks says nothing about why Revlon was so ripe for the taking and stripping. Its expensive program of buying up drug and hospital-supply businesses—begun in the mid-1970s by Michel Bergerac, the chief executive officer and a high-living alumnus of Harold Geneen's ITT college of conglomeration—was a dismal failure. As a consequence Revlon's earnings slid from $192 million in 1980 to only $112 million in 1984–85. Perelman's objective in the takeover was to sell off the low profit or losing operations and keep the lucrative cosmetics business, a strategy that worked very well. It's true, as Rifkind complains, that the costs of the deal—among them Bergerac's $35 million golden parachute, or severance settlement, duly approved by the Revlon directors, and the legal and investment-banking fees—were staggering, about $160 million! But Revlon's shareholders gained more than $500 million by dint of Perelman's—and Revlon's would-be white knight, Forstmann Little—pushing the stock up from the low $40s to a takeover settlement price of $58 a share.[10] Benefiting shareholders may not be a "redeeming virtue" in Rifkind's book, but it is in mine.

My principal objection to Brooks's fee-driven theory is that it explains neither the hostility of recent takeovers nor their timing. There's been no dearth of imaginative merger dealmakers on Wall Street since André Meyer, who made his mark in Paris, reshaped Lazard Frères in 1943. Talented merger and acquisition specialists, ever hungry for fat fees, are always poised for action. And assuming that they were making a continuous series of brilliant sales pitches for this merger deal or that, why didn't this wave of takeovers begin to rise until 1975? Why did it rise so high? And why, unlike other periods of merger mania, is it a wave of hostile takeovers? Surely something more is involved than greed, an ubiquitous and constant force but not a prime mover in market-oriented economies.

That something more encompasses three sets of developments: (1) a palpable clash of interests between corporate managers and owner-shareholders; (2) changes in the macroeconomic environment, which is shorthand for what's happening to price levels, to interest and exchange rates, and to the volume of production and trade, both here and in the rest of the world; and (3) the impacts, which may vary greatly among industries, of those macroeconomic changes on individual companies. The second and third sets of changes interact in often complicated ways, and it is to them that I want to turn.

The year 1975 marked a decade of high and very volatile inflation as well as increases in the cost of energy far larger than those of the general price level—blows that engendered fear and uncertainty about the future. The conventional financial wisdom had been that equities, common and preferred stocks, were a hedge against inflation, that their prices would outrun the general price level. But the sharp recession of 1973–75 and the OPEC cartel shattered that illusion. In fact, the mix of inflation and economic stagnation sharply depressed the prices of all financial claims, equities, and debentures. Stock prices fell because corporate earnings were squeezed by weak demand and rising costs; and there was the depressing impact of higher interest rates, which reflected the inflation. As a consequence, investors switched from financial claims, stocks and bonds, to such tangible assets as real estate, gold, and farm commodities.

One symptom of the general malaise was that, on average, publicly held common stocks traded near and sometimes below their book value during the later 1970s. Book value—or equity per share—is the estimate of the net worth of a share of stock if all the company's debts were paid off and the remaining assets liquidated. But since fixed corporate assets, such as buildings and machinery, are carried on company balance sheets at historical rather than replacement

74

costs, book values, after a decade of high inflation, grossly under-stated equities. And stocks, on the average, were greatly undervalued in relation to what it would have cost to replace or build companies from scratch. Philip Cagan and Robert E. Lipsey—economists who took pains to adjust corporate assets and liabilities for the impact of inflation—estimate that the ratio of market price to real book value for all traded, nonfinancial stocks declined by nearly 67 percent from 1970 through 1977.[11] In other words, share prices were falling in relation to real asset values, so that it was becoming increasingly advantageous to buy existing companies rather than create new ones. But because most investors took such a dim view of the future, that was an irrelevant fact, and share prices remained low. Broadly based, conventional ratios of market prices to book values—specifically, the Standard & Poor's 400—didn't begin to rise until late 1982.[12]

Inflation was the basic cause of the undervaluation by dint of its effect on interest rates and costs. Interest rates rise in inflation as lenders attempt to avert losses of purchasing power. If it were known with certainty that overall prices would rise at an average rate of 6 percent over the next ten years, buyers of high-grade corporate bonds would demand an annual inflation premium of six percentage points just to preserve the real value of their capital. The actual or market rate of interest—upwards of 10 percent—would be comprised of the "real rate" plus the inflation premium. Now, the higher the market rate of interest, the lower the capital, or discounted, value of an income-yielding asset. If the market rate of interest is 5 percent, a security that promises to pay $15,000 a year in perpetuity has a discounted present value of $300,000—that is, $15,000/.05. But if the market rate of interest doubles to 10 percent, the present value of that $15,000 income stream falls to $150,000—or, in other words, you now have to invest only $150,000 to realize $15,000 of income. High rates of interest depressed both stock and bond prices in the years 1965–80. And relief was slow in coming with the onset of diminishing inflation—or disinflation—in 1980. The rate of inflation fell much faster than nominal or market rates of interest because badly burned bond buyers feared a rekindling of inflation, and as a consequence, real rates of interest, the nominal rate minus the rate of inflation, remain high. At the beginning of August 1988 a thirty-year U.S. Treasury bond yielded about 9 percent, and inflation was running at around 4 percent, so the real rate of interest was 5 percent—high by historical standards.

The other way in which inflation depresses stock prices is through an imbalance between the market prices of equities and the replacement values of real assets. The causal nexus is most obvious in the case of oil. Because of the OPEC cartel and inflation, the price of a barrel of crude was pushed to a peak of more than $37 in 1979. And beginning in the early 1970s the intensive exploration for new oil—under the North Sea, beneath the Alaskan ice cap, and by the drilling of two-mile-deep wells in Oklahoma—pushed up production costs. Saudi Arabia can produce a barrel of crude at a fully loaded cost of well under $1. But it runs to more than $25 a barrel for the highest-cost producers, and it's their costs that determine prices if demand is strong. When world oil prices collapsed, touching a low of $8 a barrel in 1986, production costs fell little, if at all, creating an imbalance that led traditional producers such as Gulf to spend one dollar on exploration for no more than sixty cents of prospective earnings.

One entrepreneur who was quick to recognize an opportunity to enhance the depressed price of his stock was T. Boone Pickens, Jr., the maverick chief of Mesa Petroleum, a small but profitable company. In November 1979 he put most of Mesa's reserves in a "royalty trust" and issued certificates of ownership to the shareholders. The first advantage is that such a trust doesn't pay corporate income taxes, so that the "royalties"—earnings from sales of the reserves—are taxed only once, not twice as they would be as dividends, once as corporate income and again as shareholders' personal income. A second and more important advantage was that the split-up resulted in a prompt and very sharp increase in the market value of Mesa: the combined value of the common stock and royalty trust certificates far exceeded the value of the common stock alone before the spin-off.[13] What the investors applauded was a choice. Those who believed (wrongly, in my view) that crude prices would hit $100 a barrel by the end of this century held their trust certificates, reasoning that large capital gains in the future would more than offset sacrifices of current income. Others could sell their certificates at a profit, an option they didn't have before the spinoff.

When other managers, unwilling to shrink their operations, refused to adopt that disintegrative strategy, Pickens launched hostile takeover raids on three poorly managed majors, Phillips, Gulf, and Unocal. Gulf, one of the fabled "Seven Sisters," was acquired by Socal—now Chevron—for $13.2 billion. Phillips and Unocal are still independent, but debts incurred in fending off Pickens forced them to divest assets, steps toward disintegration that were more costly and painful—to both shareholders and employees—than they need have been.

Producers of such other internationally traded commodities as copper, coal, wheat, soybeans, and coffee were in the same leaky boat. In manufacturing and service industries, profits were squeezed in the disinflationary phase of the cycle because wages and other costs remained high or crept up while it became increasingly difficult to hike product prices.[14]

You might at this point conclude that the undervaluation of stocks in relation to the replacement costs of real assets—a consequence of the great wave of inflation and disinflation ("disinflation" because deflation denotes an absolute fall of the price level)—is all that's required to account for the hostile takeovers. But to make that leap is to commit the aggregation fallacy of regarding changes of the whole as representative of each of its parts. Bear in mind that when I cite ratios of market to book values I deal with very broad averages that conceal a great deal of variation among individual stocks. Some stocks have market-to-book ratios that are far above the average, while others have ratios that are far below it. And it's the low ratio stocks, low in relation to the average for the market as a whole, that attract raiders.

Raiders don't hit highly profitable companies because their stocks sell at high multiples of earnings, both absolutely and in relation to the market as a whole. The Digital Equipment Corporation (DEC) isn't within any raider's gun sights. Instead, they target companies that, as Michael Jensen points out, have high levels of "free cash flow." A company's cash flow consists of its earnings, plus the allowances that it claims for the depreciation of buildings, producers' equipment, and other assets. Free cash flow is cash flow that is in excess of what's required to fund all of a company's viable investment projects—in financial parlance, those that have positive present values when their income stream is discounted by the cost of capital.[15] What Jensen's cash-flow theory correctly predicts is that takeovers will occur most frequently in mature, slowly growing industries—broadcasting, food, and oil—and that the targets will be companies with falling or low earnings that have little debt and ample cash, so that they can be turned around quickly by managerial surgery.

Big windfall profits have been made by spotting undervalued properties. In 1984 William E. Simon, a former U.S. treasury secretary, and a partner put up less than $1 million and borrowed the rest to buy the Gibson Greeting Card division from RCA for $80 million. Within eighteen months they took Gibson public again and realized $290 million! Coups such as Simon's, which became less lucrative as more players got into the game, led to questions about the workings of what is sometimes called the market for corporate control.

Michael Kinsley, the editor of *The New Republic,* in a column called "You Won't Find an Efficient Market on Wall Street," asked: "If $150 is the proper 'free market' market value of a share of CBS, isn't there something fundamentally wrong with a system that values a share at barely half that unless some buccaneer comes along?"[16] My first answer to Kinsley is no, there's nothing wrong with the operation of the stock market per se. I'm not at all enamored of the "efficient market" theory, the belief that prices rationally incorporate all relevant information about the future. On the contrary, I believe that the "market"—shorthand for a momentary consensus of a thundering herd—is far from rational and, from hour to hour, often wrong. That's why the market's vision of the future—with a time horizon no longer than a trading session—is constantly changing. But unless it is formulated with extreme rigidity, there's nothing in the efficient-market doctrine that rules out big differences of opinion about the prospects of a company, especially if one of them is based on a plan for its radical reorganization.

My second answer is yes, there was "something fundamentally wrong," but with CBS's management, not the market. Theirs is a textbook-like example of how not to maximize a company's present value. Overpriced acquisitions in magazine and book publishing, a "show biz" indifference to controlling costs, and bad TV ratings squeezed CBS's profits, depressed its stock price, and made it a prime takeover target. When Ted Turner of Cable News Network was unable to come up with a financially viable bid for CBS, Laurence A. Tisch of Loews stepped in as a fat white knight, thus ending the long control of founder William S. Paley. Since then, staffs have been cut and the magazine and record divisions have been sold.

Let me now elaborate on my reasons for arguing that this burst of mergers is unique. There are, to be sure, similarities with earlier waves, but I contend that we're now staring at an essentially different animal.

What distinguishes this wave are five factors:

*First, it's conflict-driven:* The conflict between corporate managers and outsider shareholders is seldom articulated, but the hostile takeovers, the restructurings, and the leveraged buyouts speak much louder than words. That conflict was absent in earlier waves.

*Second, it's a new game:* The principal objective of this wave of activity—the Philip Morris–Kraft merger being a major exception—is the profitable buying and selling, not the consolidating, of undervalued companies or pieces of companies. And, as the appearance of Sir James Goldsmith and Robert Maxwell as well as Japanese and German investors suggests, it's an international game. The decline of the dollar against the yen, the deutsche mark, and other currencies, which began early in 1985, made America a bargain basement for foreign investors, just as their countries were fair game for our hunters in the 1950s and 1960s, when the dollar was strong.

Well-established businesses, once thought of as enduring if not immutable institutions, now change hands and vanish as identifiable entities with unprecedented frequency and celerity. It's still much more time-consuming and expensive to acquire and disassemble an operating company—a Beatrice, a Bendix, or a Kraft—than it is to arrange the mortgage-financed sale of a big office building. But the gap between the two transactions is narrowing. It may be wishfully premature to speak of a market for corporate control. Yet the mindset that increasingly regards companies as assets, casually to be bought and sold, is becoming more pervasive.

Two factors that strengthened that mindset and increased the momentum of the current wave were deregulation and antitrust policy. The consequences of lifting federal regulation of the airline industry and, to a lesser extent, interstate trucking were: (1) the onset of vigorous price and route competition; (2) trouble for the inefficient, high-cost carriers once the umbrella of protective regulation was folded; and (3) a series of mergers, route abandonments, and restructurings, all part of an adjustment to a new environment.

Antitrust laws, as I have already noted, were originally enacted for the purpose of blocking mergers, and the Hart-Scott-Rodino Act—legislation requiring Justice Department approval of changes of control—is routinely invoked by lawyers struggling to fend off hostile takeovers. But federal antitrust enforcement, except for price-fixing conspiracies, was greatly relaxed over the past two decades, and under the Reagan administration it fell into a state of innocuous desuetude. The dramatic 1982 breakup of AT&T, once the world's largest corporation, was not reflective of antitrust policy but was largely the result of a political miscalculation and conflict among Bell System bureaucrats and federal regulators.[17]

*Third, open season on managers:* Along with a fraternal solicitude for the sensibilities of entrenched managers, the taboo against hostile takeovers is now irrevocably broken. Earlier mergers, with few exceptions, were polite, if not friendly, transactions among men of the same industry and their bankers. But many of the more spectacular deals in this wave are hostile, initiated by rank outsiders, people beyond the established managerial pale. Until he gained prominence as a raider, T. Boone Pickens was a minor independent in the oil industry. Raiders such as Icahn, Perelman, the Belzbergs, and the Basses are investors without real roots in any industry. In fact, most of the recent deals aren't *mergers* at all but divestitures, buyouts, and recapitalizations.

*Fourth, new institutional players:* To a hitherto unprecedented degree, pension funds, savings and loan associations, employee stock-ownership plans, mutual funds, and large investment banking houses are involved as major players in leveraged buyouts and leveraged recaps, as well as hostile takeovers.

*Fifth, bonded innovation:* It is hardly a coincidence that the current wave gathered force simultaneously with the development of the high-yield or "junk" bond market, which I will presently analyze. Higher leveraging, a consequence of the development of the junk-bond market, is forcing radical changes of long-established managerial policies.

It's to the financial developments that I now turn.

At the end of September 1988, the public and private employee pension plans in the United States, covering some 60 million people, held nearly $1.7 trillion of assets. Equities—shares of stocks—accounted for more than $700 billion, and bonds for about $570 billion with the remainder in mortgages, short-term claims, and cash. That $700 billion of equities came to more than 24 percent of the total market value of outstanding equities.[18] Clearly, pension plan members have a vital stake in the profitability of U.S. corporations and, therefore, in the outcome of struggles for control.

As fiduciaries—charged by law with protecting the interests of plan members—managers of pension funds have two principal concerns. They must preserve capital by avoiding large losses, such as that suffered by the big College Retirement Equities Fund (CREF) when the Continental Illinois Bank foundered in 1984 and its common stock became all but worthless. At the same time, they must take care that the returns on investment—interest, dividends, and capital gains—are sufficient to fund the benefits due pensioners.

There are two types of pension contracts in the United States: those that define the contributions to the plan but pay variable benefits—the chief of which is the Teachers Insurance and Annuities Association–College Retirement Equities Fund (TIAA-CREF)—and those that define the benefits. Benefit-defined plans, which now account for about four-fifths of all pension-plan assets, make retirement payments that are tied in one way or another to an employee's years of service and level of pay—usually some percentage of the highest level of earnings. Defined benefits were for long the rule in the government sector, and they became dominant in private plans when General Motors went that route after spirited negotiations with the United Auto Workers, just after the Second World War.

My dwelling on that distinction between pension plans is to underscore an important point. Defined benefits rise with inflation. The link between the level of benefits and price level—which depends on the rate at which wages and salaries rise and the particular pension formula—may not be tight for short-lived inflations. But after fifteen years of high inflation, 1965 through 1980, levels of defined benefits, both currently paid and prospective, grew rapidly. As a consequence, pension-fund managers and their advisers came under great pressure to achieve higher returns on their investments, since shortfalls in the income of pension funds must be made up out of the current earnings of the parent company. A former chief executive of a large retail chain finds that wryly paradoxical. "I used to bitch," he told me, "about the shortsightedness of a market standard by which we were supposed to hit our forecasted earnings quarter in and quarter out. But at the same time, I was beating our fund manager over the head to push for higher returns so as to cut our pension costs."

The imperative of higher investment returns turned a number of pension-fund managers from passive spectators into active takeover players. In 1987 TIAA-CREF invested about $600 million in leveraged buyouts. Two big state employee funds, those of California and Wisconsin, were partners, at $20 million a share, in one of Kohlberg Kravis Roberts & Company's more successful leveraged buyouts. Harrison J. Goldin, New York City's comptroller, its chief pension-fund officer, made no secret of his willingness to benefit municipal retirees by joining forces with corporate raiders.[19]

But there's a flip side of the public-sector coin which came up during the 1988 struggle over control of the Koppers Company, Inc., a big Pittsburgh-based producer of building materials and chemicals, with Beazer PLC of Great Britain. In a blustering letter to the chairman of Shearson/American Express, an active equity partner in the proposed deal, G. Davis Greene, Jr., treasurer of the Commonwealth of Pennsylvania, took up arms "against a hostile action that can potentially have a significant adverse impact on jobs in this state." He suspended all Pennsylvania treasury business with Shearson Lehman Hutton, Inc.—which he said amounted to more than $7 billion in 1987–88—and threatened efforts to cut off brokerage business from Pennsylvania employees' pension funds as well as their divestiture of American Express stock. After a three-month struggle Beazer finally got control of Koppers, but the deal wasn't done before it agreed not to move the headquarters for at least three years, thereby fending off a suit by the city of Pittsburgh. Shearson paid a price—both in public relations and in a potential loss of state business—for its share in the victory. In the heat of the battle, Koppers employees posed for pictures cutting their American Express cards in pieces.[20]

While state and local governments take strong stands against corporate raiders, Washington's weight is thrown on the other side of the battlements. Under the Employee Retirement Income Security Act (ERISA), passed by Congress in 1974, the Department of Labor's Pension and Welfare Benefits Administration (PWBA) provides insurance coverage and enforces regulations to ensure that pension-plan participants actually receive what was promised them. One of the areas covered by ERISA is the voting and tendering of shares administered by pension trustees.

A test of ERISA's power in takeover battles came in 1982 when William M. Agee, the highly visible chairman of Bendix, a manufacturer of auto parts and aerospace products, made a hostile tender for Martin Marietta, an aerospace, cement, and aluminum company. That move raised the curtain on what became a widely viewed takeover farce, one that further tarnished the image of corporate managers. Mounting a Pac Man defense, a term of video gaming, Martin Marietta countertendered for Bendix's stock. And after much sound and fury between the boardroom princes and their retinues of lawyers and investment bankers, a friendly, negotiated settlement was reached when a third party, the Allied Corporation—led by Edward L. Hennessy, Jr., another ITT alumnus—bought control of Bendix, which had already acquired about 70 percent of Martin Marietta's shares. Hennessy and Thomas G. Pownall, president of Martin Marietta, then reversed the countertender transactions—Martin Marietta held some 50 percent of Bendix—by swapping Bendix for Martin Marietta shares. In the end, Bendix was dead as an independent entity while Martin Marietta is counted among the living.

Almost a quarter of Bendix's stock was held by a Salaried Employee Saving and Stock Ownership Plan (SESSOP) administered in trust by Citibank, and there was a question of whether the stock would be tendered to Martin Marietta, which was offering a price considerably above market. At first the Citibankers, reluctant to become embroiled in a takeover fight, declared that they wouldn't tender the shares. But Martin Marietta's pension lawyer doggedly brought the matter before a PWBA official in the Labor Department who told her that "Citibank can't do nothing"—that as a fiduciary it had to tender the Bendix shares to Martin Marietta. Citibank, over Agee's protests, tendered the shares, and when the curtain came down, the SESSOP members and other Bendix shareholders reaped a windfall harvest. The Bendix shares, which were selling at only $45 when Agee lunged, were bought by Allied for $80.[21]

But the Bendix precedent didn't prevent other chief executives from throwing the weight of their pension-fund votes on the side of incumbent management—acts of high-echelon solidarity that clearly conflict with the interests of pensioners. In 1986 Hicks B. Waldron, chief of Avon Products, Inc., the big home-marketer of cosmetics, reviewed the decisions to vote against management by its $430 million pension fund and ordered that all five of them be reversed. His view was that "fifty resolutions that seek to eliminate poison pills is fifty too many," and Avon's retirement board—of which Waldron wasn't a member—obediently complied.[22] News of Waldron's high-handed pressure, and similar pressure in other corporations as well, did not sit well with the viligant PWBA. While alleging no impropriety, the Labor Department told Avon—in a February 1988 letter it circulated widely—that pension-fund managers, and they alone in their fidiciary capacity, are to decide how to vote proxies in the interests of retirement plan members, that efforts by corporate managers to influence those fiduciary decisions violate ERISA.[23] It's doubtful that the courts, which are susceptible to the business-judgment defense by corporate directors, would have acted so resolutely to protect the interests of pensioners by giving fund managers the unchallengeable option of voting against incumbent managements. Surely the PWBA is one agency that gives lie to the notion that all federal bureaucracies are suspect.

## Milken, Drexel Burnham, and the Junk-Bond Revolution

It's difficult to imagine the current wave of takeovers and buyouts—at least on anything approaching its actual volume—in the absence of Drexel Burnham Lambert and the junk-bond market. The spectacular rise of both institutions—they are essentially two sides of the same financial coin—is the story of one young man's brilliant success.[24]

In the summer of 1962, a twenty-two-year-old Wharton School student named Michael Robert Milken—who hailed from Encino in Los Angeles' San Fernando Valley and was a 1968 honors graduate of the University of California at Berkeley—took an internship at Drexel Firestone, then a second-tier investment house, which descended from a business founded in 1838 by Francis Martin Drexel, an Austrian immigrant and an established Philadelphia portrait painter. In 1973 Drexel Firestone would be merged with Burnham and Company—a small, third-tier New York brokerage established in 1935—to form Drexel Burnham, and beginning in 1976 Drexel Burnham Lambert would be nurtured by infusions of Belgian capital from the Compagnie Bruxelles Lambert.

Milken's first task—accomplished with an arrogant impatience of slower minds—was to save Drexel Firestone some $500,000 of interest charges annually by speeding up the delivery of bonds to its customers. But that was the last time he engaged in any matter so mundane. The insights that led to what is now known as the junk-bond market came when he directed his keen intellect and enormous energy to "fallen angels," corporate bonds that were downgraded to below-investment-grade quality by Standard & Poor's or Moody's, the principal rating agencies. On quality scales running from AAA downward to C, bonds graded BB or Ba and lower are designated as speculative, or "junk."

In analyzing and trading those junk bonds, Milken reconfirmed the basic research findings of W. Braddock Hickman and the subsequent work of Thomas R. Atkinson: namely, that in the first six decades of this century the yield differentials between junk and investment-grade issues—the amount by which the returns on junk bonds exceeds those on AAA bonds, running to about four percentage points, or 400 basis points—were far larger than the experience-based risks of default.[25] There was, in other words, gold in the junk heaps: by buying and holding the fallen angels in well-diversified bond portfolios, investors could realize much higher returns, net of losses on defaults, than they could by exclusive reliance on the quality issues.

Milken also concluded, rightly, that there was something wrong with conventional bond ratings. Highly conservative standards of safety and prudence had been established in the wake of defaults in the 1930s. A more fundamental objection is that bond ratings rest far more on past and present debt ratios of companies—static, one-shot appraisals of their financial condition—than on the growth of their cash flow. By Moody's and Standard & Poor's criteria, fewer than 10 percent of all U.S. corporations, only the giants, are eligible to issue investment-grade bonds, and Milken saw that narrow view as an enormous opportunity. Why couldn't medium-sized, or even small, companies raise capital by issuing bonds of less than investment grade? Unlike commercial bank loans, such bonds would not impose restrictive convenants—for example, limitations on how much a company might expand its operations—on the issuers. So long as the cash flow of the issuers continues to grow, the interest and provision for retiring the bonds are covered.

Contrary to what was once the conventional financial wisdom, the advantages of substituting debt for equity are considerable. Greater reliance on debenture capital helps to resolve the free-cash problem of companies in slow-growing industries. Interest charges on debt soak up funds that would otherwise be squandered on unprofitable efforts to diversify through acquisition. With lower levels of free cash flow, conflicts of interest between managers and outside shareholders are diminished. Moreover, interest payments—unlike dividends on common stock which may be drastically reduced or eliminated—are a contractural obligation, a burden that compels managers to increase operating efficiency and attempt to maximize the present value of the company. A sizable debt burden makes managers behave more like old-fashioned owners than like conventional corporate officers. The reason is that with a reduction of equity capital, insider-managers can hold larger proportions of the voting stock, thus creating personal incentives that are absent in large corportions, where top management typically owns a minute fraction of 1 percent of the outstanding shares. Finally, interest payments, unlike dividends, are deductible from corporate income taxes. So if the effective corporate income tax rate is 45 percent, the after-tax cost of a dollar of interest paid is only 55 cents.

Greater reliance on corporate debt also holds attractions for investors, not the least of which are higher bond yields. In the spring of 1988, the yield on a seven-year junk bond was, on the average, more than 4.5 percentage points above that on a seven-year U.S. Treasury security, a premium that more than compensated for the risk of default. On every $1,000, junk bonds yield an extra $45.

Aside from the initial disdain of his more genteel colleagues at Drexel Firestone, Milken's greatest hurdle in developing the junk-bond market was fear. Institutional investors—portfolio managers in mutual funds, insurance companies, pension plans, and savings banks—had to be persuaded of the safety of new, high-yield bonds that were being derisively dismissed as "junk" by members of the financial establishment. Barriers still remain. A ruling by James Corcoran, the superintendent of insurance, prohibits New York State insurers from investing more than 20 percent of their assets in junk bonds. Other state insurance regulators sounded alarms, even though—as I explain below—there is no evidence that junk bonds expose fiduciaries or other institutional investors to inordinate risks.[26]

Milken overcame the resistance to junk bonds, not only by meticulous care in selecting companies and analyzing the issues that he sold, but by assuaging buyers' fears through constant tutelage and hand holding. By the mid-1970s his department was the biggest money maker in Drexel Burnham, and by July of 1978 he had sufficient clout to move his junk-bond group to Beverly Hills, where he operated with great autonomy.

During the next eight years—until November 14, 1986, the day Ivan Boesky pleaded guilty to insider trading—Milken's star ascended. He became, without doubt, the single most important figure in American corporate finance. He could place billions of dollars of new junk bonds with astonishing rapidity, and his extensive network of bond issuers and bond buyers—those for whom he floated junk-bond loans also invested in his other issues of junk bonds—made Drexel Burnham the country's fifth largest and most profitable investment house. By the mid-1980s, a Drexel Burnham letter, stating that it was "highly confident" of providing funds, was all that was necessary to complete a hostile takeover, a restructuring, or a leveraged buyout.

Samuel J. Heyman of GAF went to see Milken early in December of 1985, just before his effort to take over Union Carbide. "He gave me his personal assurance," Heyman said, "that he would be able to raise the financing, and he reviewed with me a list of individual and institutional investors . . . he thought would be likely purchasers of the Carbide issue. Within three weeks of that meeting, Mike delivered to me, on New Year's Eve, signed commitments for three and a half billion dollars from substantially the same list he had earlier predicted would be interested in the deal."[27]

Milken's customers and his circle of contacts was literally a directory of the movers and shakers in the current wave of corporate change. It included, to name only a few, Carl Icahn, Boone Pickens, Rupert Murdoch, Armand Hammer, Ted Turner, Ronald Perelman, the Belzberg and Bass families, Samuel Heyman, Saul Steinberg, and Sir James Goldsmith. Milken's growing power was celebrated in extravagant party-seminars, known as the annual "Predators' Ball." But despite an exalted status, he continued to work with demonic energy so that junk bonds underwritten by Drexel Burnham could be readily traded at all times. His work days began at between 4 and 4:30 a.m. Pacific time—in order to trade with New York and other markets—and ended at 7:30 p.m. Both issuers and investors avidly sought and patiently awaited his counsel.

After a speech to a meeting of money managers in 1986, a long-time client, unable to see Milken in the press of the crowd, asked his assistant where he was. "The King," she replied, pointing, "is over there."[28] With Boesky's conviction in November 1986, and persistent rumors of his links to Drexel Burnham Lambert, that regal aura began to fade.

Milken's spectacular success rested on the simultaneous fulfillment of two needs in the investment marketplace: (1) for higher yields by pension-fund and other portfolio managers and (2) for a permanent means, as opposed to commercial-bank bridge loans, of raising billions to finance hostile takeovers and leveraged buyouts. What he did in masterly fashion was match up junk-bond issuers with investors. Big purchasers of new junk bonds—pension plans, savings and loan associations, insurance companies, and mutual funds—were, in reciprocation, invited to participate in the lucrative takeovers and leveraged buyouts that Drexel Burnham was also underwriting. It became, in short, a one-stop takeover, buyout, and recap shop, advising raiders on targets and strategies, then following through by providing ready buyers for the junk bonds that were issued by the reorganized companies.

Early in 1984, to cite a most striking example, Drexel Burnham sent a memorandum to its junk-bond customers proposing to raise $1.5 billion for the hostile takeover of a target it code-named the Gray Oil Company. Gray was Gulf Oil, and the raider, code-named the Gray Investor Group, was T. Boone Pickens's Mesa Petroleum.[29]

Needless to say, Drexel Burnham's fees and commissions, collected on both sides of the deals, were enormous. By the autumn of 1987 Michael Milken—who plowed back his own huge bonuses and those of his staff into a number of lucrative investment partnerships and other ventures—was listed by *Forbes* among the four hundred richest people in America, and may well be, or was, a billionaire.

By dint of Milken's indefatigable labors, new issues of junk bonds grew dramatically, from a total of barely $2 billion in 1980 to a peak of $32 billion in 1986, and then declined—to $29 billion in 1987 and

$27 billion in 1988. Other investment houses, many of which were initially disdainful, are now players in the junk-bond market where transactions—the buying and selling of newly floated as well as outstanding issues—were running at an annual rate of about $180 billion in the late autumn of 1988. With increasing competition, Drexel's share of all new issue underwritings fell from a peak of nearly 70 percent in 1984 to around 50 percent in mid-1988. Then—doubtless because of increasing concern over an imminent criminal indictment—Drexel's share plummeted to 21 percent, falling behind Morgan Stanley & Co., in October and November of 1988.[30]

During its period of dominance, Drexel lobbied against legislation that would have permitted commercial banks to underwrite junk bonds, thus breaching the cartel-like compartmentalization of the U.S. securities markets that was ushered in by the Glass-Steagall Act of 1933. Drexel's chief, Frederick H. Joseph, shamelessly argued that junk bonds were too risky for commercial banks, oblivious to the billions that his company had sold to savings and loan associations, which are hardly better able to bear the risk. Hearing about the riskiness of junk bonds from Drexel, quipped Representative Barney Frank of Massachusetts, "is like getting a lecture on religious pluralism from the Ayatollah."[31]

From the outset junk bonds were anathema to the opponents of hostile takeovers. Among the disasters they freely predicted was a financial panic precipitated by junk-bond defaults. But it didn't happen. Only a few major issues defaulted, and after dipping by about 10 percent, junk-bond prices recovered nicely after the October 1987 crash.[32]

In September 1988 Michael Milken, Drexel Burnham, and others were charged in a 184-page civil complaint by the Securities and Exchange Commission (SEC) with a broad array of securities law violations that includes participation in an insider-trading conspiracy with Ivan Boesky, fraud against clients, and the manipulation of stock prices.[33] Drexel Burnham settled the case against them and avoided a criminal indictment under the 1970 Racketeer Influenced and Corrupt Organization Act (RICO) when they pled guilty to six counts of felony and agreed to pay $650 million, $300 million as a fine to the government and $350 million into a restitution fund that will satisfy judgments in class-action and other suits by those claiming injury. It was a deal—said to have been opposed by Frederick Joseph in a split vote of the directory—under which Drexel Burnham sacked Michael Milken. At the end of March 1989, Milken—who defiantly denied any wrongdoing—was indicted on ninety-eight criminal counts, for which the federal government laid claim to $1.2 billion of his assets.

The king of junk bonds was dethroned. But the changes Milken effected remain as a monument to his imagination and determination. They were succinctly, if inelegantly, summarized by Stephen Weinroth, a Drexel Burnham corporate finance partner: "I think the systematic realigning of corporate America, and putting parts of companies in the hands of guys who have major equity stakes in those companies, is the best thing we have done for our society."[34]

## Takeover Defenses: Cui Bono?

A question that's seldom raised about defenses against corporate takeovers is that of cui bono?—in whose interests? toward what end?

The short answer is that defenses against raiders are almost invariably waged to protect the positions of managers—their income, their perquisites, and their power—who in turn dominate the directories of most large corporations.[35] It's difficult to reach any other conclusion when the incumbent directors decide that the best interests of shareholders are served by denying them premiums that may run upward of 50 percent over the market price of their stock. The typical rationale for that position—one that the courts have upheld under the "business judgment rule"—is that the raiders are incompetent and that the incumbent managers, if only given more time, would achieve a much higher present value of the company than their challengers. But when shareholders are denied a choice of selling their shares at a premium price—as they are when poison pills and other defenses are adopted by boards of directors without their consent—they are compelled to accept a bird in the bush for one in the hand. Another defensive tactic is the often disingenuous invocation of social responsibility, claiming that the battle against the takeover is in the interest of the labor force and the community. Both positions conflict sharply with the only responsibility that corporate directors are charged with under common law, their fiduciary obligation to protect the interests of the owner-shareholders.

What has typically happened since Inco-ESB is that a raider, after exhaustive, secretly conducted financial research, identifies a target, an undervalued company. It is a company whose shares can be acquired at a price judged to be low in relation to what they might be worth if the business were reorganized under new managers and made more profitable, or low in relation to what might be earned by selling off the business or lines of businesses, piece by piece. After secretly acquiring just under 5 percent of the target company's stock—the legal limit under the Williams Act beyond which a public disclosure must be made within ten days—the raider offers to buy all or most of the target's stock at a price well above the market. Once the tender is announced, if not before, risk arbitragers, people betting that a deal of some sort will be made at a higher price, begin buying the targeted company's stock. In the spirit of a bazaar, the first tender is routinely rejected by the target's directors, in effect, its managers, as ridiculously low. And if subsequent, sweetened offers are also rejected, one of the following sets of scenarios will unfold:

1. The beleaguered company is "rescued" by a white knight, an investor or another corporation which usually tops the raider's offer. Gulf Oil escaped the embrace of Boone Pickens only to disappear into the maw of Chevron. More recently, Eastman Kodak played white knight to Sterling Drug by offering a cool billion dollars more than Hoffmann-La Roche.

Since manager-directors reflexively resist hostile tenders, one of the important issues to emerge in court-made corporate law is whether a company is for sale. If a court deems it to be for sale— and there is the rub—the manager-directors must sell control to the highest bidder, not to some favored purchaser who might offer less and promise to continue their employment. The issue arose in the 1985 takeover of Revlon by Ronald Perelman's Pantry Pride. The

Revlon board attempted to evade Perelman's grasp by accepting a friendly "lockup" bid for its two most valuable divisions at a price far below their estimated market value. Perelman sued to break the lockup and won in the Delaware Court of Chancery, which ruled that because Revlon was for sale its directors were obliged to obtain the highest price. Other courts went along with the dictum that once a company is up for sale, the directors must take on the role of honest auctioneers, charged with getting the best price for the shareholders. The issue that continues to be fiercely litigated is whether a company is really up for sale.[36]

2. Rather than surrender passively or be rescued, the would-be victim can defend its independence. One not very brave way out is the payment of tribute, or "greenmail," to the raider by buying back his shares—and his alone, in what the SEC calls a "targeted share repurchase"—at a price well in excess of the market. In 1984 Saul Steinberg of Reliance Capital Group, who grew rich as a 1960s wunderkind through his creative accounting for the leasing of computers, reaped more than $30 million in greenmail from his sortie against Walt Disney, the film and theme-park company.[37] Steinberg, no paragon of virtue, drew showers of brickbats while the real culprits, Disney's managers, who doled out shareholders' money to save their skins, were hardly scathed. The 50 percent tax penalty on greenmail that took effect at the end of 1987 has discouraged but not abolished the practice.

Second, there is the scorched-earth strategy of deliberately depressing the value of the target by selling off its "crown jewels" or acquiring "dogs" so that the raider will no longer find it attractive. It's a course of action that is blatantly inimical to outside shareholders' interests and ultimately self-defeating for the directors who adopt it. But it's legal.

Third, there's the parachute defense. Boards of directors award "golden parachutes," lump payments that run into double-digit millions to top managers who are displaced in takeovers, and "lead parachutes" to the lower orders, provisions that oblige the raider to maintain the existing work force. The costs of parachutes, which are borne by shareholders, are hardly a deterrent to hostile takeovers.

Fourth, there is the "poison pill." Devised in 1982 by Martin Lipton of Wachtell, Lipton, Rosen & Katz—the leading legal strategist for managements under attack who reportedly charged Kraft $20 million for two weeks' work in the Philip Morris merger[38]—it is a kissing cousin of the ploy that Jay Gould and his partners devised to fend off Vanderbilt. Assuming that the pill stands up against legal counterattack—and in 1988 the Delaware courts greatly weakened it as a takeover defense—the pill is poison because it compels the raider to swallow a much higher price for the target company or back off.

With the simplest, or Jay Gould, poison pill, the target's shareholders are issued rights to additional shares of the company's common stock, usually at a nominal price, when there is a tender offer for control or a raider's accumulation reaches a specified proportion of the total shares outstanding. So unless a court invalidates the pill—something, happily, that has been happening with increasing frequency—the raider has to purchase the extra shares, perhaps twice as many as were originally outstanding.

A flip-over pill gives the target's shareholders the right to exchange their preferred shares for the raider's convertible preferred at a most advantageous price. In order to secure control in the face of such a pill, the raider must first buy the target's newly issued preferred shares, exchange them for his convertible preferred at a fixed, unfavorable rate, and then, if the price of his common stock rises above the conversion price, suffer a dilution of earnings per share. More discriminatory pills give the target's shareholders rights to convert directly into the raider's common stock at half its current market price, what's called the forced equity provision. And to wound an acquisitor already burdened by debt, a pill may provide that its preferred stock be convertible into short-term notes rather than common shares.

According to a precedent-making decision of the Delaware courts—discussed later—the adoption of poison-pill provisions by company directors does not require the approval of the shareholders.

At worst, a poison pill restricts the alienability of common stock by preventing the target company's shareholders from selling their stock to raiders without the approval of the board of directors. Or its mere adoption may discourage potential raiders and thus depress the price of the company's stock.[39] That's why the nation's largest ($60 billion) pension fund—the Teachers Insurance and Annuities Association–College Retirement Equities Fund, or TIAA-CREF— consistently opposes poison pills. At best—as exemplified by the 1988 contest between Campeau and R. H. Macy for the control of Federated Department Stores—the target company's management, with court approval, uses the threat of its poison pill to conduct an auction among rival bidders which assures the shareholders a higher, if not the highest, price.

Last, there's the save-our-way-of-life defense: sounding dire warnings that jobs will be lost and that the target company's home community will collapse if the raider succeeds. Its object is to mobilize a broad base of hometown political and shareholder support. Bartlesville, Oklahoma, used that demagogic tactic to turn back Boone Pickens's assault on Phillips Petroleum, its principal employer, in 1984. Yet in the end, the Phillips shareholders forced a financial restructuring in which the company borrowed money to retire 50-percent of its stock at a price far above the market, close to that offered by Pickens. And Phillips's staff was sharply reduced when businesses were sold off to retire debt. In a more insidious episode, Sir James Goldsmith, the Anglo-French investor, was pitted in 1986 against a poorly managed Goodyear Tire & Rubber Company which was nonetheless solidly supported by organized labor and an aroused Akron, Ohio, community. After a heated hearing before a congressional committee that was replete with xenophobic overtones, Goldsmith retreated, his pockets bulging with $93 million of greenmail plus banking and legal fees.

Since then more than half the states have passed antitakeover laws, some more restrictive than others, and because of the weakness of the U.S. dollar, which lowers the cost of takeovers to foreign investors, there has been increasing talk about the need to protect "sensitive" U.S. industries—whatever that may mean—by new legislation. Felix Rohatyn, who takes that protectionist tack,[40] seems to have forgotten how U.S. multinational corporations, among them his client ITT, took full advantage of just such opportunities all through the 1960s, acquiring properties at low prices in the very countries that cooperated, under the Bretton Woods international monetary regime, in supporting a much overvalued dollar.

There is another set of scenarios in which companies—either to fend off potential raiders or to satisfy the awakened entrepreneurial aspirations of their managers—are reformed in very radical and usually salutary ways.

In leveraged buyouts—also known as "going private"—a small group of investors which sometimes includes key managers, buys the shares of the company from the public. At first, leveraged buyouts were friendly transactions, initiated by senior corporate managers, the insiders, often with "lockout options" which excluded other bidders. While the prices paid to the outside shareholders were always above the market, retrospective questions about their fairness are raised. For example, in 1984 John Werner Kluge, chairman of Metromedia, a communications conglomerate, took the company private at about $40 a share, an 85 percent premium over the market price. Then, shortly afterward, he sold part of his holdings at more than $200 a share, for a gain of more than $3 billion. Did the market for the Metromedia assets undergo a dramatic and extremely rapid change? Or did Kluge, as an insider, know something that he should rightly have communicated, as a part of his fiduciary responsibility, to the majority of the shareholders, who were not part of management? A number of legal actions to block buyouts have been taken by irate shareholders, charging insider-managers with deliberately withholding material information to acquire assets on the cheap, thus violating their fiduciary obligations as corporate officers. In April 1987, a New York court of appeals ruled that shareholders could sue two investment houses—Bear Stearns and what is now Shearson Lehman Hutton—over the objectivity of "fairness opinions" written at the behest of Metromedia's directors prior to the buyout.[41]

What has to be recognized is that there is an inherent and irresolvable conflict of interest in any management-led buyout. If managers faithfully discharge their fiduciary obligations to the outside shareholders, they must, perforce act against their own interests as the new owners. Suppose that manager-directors who want to buy out a company at $50 a share have reason to believe that another group will pay $60. They have a fiduciary responsibility to negotiate the higher price in the interest of their shareholders, but they benefit if the deal goes through at $50 a share. And since there are few saints in boardrooms, it's not hard to predict whose interests will be served.

The only workable solution to the problem of fairness in management buyouts—one that's increasingly resorted to because of the threat of litigation—is competition among bidders. As Bevis Longstreth, a distinguished New York lawyer and former SEC commissioner, put it: "How do you know if the price is fair if you haven't tested the market?" It's a question that made a strong impression in the boardroom of the GAF Corporation. Its chairman, Samuel Heyman, offered to buy out the shareholders for $1.4 billion, a price deemed fair by Salomon Brothers, which received a fee for stating that opinion. But the outside directors, no doubt mindful of their liability in the event of litigation, disagreed and told Salomon to go out and find other bidders. Seven months later the GAF board accepted Heyman's significantly higher offer.

Public scrutiny and competition also protected the shareholders and exposed the blatant cupidity of the insider managers in the record-breaking, $25 billion buyout of RJR Nabisco. Under the initial plan—hatched by the company president, F. Ross Johnson, and Shearson Lehman Hutton, his bankers—the six top RJR Nabisco executives, assuming that their five-year financial goals were attained, stood to realize $2.5 billion on personal investments of only $20 million. Their plot was foiled when the board of directors, frightened by the publicity and fearing shareholder suits, accepted a counteroffer from Kohlberg Kravis Roberts & Company, a house specializing in leveraged buyout partnerships.[42]

Buyouts are largely financed by issuing debt, notably junk bonds, the payment of the interest and principal of which is secured by the cash flow—the earnings plus the depreciation allowances of the reorganized company—or by selling off some of its businesses. Companies capitalized principally by debt, as opposed to equity, are "leveraged" because changes in their revenues, up or down, have disproportionately large, hence leveraged, impacts on per share earnings of their common stock.[43] Once a company is heavily in debt, it's no longer an attractive takeover target because raiders can't finance the deal by borrowing against its cash flow.

The dollar value of buyouts—some were not leveraged—rose from $636 million in 1979 to a peak of $125 billion in 1988, more than 4 percent of the market value of all equities.[44] Kohlberg Kravis Roberts (KKR) set a record for a single transaction in 1985 when it bought Beatrice, a big but not very profitable consumer-products conglomerate, for $6.2 billion, and then it eclipsed that feat by taking RJR Nabsico private for a cool $25 billion in December 1988. Most of KKR's buyout partners were large pension funds. But in a growing number of smaller transactions, Employee Stock Ownership Plans (ESOPs), which enjoy favorable treatment under the federal tax laws, were the buyers.[45]

The final scenario is the leveraged recapitalization or "recap."[46] There managers—either preemptively or more often in response to a challenge—preclude a takeover by bestowing a windfall on the shareholders, usually a large, special dividend, that is more or less equivalent to what they would have realized by selling their shares outright. This is done—as I've already explained in the saga of Phillips Petroleum—by borrowing and/or selling off assets to retire the equity, the common and preferred stock, at prices substantially above the market.

In principle, leveraged recaps simultaneously satisfy several competing interests. Shareholders, in the case of challenges, come away with about what raiders would have paid them, since the management insiders can't satisfy them with less. And they have the option of continuing as investors in the recapitalized company, receiving new stock certificates called "stubs." There are even greater advantages for the managers. First, if the recap is a preemptive action, the insiders aren't obliged to meet competing offers from outsiders. Second, the managers retain control, which they would have lost in the event of a hostile takeover, without having to make the large personal investments that are required in leveraged buyouts. In fact, corporate officers in many leveraged recaps are given equity stakes. Third, by taking the recap rather than the leveraged-buyout route, insiders avoid shareholder charges of deliberate deception and self-dealing.

Among the largest leveraged recaps was the Allegis Corporation—the parent entity of United Airlines, Hertz car rental, and major hotel chains, none of which were very profitable. In May 1987, rather than be taken over by Coniston Partners, Allegis took on $3 billion of debt so that it could make a per share payment of $60 in cash to its shareholders. It then sold off assets to retire debt. At about the same time Harcourt Brace Jovanovich—a major book publisher, a theme-park operator, and an insurer—went the same route after a highly publicized takeover attempt by Robert Maxwell, the British publisher, who in the following year staged a successful raid on Macmillan. Harcourt chief William Jovanovich's loudly voiced attacks on Maxwell were more becoming to a nineteenth-century proprietor than to a contemporary corporate executive charged by law with protecting the interests of the outside shareholders. But after a flurry of litigation, he was compelled to go the debt-and-divestiture route. The cash paid the shareholders brought them that much closer to what they would have realized in capital gains and dividends from a well-managed, value-maximizing company, and Jovanovich was hurt only by having to adjust a very large ego to a considerably shrunken empire. He retired as CEO to become chairman of Harcourt in December 1988.

What is significant is that once recapitalized, the stock or stubs of such companies tend to outperform the broad stock-market averages.

Before turning to other matters, let's look briefly at the dimensions and immediate consequences of this wave of makeovers—takeovers, buyouts, and recapitalizations. There are two ways of measuring such activity, (1) the number of completed deals and (2) their dollar value. To be meaningful both measures must be expressed in relative terms: the number of makeovers per 10,000 companies and their dollar value as a percentage of the total market value of the outstanding common and preferred shares of all publicly traded companies.[47] The number of transactions in 1988 ran at around 9 per 10,000 companies, down from a 1969 peak rate of 25. But the dollar value of activity moved to new high ground, surging to a peak of $268.3 billion in 1988, a total equal to nearly 9.3 percent of the market value of all publicly traded companies.[48] If that pace is sustained, much of the corporate sector will be affected.

Michael C. Jensen estimates that for the decade ending in late 1987, "the functioning of the market for corporate control" benefited shareholders by $400 billion, or 51 percent of the cash dividends paid. In addition to premiums paid over the pre-makeover announcement prices of shares, a comprehensive total would include the boosting of share prices by threatened takeovers, leveraged recaps, and the effective efforts by threatened managers to improve earnings. It's likely that more than $120 billion of net makeover benefits were realized in 1988.[49]

In accounting for benefits to investors, the losses suffered by bondholders must be deducted from the gains enjoyed by shareholders. Because of the large issues of new debt created to finance buyouts and recaps, the prices of outstanding corporate bonds are depressed. RJR Nabisco's investment-grade bonds fell sharply on management's announcement of the leveraged buyout, a development that elicited legal action by institutional purchasers who claimed that they had been duped at the time of purchase. And while the bondholders' losses are small in relation to the shareholders' gains, they can't be ignored.

As the number and size of hostile takeovers and leveraged buyouts increased, so too did the intemperance of the attacks. In 1985, Felix Rohatyn observed darkly that "the takeover game as it is practiced today is a little like the arms race. You have to stop it before its gets out of control." Lane Kirkland, president of the AFL-CIO, roared that it is "an outrage and a bloody scandal." William Proxmire, then a U.S. Senator from Wisconsin, intoned that "the rising tide of hostile takeovers threatens the foundation of the American business system." And an indignant Martin Lipton, smarting from his defeat in the Revlon–Pantry Pride fight, wrote a luridly entitled memorandum to his clients, "Rape and Pillage in the Corporate Takeover Jungle." He told them that "this year has witnessed the demise of the few remaining restraints on corporate raiders. They have been let loose to take over and bust up American corporations at will."[50]

Unable to garner support for antitakeover legislation in either house of Congress, the corporate establishment took the regulatory route and in late 1985 persuaded Paul A. Volcker, then head of the Federal Reserve System—known as the Fed—to support a restriction on junk-bond financing under Regulation G, its authority to impose margin requirements, the proportion of cash that an investor has to put up for the purchase of a security.[51] What the Federal Reserve Board did, in a 4–3 vote, was to decree that the junk bonds issued by a "shell corporation"—an entity with no business operations, no cash flow, and no purposes other than acquisition—are "indirectly secured" by the stock of the targeted company and therefore subject to credit margin requirements. So under Reg G, junk bonds issued by shell corporations cannot exceed 50 percent of the purchase price in a hostile takeover; the balance must be paid in cash.

In addition to the tortured logic of decreeing junk bonds to be secured by stocks rather than a company's assets and cash flow, the Fed's fastening on shell corporations made no financial sense. Why are consortiums of wealthy individuals and financial institutions that engage in highly leveraged takeovers less creditworthy than operating companies?

The Fed's action—the ostensible purpose of which was to damp what was said to be, but in fact was not, an excessively rapid growth of corporate debt—was solidly supported by the AFL-CIO, the National Association of Manufacturers, the Business Roundtable, a lobby of chief executives of the two hundred largest corporations, and, among the securities houses, Salomon and Shearson Lehman. Opponents, in addition to Drexel Burnham and raiders such as Pickens, included Merrill Lynch and Prudential Bache. As it turned out, the Fed's move proved innocuous, and 1986 was a banner year for hostile takeovers and leveraged buyouts. Raiders simply avoided the use of shells, and even if they hadn't, Reg G could have been circumvented by issuing preferred stock—in the eyes of the law, equity—instead of junk bonds. Koppers invoked Reg G as part of its unsuccessful effort to fend off a hostile takeover by Beazer.[52]

In addition to adopting poison pills, defenders of the managerial status quo were also successful in rallying the support of state legislators with the save-our-way-of-life argument against changes of corporate control. In April 1987, the Supreme Court in *CTS Corp.* v. *Dynamics Corp.* upheld the constitutionality of a crudely protectionist Indiana law that prevents out-of-state bidders from acquiring locally chartered companies. In the absence of federal legislation, the Court did not preempt Indiana by invoking the clause of the Constitution (Article I, section VIII) that empowers Congress to regulate interstate commerce. Twenty-nine states now have antitakeover laws, the most important of which is that of Delaware, where more than half of the five hundred largest U.S. corporations are chartered. Passed in February l988 and based on a New York State law enacted in 1985 at the behest of CBS in its struggle against Ted Turner, the Delaware statute, if upheld by the courts, could greatly impede hostile takeovers.[53] Under its provisions, a raider must wait three years before voting 15 percent of a company's stock to effect a hostile takeover unless: (1) all the stock is acquired in the same transaction that pushed the raider's holdings over 15 percent, a restriction that practically precludes purchases on the open market; or (2) the raider buys at least 85 percent of the target's stock and wins the approval of the majority of the "non-interested" shareholders—the remaining 15 percent of the shares, less those held by managers and ESOPs—a provision well crafted to encourage holdouts.

Boards of Delaware corporations could have opted out of the statute within ninety days of its effective date, a provision that addressed the concerns of critics who pointed out that similiar restrictions significantly depressed the stock prices of New York and New Jersey companies. But few did. A vast majority chose to entrench themselves at the cost of lower share prices and thus losses of shareholders' wealth.[54]

Even before the enactment of antitakeover laws, the courts' adherence to the business-judgment rule clothes directors with an immunity so broad as to encourage the abuse of the shareholders' interests. In 1977, the board of directors of Marshall Field & Company, when threatened with a takeover by Carter Hawley Hale, another department store chain, pursued a defensive strategy that was never disclosed to the shareholders. Cash reserves were depleted, and stores, acknowledged by internal memoranda to be "dogs," were deliberately acquired so as to diminish Marshall Field's value as a takeover target. At the same time, false statements about Marshall Field's earnings were made. Shareholders, believing that management had violated its fiduciary obligations, attempted to bypass the obstacle of the business-judgment rule by filing a suit in the Northern District of Illinois, where they charged breaches of federal securities laws. The court peremptorily ruled that none of the alleged abuses came under federal law and that under Delaware's business-judgment rule the board was immune from liability. On appeal, the U.S. Court of Appeals not only affirmed the lower court but went on to rule that even if it could be demonstrated that the directors had deliberately reduced the value of Marshall Field to maintain their control, the shareholders still could not prevail under Delaware law. In a partial dissent, Judge John Cudahy aptly remarked that the decision provided directors with "an almost irrebuttable presumption of sound business judgment, prevailing over everything but the elusive hobgoblins of fraud, bad faith or abuse of discretion." And he added that "unfortunately, the majority here has moved one giant step closer to shredding whatever constraints still remain on the ability of corporate directors to place self-interest above shareholder interest."[55]

Directors' self-interest was also placed above shareholders' interests in the landmark 1985 Delaware case, *Moran* v. *Household Intl., Inc.*[56] which upheld the legality of poison pills. That decision limited the rights of Household's shareholders in a very fundamental way: it said, in effect, that the directors could prevent the outside shareholders from selling control of the company without their approval unless the premium over the market value of the stock that the raider paid was roughly equivalent to the cost of acquisition that would have resulted from the activation of the poison pill—about $6 billion, or what would have amounted to more than a tripling of Household's share price at the time the pill provisions were adopted. All of that in the name of the business-judgment rule!

Two more recent cases of directorial abuse come to mind.

In the early summer of 1987 it was painfully apparent that the once highly profitable Salomon Brothers had fallen on hard times. The sharp rise of interest rates in the spring of that year inflicted large losses on the major securities traders. And Salomon—which (astonishingly, for a company with seventy-eight hundred employees) had no formal budgeting system—could not control the costs of its recklessly ambitious overseas expansion. With its stock trading in the low 30s during September, down from the 50s in 1986, Salomon was viewed as a takeover target despite disagreement about whether a successful raider could retain the staff talent on which a securities business is dependent.

Matters came to a head when Harry Oppenheimer, the South African mining magnate, put his 21.3 million shares of Salomon stock, 14 percent of the total outstanding, up for sale. Ronald Perelman, Revlon's raiding chairman, offered to buy it for $38 a share, $6 or nearly 19 percent above the market. But the last thing that Salomon's chairman—John Gutfreund, a not very endearing man—wanted was a raider as major shareholder, particularly in light of reports that Perelman planned to bring in Bruce Wasserstein, then the mergers-and-acquisitions star of First Boston, to turn the troubled company around. In a stealthy move, Gutfreund bought the Oppenheimer block, financing the purchase through the issue of $700 million of 9 percent, cumulative preferred stock that is convertible to shares of common—the equivalent of a 12 percent stake in Salomon—to Warren Buffet of Berkshire Hathaway, an Omaha-based investment company. Of course, Gutfreund's good friend Buffet disavowed any intention of seeking control or greater influence over Salomon—a commitment that wasn't very painful in view of the $63 million of annual dividends that Berkshire Hathaway will collect, tax free.

Salomon shareholders—cheated out of the perhaps $10 per-share premium they would have realized had the company been put into play for a takeover—were furious and some twenty lawsuits were filed against the board. But I doubt that they will succeed. Meanwhile, Gutfreund's troubles multiplied. In October 1987, Salomon got caught with a commitment to underwrite a huge new issue of British Petroleum stock at a fixed price far above the precrash level. And there were a series of high-level executive defections, deep reductions in staff, closing of offices, and reorganizations that dragged on through 1988.[57]

If a prize were awarded for boundless effrontery, Texaco's board of directors would win hands down. Because of their egregious errors Texaco lost a $10 billion suit to Pennzoil for breaching its 1984 contract to buy Getty. As a result Texaco went into voluntary bankruptcy until a $3 billion settlement was reached. Yet the directors—despite fifteen shareholders' suits hanging over them—insisted on writing poison-pill provisions into the Chapter 11 reorganization plan. Their move came just when spirited bidding was beginning to raise the price of Texaco's shares.[58]

When all the costs of the great Texaco fiasco are tallied up—forgone business opportunities, the three-year depression of the price of the stock, the $3 billion settlement, legal fees, interest, and the cessation of dividends during the bankruptcy—the loss to the outside shareholders comes to more than $5 billion. And yet despite efforts by Carl Icahn and Boone Pickens to unseat them, Texaco's manager-directors remain in control. George Custer died for his bad judgment at the Little Big Horn and Friedrich von Paulus surrendered in disgrace at Stalingrad. But in corporate wars, generals are more likely to be rewarded than punished for their shortcomings.

## The Brotherhood of Felony

Notwithstanding the efforts at Marshall Field, Phillips, Unocal, Salomon, and Texaco, the deadliest blows against hostile takeovers and a legitimate market for corporate control have been struck by the arbitragers, lawyers, and investment bankers whose greed led them to violate the prohibitions against insider trading and market manipulation. What Ivan Boesky and his co-conspirators did was create a popular impression that there is something inherently crooked about efforts to change corporate control, in my view an offense far more serious than those for which they were convicted.

Trading on information available only to insiders—manager-directors, outside directors, independent lawyers, investment bankers, arbitragers, and others who do business with the corporation—is an old and still pervasive practice. The canons of nineteenth-century business morality did not bar corporate officers, often founders, from profiting by timely purchases or sales of their company's stock and passing valuable tips along to others.

But centuries before the establishment of the Securities and Exchange Commission in 1934, there was redress under common law for people who were injured by transactions in which important information was deliberately concealed or falsified. Vendors who deliberately withheld the fact of a stallion's sterility, the fissures in the foundations of a house, or the rot in the timbers of a ship were liable. So are those who misrepresent—that is, lie. In 1909 the information principle was extended to securities transactions by the U.S. Supreme Court in *Strong* v. *Repide,* a landmark insider-trading decision.[59] The defendant, Repide, was the general manager and a majority shareholder (about 75 percent) in a corporation that owned land in the Philippine Islands that had lost much of its market value because of a failure to combat guerrillas in the area. He was empowered to sell that land; and in the course of negotiating its sale to the U.S. government at a very favorable price, he employed an agent, who did not disclose the identity of his principal, to buy shares from the unwitting plaintiff, Strong, a holder of a small minority interest, for about one-tenth of their value after the government purchase. She sued, and the Court in upholding the decision to grant her relief held that the manager's concealment of his identity as the buyer of the shares was "strong evidence of fraud." The defense's argument that pending government purchases of land in the surrounding areas were subjects of common gossip and newspaper stories was rejected because only the general manager was in a position to know with certainty that the sale of the company's land would be consummated.

The reason why insider trading is a crime—according to recent court decisions[60]—is that it entails the theft or misappropriation of valuable information. Henry G. Manne, dean of the George Mason

University Law School and a long-time critic of the SEC's prohibition, would legalize what is now a crime by permitting corporate officials to appropriate and trade freely on inside or proprietary information. It would be his way of rewarding "entrepreneurship."[61] But even if corporate insiders were in any meaningful sense entrepreneurs, the difficulty with that approach is that the rewards could prove perverse and in conflict with the interests of the outsider shareholders. Should we reward the incompetent managers who are responsible for a large but as yet unannounced drop in a company's earnings by permitting them to profit by selling its stock short? And if good news is in the offing—say, the announcement of a major technological breakthrough—should managers be permitted to gain at the expense of the outside shareholders through share purchases in advance of a public announcement? I say "at the expense of the outside shareholders" because those of them who sell prematurely are deprived of the profits they would have realized. The size of their losses—or transfers of wealth from outsiders to insiders—hinges on conjectures about their behavior as investors.[62] Rewarding insiders at the expense of outsiders would, of course, be perfectly consistent with the currently degraded status of shareholders. But that's hardly a good reason for lifting the ban on insider trading.

The offenses for which Boesky and his information vendors were convicted centered on hostile takeovers. Dennis B. Levine, a young Drexel Burnham dealmaker, whose apprehension in May 1986 brought the scandal to light, traded on stolen information for his own account and also sold tips to Boesky. Boesky was engaged in risk arbitrage, trading for himself and his partners—wealthy individuals and financial institutions, among others, Drexel Burnham Lambert—in huge blocks of shares in companies targeted for takeovers on the speculation of a sharp increase in their price. His payments to Levine for the stolen information were scaled to the profits realized. Martin A. Siegel,—once Kidder, Peabody's star strategist, who with Martin Lipton fashioned Martin Marietta's Pac Man defense against Bendix—sold Boesky a tip on the outcome of that battle in the summer of 1982, just after he had lost more than $60 million on an oil takeover that fell through and narrowly averted bankruptcy.[63] During 1983, Siegel provided Boesky with information on the Diamond Shamrock's bid for Natomas oil and a most valuable tip, based on personal consultations, that Gordon Getty, unhappy with the management, wanted to sell Getty Oil, then controlled by a family trust.[64]

As the federal law enforcement agencies unraveled the conspiracies, there was little honor among the well-heeled thieves. In return for being permitted to "cop a plea," admit guilt to a lesser charge, the felons informed on their confederates. Levine fingered Boesky in return for a lighter jail sentence, and Boesky was permitted to plead guilty to the rather trivial charge of filing false documents with the SEC in consideration for a $100 million fine, paid in securities, and information leading to the indictments of Martin Siegel, Michael Milken, John A. Mulheren, Jr., a gifted arbitrager who once headed Jamie Securities, and Boyd L. Jefferies, formerly chairman of the Jefferies Group, a Los Angeles house that specializes in brokering large blocks of securities—in transactions made off the organized exchanges in what's called the "third market"—for institutional investors. Siegel, in turn, bought leniency with testimony that led to the indictments of three big-time arbitragers, Robert M. Freeman of Goldman, Sachs, Richard Wigton of Kidder, Peabody, and Timothy L. Tabor, formerly of Merrill Lynch. Jefferies became a principal witness in the government's stock manipulation cases against: the GAF Corporation, a chemical maker, and its vice chairman, James T. Sherwin; Paul A. Bilzerian, a raider who took over the Singer Company; and Salim B. Lewis, an investment banker. Finally, several of Michael Milken's closest associates at Drexel Burnham, Charles Thurnher, Cary Maultasch, Terren Peizer, and James Dahl, turned against him in order to avoid criminal prosecution.[65] Unlike most of the Mafia, denizens of the securities markets don't obey the rule of *omertà*, silence.

To recapitulate: What happened was that property, which is what insider information is, was stolen with impunity by investment bankers and lawyers who then sold and/or traded on it to make a great deal of money. Public confidence was undermined by the suspicion that the entire equities market is rigged, and investment banking got a bad name.

I stress theft of information—which is the essence of the "misappropriation" theory of insider trading that the courts tend to favor—and its use to commit fraud on the market because I want to distinguish between takeover practices that are clearly intolerable, either under common law or prevailing mores, and those that are neither black nor white but gray.

First, there is a gray area that exists because of sharp inequalities among investors that would be difficult, if not impossible, to eliminate by legislation or regulation. Large investors, wealthy individuals or institutions, can not only buy newly issued securities at lower prices than small investors, but they also have much greater access to what some might regard as inside information. When big investors put questions to company managers they get prompt and usually candid replies for fear that their dissatisfaction could result in a dumping of stocks and bonds, and hence, lower prices. Individual investors, unless sitting on enormous holdings, have no clout and are lucky if they get the time of day.

Then there is the uncertainty about the very meaning of insider trading and information. Contrary to what the uninitiated might infer from the headlined cases brought by the Justice Department, neither Congress nor the SEC has ever defined insider trading.[66] Hardly a model of legislative draftsmanship, rule 10b-5, following the reasoning of *Strong* v. *Repide,* is aimed at fraud on the market. It states that it is "unlawful for any person" to defraud in a securities transaction by making "an untrue statement of a material fact or to omit to state a material fact" as Repide did in denying Strong her profit.

But just what is a material fact? Is it confined to knowledge of an imminent acquisition or some other favorable event? If it's so broadly defined as to encompass any information that enables a trader to realize a profit on securities transactions, a specific law against insider trading could do much more harm than good. The reason is that professional portfolio managers and traders produce information that could be deemed "material" by dint of their ongoing research and securities analysis, their experience, active participation in markets, and intuitions. Amateurs seldom, if ever, produce such information. Thus, pushing the materiality line of reasoning to its logical extreme leads to bizarre indictments of people who have more information than others, information that was not stolen. Such an environment would discourage legitimate research and analysis, impairing the efficiency of security markets and injuring all investors.

Another gray area is risk arbitrage, buying up shares in expectation of their appreciation on the consummation of a change of control. Risk arbitrage would be neither so important nor so lucrative were it not for the Williams Act of 1968. That law was designed to slow takeovers by compelling raiders to disclose both their holdings and their intentions—whether or not they're seeking control—by filing a 13d report with the SEC within ten days of acquiring 5 percent or more of a company's stock. But its effect was to create new opportunities for risk arbitragers and thus speed rather than slow takeovers. What happened is that raiders, with a critical assist from arbitragers, turned both the 5 percent cutoff and the ten-day window to their advantage. By buying just under 5 percent, raiders can delay filing their 13d's until arbitragers begin accumulating the target's stock. The rise of the price attracts the attention of other sophisticated investors who hope to take a free ride,[67] and with rife rumors and a rising stock price the target company is put into play. Once the 5 percent threshold is exceeded, the predator still has ten days before he must disclose his hand.

Now you don't have to be paranoiac to suspect constant communication and cooperation, if not outright collusion, among raiders, arbs, and securities dealers in putting a company into play and greasing the skids for its takeover or buyout. Frederick Joseph, chief of Drexel Burnham, publicly disclosed a practice that neatly complemented Michael Milken's operations and subjected the firm to strong criticism. In 1984–85 top clients were sent sealed envelopes with the details of a series of Drexel Burnham's prospective tender offers. They were asked to participate in the financing of those takeovers but were warned that they shouldn't trade on the information in the envelopes.[68]

What can be inferred from Drexel Burnham's disclosure and the SEC's silence is that the dissemination of what was insider information, as opposed to trading on it, is not an offense. But the same can't be said for stock parking—placing shares with other parties to conceal their actual ownership, usually by a nominal sale with an obligation to repurchase at an agreed-upon price. The objective may be the evasion of the SEC's capital requirements for securities traders—the amount of cash or near cash they must have on hand—or more likely and importantly, the manipulation of markets, moving a share price up or down. Boyd L. Jefferies pleaded guilty to both charges in connection with Ivan Boesky's operations. By parking shares with Jefferies, and perhaps others, Boesky bolstered their price by keeping them off the market and at the same time controlled a larger block than permitted by the working capital invested in his company. Later, Princeton/Newport L.P., a small arbitrage house that did business with both Drexel Burnham and Goldman, Sachs, was indicted for criminal conspiracy to manipulate markets under the RICO Act. A substantial portion of its assets were impounded and in December 1988 the firm was liquidated when fearful investors withdrew their capital.[69] Drexel Burnham Lambert, too, might have suffered an impairment of capital and a crippling loss of business had they refused to plead guilty to six counts of felony and been indicted under RICO.

Today's spate of insider trading and share price manipulations harks back to the investors' pools and rings of colluding brokers that flourished in the first three decades of this century.[70] And the irony is that it was Congress that set an ideal stage for abuse by passing the Williams Act with its 5 percent raiders' threshold and ten-day pre-filing period. Henry Manne is right in urging the repeal of that act. But I don't agree with him that "the SEC should be stopped by Congress from its maniacal crusade against insider trading" because of "the enormous losses that more than a hundred million investors and savers will experience."[71] Zealous SEC investigators and Justice Department prosecutors—bent on making headlines as well as careers in private law practice and politics—such as Rudolph W. Giuliani, might impede a few takeovers or makeovers by captious charges and intimidation. But that's hardly a good reason for countenancing insider trading and market manipulation. Changes of corporate control are perforce marked by conflict but they need not be accompanied by fraud.

## Makeovers: Pluses and Minuses

Do corporate makeovers really enhance economic efficiency, or are they simply moves in a financial shell game that line the pockets of raiders, insiders, lawyers, and investment bankers?

To answer that question, consider the objections of an informed, eloquent critic who has no ties or allegiences to incumbent corporate management. Benjamin J. Stein is a lawyer and journalist who went before the SEC and blocked the leveraged buyout of an investment company—founded by the pioneering conglomerator, Royal Little— in which he owned shares only to be frustrated when the self-dealing managers achieved their end by a thinly disguised subterfuge. They agreed to a friendly acquisition by another company under terms which rewarded them with a $32 million consultants' fee.[72] It was, to be sure, a scandalous business, but it hardly justifies Stein's sweeping attack: "Wall Street and the leveraged buyout phenomenon are turning American industry into a vast junkyard of corporate spare parts, and this is hardly what we need to compete in the world market."[73]

That "junkyard" line is one of which a wordsmith alumnus of Richard Nixon's White House can be proud; yet Stein's statement is no more valid than the more pedestrian fulminations of a Drucker or a Rohatyn. The image of divested businesses as dead businesses, analogous to auto engines lying on the ground in a junkyard, is mischievously misleading. Except for mature or declining industries from which companies were routinely withdrawing long before the advent of hostile takeovers or buyouts, plants and equipment are not idled or scrapped in corporate makeovers. As a legal entity, the Electric Storage Battery Company, along with its Willard and Exide brands, vanished. But its plants are still operating around the world under other corporate names. Most recent divestitures—those by

Revlon, Mobil, and Exxon—were essentially damage control moves to stanch losses and get out of businesses acquired in misguided programs of diversification. The fact that the properties were sold to operating companies indicates that they didn't wind up in junkyards.

The point that most critics of makeovers ignore is that efficiency and profitability are increased through divestitures and the restructuring of companies that are too big—of greater than optimal size. Similarly, the research that they cite fails to distinguish between mergers, combinations which make big companies bigger and less efficient, and breakups and restructurings which make them more efficient and more profitable.[74]

Ennius Bergsma, who heads McKinsey & Company's practice in corporate finance, observes:

We may be getting close to the point where just the cost of being a large diversified enterprise is starting to outweigh the benefits of scale and synergy. If you were to look at headquarters as if it were a portfolio manager, you would relate its costs to the market value of the equity that it oversees. McKinsey did that for the Fortune 25 using the "unallocated costs" in the companies' 10Ks. Those pre-tax expenses on average represented almost 2% of the market equity value. (This doesn't even include a number of related allocated costs—for meeting reports, etc.)

For the major mutual equity funds, the management fee is on average 0.7% of net assets, the market value of portfolio investments. In other words, the corporate center at a minimum of 2% is at least three times as expensive. In reality it's probably six times as much.

Divestitures and restructurings can narrow not only the headquarters cost gap but others—not so easily identified—in production, purchasing, and marketing. Bergsma concludes that "contrary to popular belief—that restructuring is merely paper shuffling and financial legerdermain—our analyses show that more than 80% of the gain from restructurings is generally attributable to improved performance, i.e., to better-managed companies with less overhead and more efficient asset use."[75]

Bergsma's findings are buttressed by the far more comprehensive research of Frank R. Lichtenberg of Columbia University's Graduate School of Business. Lichtenberg and an associate used Census Bureau data to measure the total factor productivity (TFP) of more than eighteen thousand relatively large U.S. manufacturing plants between 1973 and 1984. Productivity is output per unit of input. For an auto assembly plant, the output is the number of cars or trucks that come off the line, and the total inputs are composite units of labor hours, materials, and invested capital—which is why it's called TFP. The higher the productivity—which is the ratio of outputs to total inputs—the more efficient the plant.

Now to the nub of the research. Some thirty-four hundred—or about 19 percent—of those plants changed ownership at least once during the eleven-year period. So there was an objective basis for measuring the impact of ownership changes on manufacturing efficiency. What Lichtenberg found was first, that the least productive plants in an industry were those most likely to change hands—exactly what we would expect. Second, and more importantly, he found that on the average the productivity of those plants that changed hands between 1974 and 1980 grew significantly faster than those that didn't. Lichtenberg is careful to point out that bad matches between plants and new owners can depress rather accelerate the growth of productivity. But his finding of a positive relationship between ownership change and the growth of productivity surely flies in the face of critics who contend that takeovers are destroying American industry.[76]

Also without substance is the charge that takeovers and restructurings are somehow responsible for the decline of America's international competitiveness. There's no credible evidence that reorganized companies are sacrificing long-term growth to short-term profits or that research and development have suffered as a result of takeovers. Since U.S. shares of overseas markets began shrinking long before 1975 (I'll buttress that assertion in the next chapter) it's fair to ask why the ousting of managers who presided over that decline and/or the restructuring of their companies poses a threat to our economic viability. Logic points to the opposite conclusion, that shaking out complacent managers and restructuring inefficient companies enhance the U.S. position in the world arena.

But what assurances are there that the new managers will be less complacent than those they replace? None, but as I've already explained, the heavy debt incurred in the financing of many makeovers subjects managers to a salutary discipline that is absent in companies that are largely financed by equity capital.

But what of those dire warnings about "the mortgaging of corporate America"? Is corporate solvency threatened by a plethora of debt? I think not.

One of the points on which most students of corporate finance agree is that it makes little difference over the long haul whether a company is financed by equity or debenture capital, by issuing common stock or bonds. In either case the cost of capital—what the corporation really pays for it—tends to be the same. Investors buy common stocks with the expectation of a certain rate of return—a combination of dividends and capital appreciation. If they are disappointed, they'll switch to bonds, and it's such switching back and forth—what securities analysts call portfolio adjustments—that tends to equalize the returns, corrected for risk, between equities and debentures.

There's an impression that start-up companies in exciting, high-technology fields, such as genetic engineering, the new ceramics, and superconductivity, have access to free equity capital. But that's an illusion. Venture capital funds that finance most startups are experienced and carefully calculate their risks. Their holdings of both equity and debentures are sufficiently large for them to exercise control, so that they can shut a new venture down if there are no reasonable prospects of a marketable breakthrough in technology or merge it even though it's successful. For typical high-tech entrepreneurs, the humiliating loss of control over their brainchildren—to which may be added the insult of being sacked—is a terrible price to pay for equity capital.

There was a time when the antipathy toward corporate debt made better sense than it does today. Under the rules of the gold standard, in force from the early 1870s until the Great Depression of the 1930s, monetary authorities in the industrial countries deflated—they shrank the stock of paper money and thus restricted the availability of credit—whenever a fixed convertibility between their currencies and gold was threatened. Such restrictions were usually triggered when gold flowed out of a country in anticipation of a currency's depreciation—a fall in its value in relation to other currencies. In times of monetary restraint, businesses and individuals with heavy burdens of debt got wiped out as interest rates soared and the difficulties of refinancing, rolling over old debt by new borrowing, increased. The great American economist Irving Fisher—who was all but bankrupted as a result of stock speculations and the 1929 crash—captured the dynamics of the process in his "debt-deflation" theory of the business cycle. Heavy debt and efforts to retire it in the face of a sharply falling stock of money made deep depressions inevitable.[77]

Fisher's general proposition is still valid, as farmers in the Midwest and oil drillers in the Southwest are painfully aware. If you're heavily in debt, you get into deep trouble when the price of your product—and hence, your income—falls much faster and farther than your interest costs. But what greatly troubled Fisher, and properly so, was *deflation:* the drastic shrinkage of the money supply that caused the *price level,* the average of *all* prices, to plummet and the real output of goods and services to drop by more than 30 percent from the 1929 peak to the nadir of the Depression in 1933. A deflation hasn't recurred since the 1930s, nor is it likely to. The reason is that under the post-Depression fiat or paper money standard, currencies are no longer convertible to gold or any other commodity; and so the once deliberate *shrinkage* of money supplies by governments is now unnecessary. Today governments slow money growth only in order to check inflation. That's why individual commodity prices—oil or copper or wheat—may plummet, but *not* the *price level.* And it's also why we've suffered brief recessions of output and employment since the 1930s, but not a deep and prolonged depression with more than a quarter of the labor force unemployed.

Federal Reserve policy is the reason why Black Thursday, October

24, 1929, was the first act of a tragedy while Black Monday, October 19, 1987—frightening to be sure—was an endurably painful blow. After the 1929 crash, the Fed pursued deflationary policies under which the money supply fell more than 30 percent by 1933. In 1987, by contrast, the Fed and other central banks around the world, flooded the financial markets with liquidity, and we've yet to see signs of recession, let alone a depression.

Can it happen again? In theory, a deep depression and deflation could be precipitated by the widespread hoarding of cash—the refusal of households and businesses to spend—a drop in the turnover or "velocity" of money, which would be tantamount to a sharp reduction of its supply. But I find it difficult to imagine what would trigger such a scenario, especially in light of the inflation that has plagued the world under the fiat money standard. If you believe that the purchasing power of money is about to be eroded by a burst of rising prices, the last thing you would want to do is hoard it. Hoarding makes sense only if you believe that prices will plummet, thus enhancing the purchasing power of money.

I cite these changes in the monetary order so as to place the corporate debt question in perspective. Bankruptcy will be both a danger and a problem so long as fallible people conduct autonomous business enterprises in unfettered markets. But governments no longer induce *epidemic bankruptcy*—which differs from individual bankruptcy in much the same way that a fall of the price level differs from the fall of some commodity prices—either by acts of omission or by acts of commission. If anything, they are overly anxious about preventing them, Chrysler and Continental Illinois being cases in point. In light of that, the preoccupation with corporate debt is often misplaced. What is important (as mortgage lenders, commercial banks, and junk-bond investors know well)—is not the ratio of debt to net worth, which may look high, but whether future cash flow will be sufficient to cover the service charges. So long as governments avoid actions that depress levels of income and, hence, cash flow, the likelihood of a debt-default panic—the specter of which still haunts the financial markets—is remote.[78]

One of my reasons for optimism on that score is the development of what is known as strip financing. It is a deal in which different securities of the same company—common shares, preferred shares, convertible shares, and various debentures—are, in effect, stapled together so that an investor who buys, say, 0.5 percent of one type has to buy 0.5 percent of all types. Each strip of securities specifies a holder's rights in the event of default on dividend or interest payments—such as the right to take the company into bankruptcy or to gain board representation. And if the senior securities in the strip —preferred stock, notes, and bonds—go into default, stripholders are granted new rights to intercede in the company's affairs. By eliminating conflicts among investors that surface in the bankruptcies of conventionally financed corporations—for example, disputes as to which bondholders have first claim on the assets—the reorganization of strip-financed companies should be accomplished quickly and cheaply.[79]

There is a preponderance of winners over losers—benefits over losses, however they are reckoned—in this current wave of changes of corporate control. Among the big losers are manager-directors who either are displaced by hostile takeovers or can't participate in buyouts. Yet with golden parachutes and big retirement benefits, they are more likely to suffer losses of status than income. But the same can't be said of ordinary workers, especially those who are too young to retire and cushioned only by unemployment benefits. Although it's hardly any consolation, many of those same jobs would eventually be lost, even in the absence of takeovers, because of the backwash of the long wave of inflation-disinflation and the intensification of international competition.

Shareholders of target companies—especially the 60 million members of pension plans, who often don't realize that they own corporate stocks and bonds—were the big winners—by hundreds of billions— because of takeover premiums paid over the market prices of shares and the large cash payouts in recapitalizations. But holders of what were once deemed high-grade corporate bonds have suffered losses. And gains to the shareholders of raiding companies were very much smaller than those realized by the shareholders of the targets. Finally, the profits and fees of raiders, arbitragers, lawyers, investment bankers, and others were enormous—some would say obscene—even if not in relation to the size of the transactions or the gains realized by outside shareholders.

I don't want to leave the impression that I'm enamored of everything about the corporate makeover, or that it's a panacea for all of our economic problems. If the Bendix–Martin Marietta Pac Man farce had any redeeming virtues, they continue to elude me. Kodak's very pricey—$5.1 billion—takeover of Sterling Drug and Philip Morris's $13 billion takeover of Kraft are open to the same objections that I've lodged against efforts by Sears, Roebuck, General Motors, and the major oil companies to solve their free-cash-flow problems by diversification. They don't work.

It's important—although quantitatively difficult—to draw a distinction between "bust up" takeovers and buyouts—such as Pantry Pride–Revlon, Beatrice, and RJR Nabisco—and ordinary mergers. Bust-ups, many of which reflected the need to shrink conglomerates, result in smaller and more efficient organizations. General Electric's acquisitions of RCA and Kidder, Peabody, by contrast, were moves in the wrong, conglomerate direction that will one day be reversed.[80]

Changes of control—sharp blows, or threatened blows, aimed from outside of complacent organizations—are essential to revitalizing U.S. industry and resolving the conflicts of managerial control. But they alone are not sufficient. Makeovers are expensive, painful, and sometimes wasteful. That's why I turn to internally imposed reforms in the next chapter.

# 4

# WORKERS AND SHIRKERS:

## Corporate Salvation by Carrots and Sticks

It was 1959. At ease in the White House, General Eisenhower inspired national confidence without once rambling about "America standing tall" or for that matter saying much of anything at all. The United States ran a large trade and current account *surplus* with Japan; and *The Wall Street Journal,* bemoaning our ally's chronically weak trade performance, said that Toyota's decision to increase its exports of "Toyopets" beyond seven hundred was "a big gamble." Sunny, seven-room apartments on Manhattan's begrimed Upper West Side rented for less than $250 a month. And a brilliantly satirical British film delighted audiences in art-film houses.

*I'm All Right, Jack*—a prefatory obscenity was omitted from the title in those more demure times—starred Peter Sellers and Ian Carmichael and took on what until then were sacred cows, British trades unions and their managerial adversaries. Carmichael, a young army veteran, seeks a career in industry and soon becomes an unwitting foil in a conspiracy between his manufacturer uncle (Richard Attenborough) and the owner of a competing company (Dennis Price). The two colluding businessmen reason that the conscientious Carmichael, still imbued with the work ethic, will touch off a strike in Price's plant if he's employed there. With Price's plant shut down, Attenborough would fill its customers' orders at highly inflated prices, and the two conspirators would then split the spoils. Carmichael, as anticipated, quickly discovers ways of enhancing the productivity of Price's plant—such obvious moves as altering delivery schedules so that workers can't take a tea break every other hour. He infuriates the shop steward, Peter Sellers—as pompous a Labourite as ever wiped a lathe—who calls a strike. But the owners' conspiracy goes awry when the workers in Attenborough's plant walk out in sympathy with Sellers's men, and the strike then spreads to the transport unions, bringing all British business to a slow crawl. Carmichael, interviewed with Sellers on a national TV news program, assails both labor and management for their "I'm all right, Jack" readiness to put the needs of the moment before their own longer-term interests, to say nothing of those of society. But after hysterically ranting and being hauled away by the police, Carmichael concludes that he isn't the man to undo a hundred years of hostility on Britain's industrial scene. He decides to chuck it all and live with his father in a nudist camp.

My recollection of my reaction to the film—and that of academic and journalist friends who, like me, fought in the Second World War—is more vivid than my memory of its plot. It was, in effect: Poor, decadent Britain. Aren't we fortunate, after our stormy demobilization, which was over by 1948—a time of meat and other shortages, escalating prices, and strikes—to be free of such debilitating conflicts. But by the early 1960s such condescending complacency was no longer justified. Large outflows of capital—as a result of defense spending and corporate decisions to buy or build overseas plants—resulted in a deficit on account of our overall balance of international payments. Well before our massive involvement in the Vietnam War, those deficits and the weakening of the dollar—which alone among the world's currencies could be used by other governments or their central banks to purchase gold from the U.S. hoard at only $35 an ounce—were the cause of great anxiety in Washington.[1]

In the years following the Kennedy administration, the anxiety over the strength of the dollar in world markets—then viewed as a "financial" problem—became fear about the declining competitiveness of almost all U.S. manufacturing and service industries as reflected by their loss of world market shares. That problem, fitfully addressed in the 1988 presidential campaign, is not easily defined let alone resolved.

The first question to be faced in this era of multinational corporations is whose market shares are declining, those of the United States as a nation state or those of our corporations which operate in many countries? Our nation-state record—which is important if you're grappling with the politically charged issue of domestic employment—looks dismal. The U.S. share of worldwide manufactured exports declined from 21.3 percent in 1957 to a low of 13.3 percent in 1977. Since then there has been what two perceptive international economists, Robert E. Lipsey and Irving B. Kravis, describe as a slight or temporary reversal of that downward trend, with the U.S. share of the world market running at around 14 percent. But when we turn to U.S. multinationals—both parent companies and majority owned foreign affiliates (MOFAs)—there's no sign of a decline. Together parents and MOFAs accounted for 17.7 percent of worldwide exports of manufactures in 1966 and for 18.1 percent in 1984. What this—and other evidence adduced by Lipsey and Kravis—suggests is that American technology and overseas management remained competitive but that our country didn't, largely because of higher costs and our managers' reluctance to trim export prices in the face of growing competition.[2]

America's power—its ability to shape world events to its liking—has diminished since the 1940s and 1950s. But how do we distinguish between a relative decline that results from the deployment of bigger military forces by more countries, all fiercely asserting their sovereignty, and impotence stemming from the dispiriting indolence that afflicts rich and powerful countries? It's the latter that concerns those who see America slipping down the slope of degradation.

But history is full of surprises. Seemingly immutable forces and trends are ficklely reversed. After General Burgoyne's surrender to the colonists at Saratoga in 1777, John Sinclair lamented to his friend Adam Smith Britain's misfortunes in the American war, exclaiming: "If we go on at this rate, the nation *must be ruined*." Smith calmly replied: "Be assured, my young friend, that there is a great deal of *ruin* in a nation."[3] Britain's military and economic power continued to soar for nearly one hundred years after the defeat at Saratoga. Once the challenge of Napoleon was overcome, the Empire occupied a position of global supremacy until about 1870, when its power began to be eclipsed by the shifting balance of forces.[4]

Although it's fascinating—and relevant to the future of the American corporation—geopolitical prognostication isn't my strong suit. The only proposition that I wish to advance here is that as a consequence of America's postwar preeminence—the world's largest, unscathed economy from the mid-1940s to the later 1950s—our corporations are now less efficient and thus competitively weaker than they might otherwise be.

## A Debilitating Dominance: The Postwar Story

In 1950, output in the United States—our gross national product (GNP), achieved with slightly more than 6 percent of the world's population—accounted for about 45 percent of the global output of goods and services, or what's called the world gross product (WGP). Today, nearly forty-five years after the devastation of the Second World War and decades of rapid economic growth in less developed countries, our GNP is running at 22–24 percent of the WGP and our population now accounts for less than 5 percent of the world total. Clearly the United States was economically dominant in the early postwar years—in 1945 it doubtless accounted for more than half of the WGP—but in order to gain a better understanding of the postwar predicament and what's happened since, let's turn to a group of industrialized countries.

This table compares levels of economic well-being in the United States with those of eight other industrial countries over thirty-five years—beginning in 1950, the earliest year for which comparable postwar data are available. The measure of economic welfare is real output or GNP per head: the U.S. dollar value of all the goods and services produced by a country, divided by its population and adjusted, first to eliminate the effects of inflation between 1950 and 1984 and then for differences in the purchasing power of the dollar and other currencies. To be specific, U.S. output per head in 1984

## LEVELS OF REAL OUTPUT PER HEAD,
### 1950 AND 1984[5]

| | PERCENTAGE OF U.S. | | ANNUAL GROWTH RATES |
| | 1950 | 1984 | 1950–84 |
| --- | --- | --- | --- |
| *United States* | 100.0 | 100.0 | 1.91 |
| *West Germany* | 37.6 | 88.9 | 4.19 |
| *Denmark* | 55.9 | 89.4 | 2.65 |
| *Belgium* | 54.0 | 81.2 | 2.72 |
| *Netherlands* | 45.1 | 75.8 | 2.62 |
| *France* | 47.5 | 83.2 | 3.33 |
| *Italy* | 23.9 | 66.2 | 3.75 |
| *United Kingdom* | 57.4 | 73.4 | 1.94 |
| *Japan* | 17.1 | 76.3 | 5.73 |

was $15,275, and in Japan—after taking account of the difference in the purchasing power of the dollar and the yen[6]—it was $11,652 or 76.3 percent of the U.S. level.

The percentages in the first two columns show the gap between the level of real U.S. output per head and those of the other countries. At the end of 1950, five years after the end of hostilities, Japan's output, at only 17.1 percent of the U.S. level, was by far the lowest among the industrial nations—less than a third of the United Kingdom's. But by 1984 it surpassed the United Kingdom's. In narrowing the gap between it and the United States' by 59.2 percentage points, Japanese output per capita grew at an average annual rate of 5.73 percent, much faster than any of the other industrial countries.

If data were available for 1945—or other years in the 1940s—they would show lower levels of output, especially for Germany and Japan, which were dealt devastating blows. By 1950—with cold-war antipathy between the communist and anticommunist blocs growing—the recovery in Europe and Japan was accelerated by the Marshall Plan, a program under which the United States made large grants of economic assistance, all sorts of industrial goods and services that would amount to some $60 billion at todays's prices. In addition to the Marshall Plan, there were other important spurs to the recovery of West Germany and Japan. The treaties that ended the states of war and their new constitutions relieved them of the burdens of large defense establishments.

Further, under the Bretton Woods international monetary arrangements (1944), the deutsche mark and the yen were deliberately undervalued in setting their fixed exchange rates against the U.S. dollar. $100 worth of deutsche marks (DMs) bought more real goods and services in West Germany than $100 did in the United States. With an undervalued DM, West Germany, once it recovered its capacity to export by the late 1950s, had a competitive edge against the United States with its conversely overvalued dollar. Japan began to realize the advantage of an undervalued yen somewhat later. (See note 6.)

Cold-war tensions gave rise to a most significant economic change in the United States. For the first time in the country's history a large military establishment was maintained in the absence of a declared war or national emergency. Since the end of the Second World War our armed forces have on the average numbered more than two million, not a very heavy burden for a country whose labor force has more than doubled since 1945. But defense expenditures do weigh heavily. Since 1940, total defense spending dipped below 5 percent of the GNP only once—in 1950, the year in which the Korean War began and precipitated a major buildup of armaments. In 1987, defense outlays were $380.6 billion, 6.6 percent of the GNP.[7]

Leftists sometimes contend—advancing what's called the permanent war economy thesis—that massive military spending is necessary for the maintenance of high employment in a market-oriented economy.[8] Postwar experience in Japan and West Germany contradicts that dogma. But the same can't be said of the converse argument—that a large military establishment undermines the efficiency of a market economy.

The defense establishment—contracting, production, research, and the deployment of forces—falls under the rubric of barracks socialism. Members of the armed services, in their sheltered, bureaucratic world of entitlements, subsidized commissary stores, and scheduled promotions, face few of the economic risks borne by civilians. Defense contractors are also spared the vagaries of open competition—although as the 1988 procurement scandals demonstrate, they will steal, bribe, and rig bids in pursuit of bigger slices of the Pentagon melon—and are hardly private enterprises in any meaningful sense. Rather, they are captive entities, tightly controlled by regulations governing their costs and profits, protected from competition and often totally beholden to their dominant, if not single, buyer, the Defense Department. When they are bankrupt, as Lockheed was, they are not permitted to fail, and when they cheat, as General Dynamics and General Electric did, they are more likely to be admonished and fined than punished by a significant loss of business.

Because of the huge defense establishment, an important segment of our high-technology industry—aircraft and electronics as well as research and development—is exempted from the need to achieve maximum operating efficiency or compete vigorously in the marketplace. Companies that can rely on a virtually certain cushion of Pentagon orders aren't going to try as hard as those that must sell in open markets. Nor is the damage confined to the defense sector per se. Other producers suffer because of the insurmountable advantages of defense contractors in attracting and retaining the services of scientists and technicians, many of whom would be more productively employed in other pursuits. Seymour Melman, a long-time analyst of the arms race, estimates that the number of scientists and engineers engaged in U.S. civilian production during 1977 was only 38 per 10,000 in the labor force as against 40 in West Germany and 60 in Japan.[9] Finally, there's a political ambience—congressional log rolling in choices of weapons and contract awards by states, funding rivalry among the armed services and ubiquitous conflicts of interest—that's at war with economic rationality or efficiency. In one of his few eminently memorable utterances, President Eisenhower warned in his farewell address that: "This conjunction of an immense military establishment and a large arms industry is new in the American experience. . . . In the councils of government, we must guard against the acquisition of unwarranted influence, whether sought or unsought, by the military-industrial complex. The potential for the disastrous rise of misplaced power exists and will persist."[10]

In the period of America's postwar economic dominance, the failure of managers to maximize present values of their companies posed no real threat. With the rest of the world in shambles, all that was required for the success of U.S. corporations was a stable, optimistic environment. Once the most daunting of postwar fears were dispelled, confidence in the strength of the U.S. economy—and especially its corporate sector—reached a level not attained since the early 1920s. It was clear by mid-1946 that neither the demobilization of the armed forces, the sharp contraction of defense spending, nor the reconversion of industry to civilian production was going to plunge the country into another 1930s-style slump. The widely feared "postwar depression" didn't happen because there was an enormous backlog of unsatisfied consumer demand that was financed out of forced savings—the abundance of cash, war bonds, and other less liquid assets accumulated during the war. Confidence was also enhanced by a framework for labor-management peace that was established by a series of precedent-setting agreements between Walter P. Reuther of the United Automobile Workers and General Motors. In addition to generous hourly wage hikes, they provided for costly retirement, health, and unemployment benefits. General Motors, with more than half the auto market, became synonymous with corporate stability and responsibility. Its reputation was epitomized in a celebrated remark by its former president, Charles Erwin Wilson, called "Engine Charley" to distinguish him from the other Charles E. Wilson ("Electric") who then presided over General Electric. During Senate hearings on his nomination as secretary of defense in 1953, Engine Charley was asked if he could make a decision that was in the interests of the country as a whole but inimical to the those of General Motors' shareholders. He assured the Senators that he could but quickly added that such a conflict could never really arise. "I cannot conceive of one," he said, "because for years I

128

thought what was good for our country was good for General Motors, and vice versa. The difference did not exist."

Although there was much grumbling about the economy in the second Eisenhower administration—especially after the 1957–58 recession—the record, in retrospect, is an admirable one. Over the eight Eisenhower years, 1953 through 1960, real GNP grew at an annual average rate of 2.37 percent while inflation, measured by the broad price indices used to estimate real GNP, ran at 2.43 percent, a rate that would now be cause for great rejoicing. But there were portents of trouble. Real hourly earnings in that same period rose by an average 2.75 percent while total labor productivity—the increase of the hourly output of all people in business—grew by only 2.52 percent. With the growth of wages and salaries outstripping productivity gains by some 9 percent, unit labor costs rose at an average rate of 2 percent and exerted upward pressure on prices.[11] There was little buyer resistance to price hikes, particularly in export markets so long as the United States was the dominant world supplier. But as that dominance was eroded by the recovery and growth of other countries, competition—in prices as well as in product design and quality—intensified.

Had the United States been more open, more dependent on foreign trade, loud alarms would have sounded about a lack of competitiveness by the early 1960s. But because of a huge and growing internal market with exports comprising less than 6 percent of the GNP, the U.S. economy was relatively closed, and telltale signs of weakness drew little attention.

Steel is a significant case in point. In 1950 the United States accounted for more than half of the world's steel output; only thirty-one other countries even made steel then. Today there are nearly ninety steel-producing countries, and the U.S. share is under 10 percent.

In 1962, there was an antidumping action brought by six of the largest domestic steel companies against their competitors in the European Economic Community, or Common Market. The Antidumping Act of 1921 bars price discrimination in international trade—simultaneously selling the same product at different prices in one or more markets—a practice that is legal, commonplace, and desirable in domestic trade. Manufacturers who sell to discounters as well as retailers who charge list prices are engaging in a form of price discrimination that benefits consumers, and so too is the powdered-milk or aspirin manufacturer who packages the identical product under both high- and low-price labels.[12] But in the name of protecting American industry, a foreign producer cannot charge lower prices in the U.S. market than at home—in short, dump his output here—and domestic producers can secure relief if they can prove injurious dumping.

The 1962 antidumping complaint against Belgian and German steel producers and the accompanying union-supported lobbying campaign were orchestrated by Donald Hiss of Covington & Burling, whose law partners then included such luminaries of the Democratic Party establishment as Dean Acheson. Despite spending what was then a lot of money, Hiss failed to obtain dumping relief for his clients. Even if his brief before the Tariff Commission had been brilliant, the political scales would still have been sharply tipped against his clients. The reason was a bitter clash between the steelmakers and the White House. In April, U.S. Steel—quickly followed by other major producers—raised its prices in defiance of the Kennedy administration which, in a highly publicized effort to stanch inflation, had just coerced the United Steelworkers into lowering its wage demands. On learning of what he viewed as U.S. Steel's perfidy, Attorney General Robert Kennedy, zealous for maximum press coverage, dispatched FBI agents to rouse sleeping reporters before dawn. And when threats of an antitrust prosecution for a price-fixing conspiracy emanated from both the White House and Capitol Hill, the contrite steelmakers rescinded their price hikes.

The big steel producers—oligopolistic price setters since 1901, when J. P. Morgan Sr. rationalized the industry—who never before had faced real foreign competition, were willing to surrender the low-profit end of the U.S. market, products such as nails, light wires, and reinforcing bars, to the Europeans and Japanese but drew a battle line when it came to rolled sheets and pipes, on which profit margins were much fatter.

It might be argued that the decline of the big integrated U.S. steelmakers was inevitable, that they were overwhelmed not only by low-cost foreign competition but also by technology—the development of such non-ferrous substitutes as aluminum, prestressed concrete, fiberglass, and other plastics which steadily reduced domestic steel demand. But such apologetics ignore the effects of what can only be characterized as suicidal big steel policies. In April 1966 there was an elaborate public relations affair at Bethlehem Steel's large Sparrow's Point, Maryland, facility. The occasion was the dedication of their first basic oxygen furnaces (BOF). The BOF or Linz-Donawitz process was developed in this country and perfected in Austria before the Second World War. Yet Bethlehem's managers went on investing hundreds of millions of dollars in patently obsolete, low-productivity, open-hearth furnaces. Why? Why had it taken Bethlehem more than twenty-five years to adopt a clearly superior technology? The short-sighted answer is that there seemed to be no pressing need for the great expense of adopting the BOF technology when money could be made by continually hiking the prices of open-hearth steel. The fatal flaw of that strategy was that the higher prices increased imports of steel and accelerated the switch to substitutes.

In the early 1960s the domestic auto manufacturers were in better shape than the steelmakers. The "big three"—something of a misnomer, since General Motors then had about 50 percent of the market—at first emulated big steel in permitting Volkswagen of West Germany to take the low-profit, compact segment of the market without opposition. Volkswagen's only challenges came from American Motors' Rambler and belatedly from GM's Corvair, the car ("unsafe at any speed") that made Ralph Nader famous. What is remarkable, after twenty-five years, is that so little has changed on the auto front. To be sure, GM's U.S. market share is now down to around 36 percent, but the big three still can't or won't produce high-quality compacts. It's a case of what Thorstein Veblen called a "trained incapacity" to compete.

When the yen began its sharp rise against the dollar in early 1985, it was hoped that the domestic auto makers—protected by Japan's "voluntary" export ceilings at a cost to U.S. consumers of about $2,500 more per car than they would otherwise pay—would recapture lost shares of the domestic market by trimming their prices or at least not boosting them in the face of rising dollar prices for Japanese models. Instead, the big three hiked their prices in lockstep with their Japanese counterparts, and the result has been higher profits and bigger bonuses for managers and production workers but no increase in market share or employment.[13]

## A Disorderly Descent from Dominance

Had the debilitating effects of economic dominance been the only destructive force impinging on U.S. industry, managerial control would not have broken down, at least not so soon. The decisive blows were the Vietnam War and the great wave of inflation that began in the mid-1960s, events that destroyed the Bretton Woods monetary regime and set the stage for energy price hikes by the OPEC cartel and the ensuing economic stagnation of the 1970s and early 1980s.

The key to understanding the worldwide inflation that raged from 1965 to the early 1980s is the Bretton Woods monetary system that became operational in 1945 with the establishment of the International Monetary Fund (IMF). The IMF is a pool of gold and currencies from which countries can borrow to finance balance-of-payments deficits.[14] Under the original IMF rules, member countries expressed the par, or official, value of their currencies in U.S. dollars and gold, and they agreed to maintain fixed exchange rates through central bank pegging operations—buying their currencies on the foreign exchange markets when the rate fell below 1 percent of par and selling when it rose by more than 1 percent above it. Since the United States then owned more than 70 percent of the world's monetary gold—bullion and coin in the coffers of central banks—it alone agreed to peg its currency to gold at the rate of $35 an ounce, plus or minus one quarter of 1 percent. That meant that foreign central banks—not individuals—could convert their dollars into gold from the United States at the official price of $35 an ounce.

What evolved was a system built around the dollar. The dollar was pegged to gold, and other currencies were pegged to the dollar. By virtue of U.S. economic dominance, the dollar became the world's principal trading, or vehicle, currency—most foreign trade and investment transactions are still denominated in dollars. And because central banks could freely convert it to gold, the dollar also became, and continues to be, the world's principal reserve currency. Foreign central banks buy and sell U.S. Treasury bills and notes with dollars earned by their nationals, and they hold them as reserves, assets that can be readily cashed in to settle their balance-of-payments deficits.

Under the IMF rules, the pegs or fixings of other currencies to the dollar—the dollar–deutsche mark or dollar-sterling exchange rate—were adjustable but only in small steps that were approved through negotiations with the IMF. Currency revaluations were permissible when a country's international payments position was deemed to be in "fundamental disequilibrium." Under the adjustible peg, there was a general devaluation in 1949 to permit war-torn countries to cheapen their currencies and thereby improve their balances of payments; but aside from the sterling devaluation crisis of 1967, the exchange rates of the industrial countries remained fixed until the system fell apart in August 1971.

Because of the pivotal role of the dollar as both the vehicle and the reserve currency, the United States enjoyed enormous power under the Bretton Woods regime. But that power was not, unfortunately, accompanied by commensurate responsibility in the conduct of monetary policy. When rulers first began minting coins, they discovered that there was a profit, called seignorage, to be extracted by their treasuries, the difference between the cost of producing the gold, silver, or copper coins and the face, or nominal, value that they placed on the coins. The coins, in short, were deliberately overvalued. Under the Bretton Woods regime the United States—as the issuer of the world's reserve and vehicle currency—extracted a new sort of seignorage from the rest of the world by dint of a dollar that was overvalued so long as exchange rates remained fixed and few effective limits were placed on the expansion of its supply by the Federal Reserve System, this country's central bank. This new seignorage was a reflection of the overvaluation of the dollar in terms of its relative purchasing power.

An overvalued dollar purchased more real goods and services in other countries than it did at home, and that redounded to the benefit of the United States as the issuer of the world's reserve currency. Because of overvaluation, imports were cheap and, more importantly, U.S. multinational corporations could buy up businesses in other countries or establish new ones on the cheap, the same advantage that Japan now enjoys by virtue of its overvalued yen. The new seignorage—which annually ran to the billions between 1960 and the breakdown of the Bretton Woods system in 1971—was the difference between what Americans actually spent on imports and overseas investments and the higher dollar prices that they would have paid had our currency not been overvalued.

The dollar is overvalued against the deutsche mark if, at the prevailing exchange rate, $100 worth of deutsche marks buys a larger bundle of equivalent goods and services in West Germany than it does in the United States. It's undervalued if, at the prevailing exchange rate, $100 buys more in the United States than $100 worth of DMs buys in West Germany. Finally, the exchange rate is at its purchasing parity level—one that's consistent with the economic fundamentals—when $100 buys just as much in the United States as $100 worth of DMs buys in West Germany. (For more on purchasing power parity, see note 6.)

A country's currency becomes overvalued when its prices or production costs rise faster than those of its trading partners, because of a more inflationary monetary policy and/or the lagging productivity that frequently results from a failure to keep abreast of technological advances. Although the net advantages of an overvalued dollar were considerable in the 1960s, U.S. exports were increasingly disadvantaged as other industrialized countries recovered and developed new products. But the problem didn't attract much attention until the 1970s, when the output and demand for Japanese exports really took off.

Politically, the overvalued dollar was a double-edged sword. The obligation of other countries to peg their currencies to it guaranteed support for the weakening dollar through central bank purchases in the foreign exchange markets. So long as dollars were thus accumulated without protest, the United States was free to make huge expenditures for military bases around the world, installations deemed essential to the maintenance of a nuclear umbrella against Soviet attack. Washington wasn't at all shy in reminding our allies that support for the dollar was an indirect shouldering of a common defense burden and in 1967 threatened to reduce the U.S. military presence in West Germany if the Bundesbank didn't stop converting dollars to gold.[15] Bonn backed down, but fears about the future value of the dollar and opposition to its limitless accumulation by central banks persisted. In the case of France, especially under Charles de Gaulle, it was a combination of a distaste for American hegemony and a strong preference for gold as an international reserve asset. France regularly converted its accumulated dollars to gold, and other countries also cashed in dollars to diversify their reserve portfolios as their exports recovered. The result was a fall of the U.S. monetary gold stock, from nearly $25 billion in 1949 to $17 billion at the end of 1960, with the steepest decline occurring after the removal of many of the postwar exchange controls by European countries— imposed in the hope that they would speed economic recovery—and the restoration of currency convertibility in 1958.

Concern about overall U.S. balance-of-payment deficits—the result of our spending, lending, investing, and giving away much more than we were receiving in payments from the rest of the world— began with the restoration of currency convertibility. By the summer of 1962 a nervous Treasury was busily devising measures to stanch the outflow of dollars. The first of several was the interest-equalization tax, an attempt to slow U.S. lending and investment abroad by raising costs. The tax was supposed to eliminate the gap between interest rates here and higher rates abroad; or, to put it another way, the dollar cost of acquiring a foreign stock or bond was increased. So the interest-equalization tax was in fact a thinly disguised partial dollar devaluation, although saying so at the time was heresy. With the expansion of the U.S. role in the Vietnam War, which was superimposed on higher federal spending for Lyndon Johnson's social welfare programs, new measures of partial devaluation followed. When U.S. interest rates rose in relation to those abroad and thus nullified the equalization tax, it was replaced by "voluntary" foreign credit restraints, and the Pentagon was forced to "buy American" for its overseas operations even though the costs were higher—a humiliating confession of an overvalued dollar.

Political realities—including strong domestic opposition to the widened war effort—compelled President Johnson to reverse U.S. policy after the Viet Cong's Tet offensive of February 1968 and to seek a negotiated peace in Vietnam. A far less conspicuous but nonetheless critical economic consideration was a growing resistance by our allies to supporting the sagging dollar. The U.S. gold stock plummeted from $17 billion in 1961 to a low of $10.6 billion in 1968. Before March of that year the industrial countries regularly poured gold into the free London market in order to cap its market price at the official level of $35 an ounce. When it was apparent that the upward price pressures could no longer be countered, the authorities announced a two-tier system: $35 an ounce for official transactions among central banks and a free-market price for others. But that was not the end of the trouble. In November, France and West Germany reached an impasse over a currency realignment: France, not wishing to evince political weakness, adamantly refused to devalue its overvalued franc, and the Germans, concerned about the competitiveness of their exports, wouldn't budge on the upward revaluation of their undervalued DM. A resolution came in the following summer when Bonn floated the DM—ceased pegging it to its dollar par values. The DM moved upward, and the exchange markets continued to function effectively, much to the surprise of the advocates of rigidly fixed rates, who for long had equated floating currencies with chaos.

The blow that finally ended the faltering regime of fixed exchange rates was delivered by the United States in August 1971. Faced by rising inflation and an increasingly weak dollar, Richard Nixon ended gold convertibility, floated the dollar, and froze all wages and prices. It was a decision that put the world on a paper-money standard, one without the tie to gold that once served as a price level anchor and brake on inflation.

While not floating freely as they would in the complete absence of central bank intervention—it's called a dirty float—exchange rates have been flexible since 1971. With flexibility, there is no longer a mechanism—a system of rules and obligations as there was under fixed rates—by which inflation is transmitted from country to country. Other countries are no longer compelled to support the dollar by intervention that results in the expansion of their money stocks and, hence, higher inflation. But the problems of overvalued and undervalued currencies remain. Since the dirty floating of currencies began, the traded-weighted value of the dollar against ten other major currencies[16] moved in two long waves that the central banks of the world were powerless to counter by intervention in the exchange markets. It peaked in 1976, touched bottom in 1979, and then began a spectacular ascent to a much higher crest in February 1985. The dollar then plummeted until early 1988 and afterward fluctuated around a flat trend—up and down slightly from one week to the next, very much like the price of stock that is going nowhere.

The fluctuations of the dollar exchange rates reflect differences in levels of real interest rates among the industrialized countries, the financial markets of which are closely knitted by flows of capital. In the 1970s, the dollar exchange rates fell because real interest rates in the United States—that is, market rates of interest minus the rate of inflation—were lower than those of other countries. As a consequence, foreigners shifted out of U.S. investments, and in doing so drove down the dollar. But during the sharp recession of the early 1980s, precipitated by monetary restraint in 1979, inflation fell much faster and farther than market rates of interest, causing a sharp rise of real U.S.interest rates, especially in relation to those of other advanced countries. U.S. investments became very attractive, and in their rush to get back into our booming stock and bond markets, foreign investors caused a spectacular run-up of the dollar that peaked in 1985 as the real interest-rate differential began to move against the United States.

The 1979–85 run-up—an increase of about 60 percent—overvalued the dollar, further diminished the competitiveness of U.S. imports, and started a groundswell of protectionist sentiment that hasn't yet abated. Now the dollar—having overshot its purchasing power parity—is undervalued and the U.S. trade deficit is shrinking, though not nearly fast enough to please the Washington policymakers.

The 1970s and early 1980s were turbulent times of oil embargoes, Middle Eastern wars, inflation that ran as high as 12 percent, short-term interest rates that soared to a peak of 22 percent, and short but deep recessions. It was a decade of sharp deterioration in the competitive position of the U.S. economy. Hourly compensation in the business sector increased at an averge rate of 8.3 percent annually while hourly output per person in the business sector increased by an average of only 1.3 percent and—for the first time since the measures commenced in the late 1940s—actually declined during all of 1974, 1979, and 1980. To be sure, they were all recession years: real GNP fell in 1974 and 1980, while its growth declined sharply in 1979. But the very fact that hourly output per person in the business sector declined in those three calendar years and in the latter instance for two consecutive years—something that never happened in the late 1940s, the 1950s, or the 1960s—suggests both bloated labor forces and inefficient managers who could not or would not trim hours worked with sufficient speed to offset declines of output. The corporate profits record was equally dismal: pre-tax earnings slumped in 1980 and didn't exceed their 1979 level until 1987.[17]

When it was no longer possible to hike prices with impunity, managers scrambled to reduce labor costs in a variety of ways. But reactive behavior is hardly compatible with the maximization of the present value of companies. What's needed is a preemptive forward-looking strategy, and that's why in what follows I want to look at some of the ways by which corporate employees—managers and lower-level workers—are compensated and consider proposals for their reform.

## Who Gets Paid What, and Why: Workers

The economist's answer to the question of how wages and salaries are determined is deceptively simple. It is—as a first cut—that compensation should be equivalent to the employee's contribution to the revenue of the company. More precisely, one of the essential rules for maximizing the profits of a company is that pay should equal the market value of the physical product added by the last worker hired—or what's called the marginal revenue product. Let's run through a hypothetical example to see what it means.

A small bakeshop—staffed only by a husband and wife—turns out one product, a "natural" five-grain bread that it supplies to health-food stores, delis, and upscale supermarkets. They sell 700 loaves weekly for $1.40 cents a loaf wholesale, so that their total revenue is $980 a week—700 loaves × $1.40. Now suppose they hire a third baker, who enables them to increase production by 340 loaves weekly, his or her marginal physical product, but that to sell 1,040 loaves weekly against the competition they must cut their price to $1.23. Their total weekly revenue is now $1,280. The marginal revenue product (MRP) of the new baker is $300 a week—$1,280 − $980, or the marginal physical product times the marginal revenue, 340 loaves × 88.24 cents per loaf. And the weekly average revenue product (ARP)—the marginal physical product times the price or average revenue—is $418.20, with the difference between the ARP and the MRP going to cover capital, overhead, and profit. The weekly wage that maximizes profit with an output of 1,040 loaves and a price of $1.23 is $300. But as we shall see, the weekly wage that's actually paid bakers in the area is determined by forces that are external to and unaffected by our little bakeshop.

Note that the marginal revenue per loaf is lower than the price or the average revenue per loaf, and the reason is that the price is cut from $1.40 to $1.23 on all 1,040 loaves, not just on the marginal 340 as it would be if our bakeshop could somehow get away with being a perfect price discriminator—selling the same product at a different price to each customer—something than can't happen, at least not for long, among informed, competing retailers in the same market area.

If a fourth baker is hired, 330 loaves are added to weekly output. Marginal physical productivity—the size of the increment to total output—declines slightly, because nothing is added to the basic equipment and no change is made in the layout of the shop. Suppose now that it's not possible to sell 1,370 loaves weekly without cutting the price to $1.05. Weekly total revenues are then $1,438.50. So the MRP of the fourth baker is only $158.50 weekly.

In a profit-maximizing company the labor force is expanded until the MRP equals the wage rate, the marginal cost of the last hire. Hence, if the prevailing wage for bakers is $250 a week, our shop as presently configured shouldn't hire a fourth baker. But that move might make sense if the owners were soundly planning to raise productivity and lower costs through investment in new and more efficient dough hooks, ovens, and packaging equipment.

Before turning to the question of actual or market wage determination, note that our bakeshop is what's called a *price maker*. Unlike the farmer—who as a *price taker* selling into a huge international market can't possibly affect or control the price of his wheat—the bakeshop's price is inversely related to its output. Higher production can force prices down, spoil its market and narrow its profit margin unless costs are reduced. The reason for the inverse relationship between price and output is competition from other "natural" breads, conventional breads, and substitutes for bread such as crackers and biscuits. Note that the percentage rise of sales was greater than the percentage reduction of the price: a less than 23 percent cut in price boosted sales by nearly 96 percent. That stretching is what, in the jargon of economic analysis, is known as the price elasticity of demand. In the case of the five-grain bread, the price elasticity is 2.24, which means that on the average a 1 percent reduction of price will increase sales by 2.24 percent. If you know the price and the price elasticity, marginal revenue is easy to calculate. With an elasticity of 2.24 it's a bit more than 55 percent of the price. The lower the price elasticity—or the responsiveness of sales to price changes—the bigger the wedge between price and marginal revenue; the higher the elasticity, the smaller the wedge.[18]

Now back to the market for bakers. In the specialty-bread-product market our bakeshop is a price maker: it can't profitably increase production without lowering price. But in the labor market for bakers, our bakeshop is purely a price taker. It's much too small to affect bakers' wage rates in its market; and even if the business grew until it became a regional or national supplier, it would remain a price taker, because its plants would be scattered in different market areas. Bakers' wage rates are set by market forces of supply and demand, and the individual bakeshops adjust accordingly. Those that pay less than the going rate won't keep their workers for long, and those whose marginal revenue products are below the market wage rate must contend with subnormal or vanishing profits unless they take steps to either trim their work forces and output or lower costs by investing in new equipment. So the MRP wage level is a standard toward which a business will adjust over the long run.

Developments in the airline industry illustrate what I have in mind. Before the deregulation of the late 1970s, the Civil Aeronautics Board, a federal agency, determined who could enter the industry, the routes they could fly, and the fares they could charge. Two by-products of that cozy and not altogether malign cartel were comfortable profits and generous packages of pay and perquisites. Attractive young women didn't flock to the airlines because there was anything particularly ennobling about the calling of an airborne waitress but because the combination of pay and perks was irresistible. With the advent of deregulation and the cutting of fares to increase market shares, the airlines quickly discovered that old levels of salaries, wages, and perks were ruinously high. Hence the battles between unions and management—Continental, Eastern, Pan American, and other airlines. In virtually every instance unions made large concessions through pay cuts and the relaxation of work rules in order to save jobs, an illustration of what happens when a change in the nature of the game—a shift from cartel-set prices to market-determined prices—opens a large gap between market wages and levels of marginal revenue productivity.

What of the role of unions? Are they responsible for pushing wages above economic levels? I don't think that unions—except in special circumstances—have that power. Wage levels don't rise unless unions encounter managers who are compliant by virtue of a permissive business climate. Here's why. First, union membership has been falling in relation to the labor force for about thirty years. In the private sector of the U.S. economy—which is what really concerns us—the decline has been very sharp, from 31.9 percent of the labor force in 1960 to only 16.6 percent in 1984.[19] Second, save for the public sector (and there union power is limited by budget constraints), organized labor in the United States hasn't the political muscle that it does in the European parliamentary democracies. Because of the frontier and historically high real wages, the mainstream of the U.S. labor movement has been reformist rather than revolutionary and, save for the 1930s, not terribly militant. Third, with some notable exceptions, the power of unions to push up wages is not great. The best estimates are that the incomes of union workers, on average, exceed those of their non-union counterparts by at least 12 percent but probably not more than 20 percent.[20] That differential includes the important effects of the Davis-Bacon Act of 1931 and its counterparts in some thirty-five states which, in effect, mandate high union wage rates in government-financed construction.

The last point requires elaboration. A union has little power to push wage rates higher than they might otherwise be unless it has tight control over workers' entry to the industry and the employer's elasticity of demand for labor is very low.

There is a classic account of control over entry in "Old Times on the Mississippi," where Mark Twain explains how the elite riverboat pilots of the 1850s were able to push their monthly salaries—which were in addition to room and board—up to $500, about twenty-four times the earnings of preachers. Only seasoned, constantly working river pilots had timely knowledge of the daily channel changes, the new reefs or shoals that posed an ever-present danger to steamboats along thousands of miles of the river, and they arranged to share that information only with fellow members of the Pilots Benevolent Association. The association, which had the strong support of insurance underwriters, controlled the entry of apprentices or cubs as well as the certification of pilots to form what Mark Twain called "the tightest monopoly in the world." But their power waned with the construction of paralleling railroads. The American Medical Association is a contemporary counterpart of the river pilots' monopoly. As a principal player in the health-care cartel created by the federal and state governments, it raises the income of its members through control over the number and size of medical schools, the licensing of physicians, and, through affiliated boards, the certification of specialists.[21]

During the 1930s, motion picture projectionists in Newark, New Jersey, were able to make big wage gains. The union local was run by mobsters who firmly limited the number of eligible projectionists and extorted large sums for new union cards, which were pretty much confined to relatives of members. Yet even after projectionists' salaries were forced up, they accounted for a very small fraction of the total cost of operating a movie theater. Owners feared more for their kneecaps and their lives than for their pocketbooks.[22] Much the same control was achieved without guns and blackjacks by the newspaper photoengravers. In the early 1960s, the handful of engravers in the composing room of *The Washington Post* were paid much more for far fewer hours of work than any reporter in the city room. Because of their fewness, their higher salaries—unlike those of reporters, typographers, or pressmen—were a minuscule fraction of a newspaper's total wages bill, hardly worth fighting over. Today, New York City's construction scene—with its heavy Mafia presence, byzantine, corruptly administered building codes, and unabashedly complacent real estate tycoons—is one in which the building craft unions doubtless have clout. The same might be true of certain locals of the International Brotherhood of Teamsters—the national leadership of which was charged by the U.S. Justice Department with being in league with organized crime.[23] But most unions are weak, unable to push wages very far above where they would otherwise be.

Labor is a heterogeneous service. Some workers are more experienced and more efficient than others, and there are great variations in the effort that's exerted. George S. Moore, president and then chairman of what is now Citibank from 1959 to 1970, had an instant reply to the visitor's question, "How many people work in this bank?" It was "About half." Every business has its shirkers; and the bigger the organization, the bigger the proportion of shirkers.

Except in isolated areas or where very rare skills are required, businesses are price takers in their labor markets. Unlike most product prices, which are inversely related to the volume of output, wage rates aren't directly affected by a single company's decision to hire more people. They tend to move slowly, which is why some analysts speak of an implicit wage contract between employers and employees. Policymakers and economists have long complained of the downward inflexibility, or stickiness, of wage rates, especially in the manufacturing sector. They reason that if wage rates fell freely, unemployment, an excess supply of labor, would be eliminated by a clearing of the labor markets—bringing demand and supply into balance. With flexible wage rates and product prices, the overall economy would be more stable because the adjustment to changes—such as an unanticipated drop in the demand for autos—would be made principally through wage and price changes rather than through sharp cutbacks of production and employment as is now the case. But recent analyses suggest that downward wage-rate flexibility isn't feasible. The reason is that cutting real wages in the face of involuntary unemployment lowers the morale and productivity of employed workers so that employers, many with heavy investments in training their work forces, find it unprofitable. In other words, the real wage rate that maximizes worker effort or efficiency results in an excess supply of labor.[24]

I cite this explanation of unemployment, the efficiency-wage thesis, not to pass judgment on its validity but to set the stage for the ideas of Martin L. Weitzman, an economist at the Massachusetts Institute of Technology and author of *The Share Economy,* a widely read book that challenges the prevailing hourly-wage system in a fundamental way.[25]

Weitzman proposes that the compensation of production workers be based on shares of a company's revenue rather than on fixed hourly wage rates. Suppose—and here I'm using Weitzman's hypothetical numbers—that the wages and fringe benefits of the average General Motors worker come to $24 an hour, which is the marginal cost of adding another hour of work. To maximize profit, GM would add hours of labor until the marginal value product per hour is $24. The average revenue product per hour is $36, with $12 going to cover overhead, capital depreciation, and profits. Imagine now that the United Automobile Workers and GM agree on a different sort of contract under which each of its some 500,000 hourly rated employees shares two thirds of GM's average revenue per worker. GM's total revenue per hour is $18 million—$36 × 500,000—and the share going to labor is $12 million—$24 × 500,000 or .667 × $18 million.

So far it seems as if nothing's changed since the workers get $24 an hour, just as they did under the old hourly wage contract, and GM retains $12. But, says Weitzman, there is in fact a most important difference. Under the old time-wage contract, GM has no incentive to increase its work force, since the marginal cost of a new hire equals his MRP, which is $24 an hour. But under the share contract, it's a very different game. A new hire adds $24 an hour to GM's total revenue, but its total labor costs, the slice going to labor, now increase by only two-thirds of $24, or $16, per hour—from an hourly total of $12 million to $12,000,016 or .667 × $18,000,024. So, if the company hires an extra worker, it stands to clear a profit of $8 an hour because the hourly pay of each of the 500,001 workers declines by $8/500,001, from $24 to $23.99998. With labor costs falling, GM now has an incentive to expand its employment and output, provided that it lowers its auto prices in relation to the competition from Ford, Toyota, Honda, and the like. Bear in mind the necessity of cutting prices, because Weitzman, I think, underestimates GM's penchant for perverse oligopolistic pricing—raising its prices to match the rising dollar prices of Japanese imports instead of cutting—and sorry record for turning out cars of poor quality. But we'll return to those issues.

What Weitzman is trying to do is break the asymmetry that characterizes GM and virtually all other enterprises, save farms, that are price makers in their product markets but price takers in their labor markets. He wants them to be price makers in both markets. In place of fixed, hourly marginal labor costs—a flat wage rate determined in the market and unaffected by the number of people hired—labor costs would fall under the share approach. There would be a wedge between average and marginal costs, paralleling that between average and marginal revenue in the product markets. The more hires, the lower the average and marginal labor costs. Much the same results would follow from a heavy reliance on bonuses rather than straight wages. With fixed rates under the present time-wage system, there is a chronic tendency toward an excess supply in the labor market. Under a share or bonus system—Weitzman contends—there would be an excess demand for labor and therefore much fuller employment, provided that reductions of product prices paralleled the fall of labor costs.

Because prices exceed marginal costs—and therefore may be above market clearing levels in all but the perfectly competitive farm-product markets—Weitzman sees a tendency toward excess supply:

> The idea that we live in an economy of goods and services where "demand equals supply" even as an abstraction represents a deeply erroneous perception of what political economy has taught us. In fact we live in a world where the normal condition of the product market is that supply exceeds demand, which is a very different paradigm indeed! To overlook this essential aspect is to miss a good deal of what capitalism is all about. Too many economists seem unmindful of the basic point that producers *set* prices, in systematic relation to costs, so that supply exceeds demand in 95 percent of the product markets of advanced capitalist countries. . . . We live, all of us denizens of a market economy, in a buyer's paradise.[26]

As the full title of his book, *The Share Economy: Conquering Stagflation,* implies, Weitzman looks upon share and bonus compensation systems as a means of improving the overall performance of the economy by averting the inflation of prices and stagnation of real economic growth that plagued the 1970s and early 1980s. But in my view—which isn't really antithetical—the principal contribution of a share scheme is the raising of corporate efficiency by tying pay to the fortunes of the company rather than hours of work.[27] Workers earning significant proportions of their income in shares or bonuses—as they do in Japan, an advanced country whose efficient corporations and rapid growth are the envy of the world—would no longer perfunctorily put in their seven or eight hours of work. An awareness that their incomes hinge critically on the profitability of their company would have a salutary effect on effort and the quality of work. Let's then consider some of the impediments to what would be a truly radical and promising change in the way production workers are compensated.

The time-wage system isn't inextricably woven into the social fabric. As Weitzman points out, there are alternatives—such as tips, share croppping, bonus plans, piece work, and sliding wages tied to profits. Although I wouldn't for a moment underestimate workers' suspicion of or resistance to tampering with so fundamental an economic institution as the wages system, prospects for change are far from dismal. First, in the disruptive wake of the inflation-disinflation cycle of 1965–80, the U.S. labor force became inured to change— layoffs, wage cuts, and the loosening of work rules—some of it very painful. There are now more part-time and temporary workers than ever before and the perks and fringe benefits of full-time employment, medical and dental insurance among others, are being sharply reduced. So even though they are predicated on variable rather than fixed incomes, share or bonus systems that promise steadier employment should find more favor than they would have in the 1950s, 1960s, or 1970s. Second, about one-third of all U.S. employees now receive part of their compensation in the form of bonuses, either as year-end profit sharing or as specific rewards for outstanding performance. Weitzman cites the example of Steelcase, a manufacturer of high-quality office equipment in Grand Rapids, Michigan, where about half the production workers' pay is in bonuses. There are no layoffs and morale is high.[28]

But what of product price cuts, which are absolutely essential if cutbacks of production and employment are to be avoided? Here I think that Weitzman greatly underestimates the resistance in the auto industry. Walter P. Reuther, of the United Automobile Workers, tried on several occasions in the 1950s and early 1960s to trade smaller wage hikes for pricing moderation—holding the line on the size of price increases. He did it because, unlike his counterpart in the United Steelworkers, he realized that lower prices and bigger car sales would benefit both his members and the public at large. But in the era of American hegemony, Reuther's initiatives were non-starters. Today, in a far more competitive auto market, General Motors, Ford, and Chrysler don't hesitate to offer rebates and below-market interest rates on installment loans in order to clear out inventories of their slower-moving models. That, however, is still a far cry from the straightforward, aggressive pricing policy that Weitzman envisages as indispensible to the share and/or bonus system of compensation. There's no good reason for auto prices to be so much stickier than personal-computer prices. But there's much more to the U.S. economy than autos. In addition to computers, other major consumer durables—washers, refrigerators, dryers, stoves, and, that ultimate durable, the home—are flexibly priced.

When it first appeared in 1984, *The New York Times* said that *The Share Economy* was the "best idea since Keynes." But after a little more than a year of sporadic media attention, the idea was pretty much forgotten. If anyone can revive it, it will be corporate managers, seeking not to stabilize the U.S. economy but searching for an alternative compensation system that increases profitability by enhancing worker efficiency and morale.

## Who Gets Paid What, and Why: Managers

The men at the pinnacle of America's corporate hierarchy took a beating in last fall's stock-market crash, no doubt about it. But while most ordinary shareholders are still licking their wounds, the executive-suite elite are recouping fast—in their paychecks if not in their portfolios.

Though not quite rock-star rich, they're the richest hired hands in history.[29]

That was Amanda Bennett's lead into her front-page *Wall Street Journal* story that appeared in the early spring of 1988, one that neatly reflected the feelings of almost everyone who was following the upward course of executive compensation. An accompanying chart spelled it out with precision. From 1977 through 1987, hourly wages increased by less than 80 percent, paralleling but running well below the rate of inflation, while chief executives' compensation increased by 225 percent. Corporate profits during that time were flat.

Grumblings about exorbitant executive pay, another manifestation of the breakdown of managerial control, would be more productive if they were shorter on moral indignation and longer on guiding principles. What's alarming is not that the average chief executive officer was paid $595,000 in 1987 or that Jim P. Manzi of Lotus Development Corporation, the computer software house, led the pecuniary parade with a cool $26.3 million in salary, bonus, and stock options. Although they are outrageously high for reasons that I'll explain, it's not the *levels* of compensation that will make or break the American corporation but rather the lack of any reliable link between what CEOs are paid and how well they perform.

In baseball, Dave Concepcion of the Cincinnati Reds hit .260 in 1987 and was paid $320,000 while Wade Boggs of the Boston Red Sox hit .357 and got $1,600,000, five times more for a player who really made a difference in winning games. You may object to applying the same logic to CEOs because, after all, managing a GM or an IBM entails more complexity and surely greater social responsibility than swatting fastballs. But if the name of the game is the market value of the company's shares—as I think it should be but in fact is not—then it makes sense to hold the CEO accountable for what happens in much the same way as generals and presidents earn plaudits or brickbats for performance on the battlefield or in the political arena. It is true that imputation—ascribing a result to the effort of a single person as we did in the case of the little bakeshop—becomes difficult as you ascend the hierarchy of a large organization. But at the summit, individual contributions—however significant they may be—are beside the point. What we look for in a corporate leader is the ability to orchestrate a group effort: formulating a winning business strategy and executing it with a carefully chosen, hard-driving, highly motivated work force.

Like baseball managers and football coaches, CEOs should be rewarded for boosting the present value of the company and be promptly—say, within two years—sacked when they fail. But that doesn't happen in the business corporation, because the shareholder-owners, unlike the owners of baseball and football franchises, exercise no power. Virtually all corporations are controlled by their CEOs, and it would be absurd to expect that those who serve as both judge and jury would convict themselves. In June 1988—to cite a case in point—it was announced that Fred L. Hartley, seventy-one, would step down after nearly twenty-five years as CEO of the Unocal Corporation but would stay on indefinitely as chairman of the board of directors. Hartley won a famous victory in 1985 when he repulsed T. Boone Pickens's takeover attempt, only to pursue that raider's policy by restructuring Unocal, a move that might have netted the shareholders hundreds of millions of dollars more had it come earlier and without a costly battle. Hartley's pet project is a $600 million shale-oil operation in Colorado that loses money—despite an Air Force guarantee of a high price for any jet fuel refined—and is a drag on the price of Unocal's shares. Yet he remains as chairman, wielding still undetermined but probably significant power within the company.[30]

It may not be possible to make the tenure of corporate CEOs as insecure as that of big-time athletic managers, yet surely year-to-year changes in their compensation—salaries, bonuses, and stock options—ought to be systematically related to profitability, up in good years and down in bad. But they're not. I ran a simple up-or-down test using 1987 CEO salary data from the *Business Week* "Top 1000" companies.[31] First I culled 109 companies whose return to shareholders—dividends plus the appreciation in the price of their stock—either declined or increased by less than 50 percent from 1985 through 1987. They were the underachievers, the bottom of the corporate heap. Then I looked at the changes in the compensation of the CEO and the next highest ranking executive—salaries, plus bonuses, plus the value of such long-term compensation as the present value of their stock options. Here's what I found: pay was cut in only 28 companies or less than 26 percent of the total; pay was raised in 78 companies or nearly 72 percent of the total; and in 3 instances pay was unchanged. Nor was there much of a tendency to penalize failure in the lowest subgroup, the 61 companies with either declining returns to shareholders or gains of less than 25 percent over those same years: pay was cut in 19 companies, or a little more than 31 percent of the subtotal; it was raised in 39, or nearly 64 percent, and was unchanged in 3.

One of the more egregious examples of pay moving sharply in the wrong direction was that of John S. Reed, CEO of Citicorp. His total compensation rose from $1,143,000 in 1986 to $2,679,300 in 1987, a more-than-doubling in a year during which Citicorp lost $1.1 billion because of provisions for likely losses on Third World loans. Adding stealth to injury, information on Reed's compensation over and above his $840,300 salary was scattered in the boilerplate of the proxy statement and was nowhere totaled.[32]

What should have been all sticks in 1987 was mostly carrots! But then we have to take into account the facts of life under managerial control. Autonomous corporate managers—and bear in mind that they dominate their boards of directors—will cut their own salaries only if they are fearful that irate investors would dump their shares, drive the share prices down below book value, and thus expose them to a hostile takeover or proxy fight. Among the managers of those 109 poorly performing companies, that fear obviously wasn't very great. Other, more elaborate tests than mine make the same points.[33]

There's a built-in element of circularity in thinking about corporate compensation—especially the professional counseling and board-room deliberations on the salaries and perks of CEOs and other principal executives' pay. It's the implicit assumption that whatever "comparable" companies pay is competitively determined and there-fore "right." The result is that a floor is built under offers to potential recruits that guarantees an upward ratcheting of pay levels. I was an outside director of a technologically advanced biomedical company for twelve years and on several occasions participated in deliberations about what to offer a new president and other key players. What typically happened—with or without the assistance of a professional headhunter—was that offers were confined to highly placed people in our or a closely related industry segment, managers whose virtues were extolled by former mentors and old pals of equally dubious objectivity. If anyone ever proposed breaking the mold—saving money by making an offer to a junior but very promising person— I've forgotten it. My experience—which I think was typical of what goes on—brings to mind a bit of doggerel by Herbert J. Davenport, a prominent American economist in the early decades of this century. It goes:

> *The price of pig*
> *Is something big;*
> *Because its corn, you'll understand,*
> *Is high-priced, too;*
> *Because it grew*
> *Upon the high-priced farming land.*
> *If you knew why*
> *That land is high,*
> *Consider this: its price is big*
> *Because it pays*
> *Thereon to raise*
> *The costly corn, the high-priced pig!* [34]

Robert Topel of the University of Chicago's business school said in 1988 that: "Competition is going to dictate what people make. The best measure we have of the value of what someone produces is what he was paid." [35] But the empirical evidence suggests that it isn't the case for CEOs and other high corporate executives. Rock stars who draw crowds, currency traders, and investment portfolio managers who beat the odds, all enjoy incomes that are commensurate with what they produce—big box-office receipts or high profits. The incentive bonuses usually paid to top traders and portfolio managers ensure that outcome. But the market tests for CEOs and their highly paid but less visible staff are notoriously lax, if they can properly be called tests at all. Rock singers who fail to draw crowds or currency traders who lose big money quickly find themselves walking the streets. But Thomas H. Wyman was permitted to preside over the decline of CBS for years, and when finally ousted by white knight

Laurence Tisch in September 1986, he was given $1.1 million in salary and bonus for the whole year, a lump-sum payment of $2.8 million, and a pledge of $400,000 a year for life. Richard Ferris, the chairman of Allegis and architect of a disastrous strategy that necessitated the spinning off of resort properties, was sacked in 1987 with a promise of five years' salary and bonus payments worth nearly $3 million. True, neither is likely to find further gainful employment, nor will they be driven by necessity to do so. But if failure is so richly rewarded, why should any CEO strive to avert it?

An enchantment with an ideal market mechanism blinds some economists to the defects of the real thing. There is a market for high-level managers, but a very idiosyncratic one. Headhunters—whose standard fee is a third of the quarry's proffered first year's salary whether or not she or he is actually bagged—are constantly searching for executive talent.[36] Hefty premiums over current pay are routinely paid to entice sitting CEOs and others not visibly accountable for past or unfolding business disasters to move from one company to another. But such trappings of competition don't add up to what can reasonably be deemed a competitive market. Let's look at both sides of it. The buyers—directors seeking the services of an executive from outside their company—are corporate managers, agents not renowned for their slavish devotion to the interests of the shareholders and who won't knowingly embrace a potential challenge to their power. The sellers, often CEOs who were literally anointed by their predecessors, are people of a similar mindset. What's absent in the transaction—because the shareholders, as principal buyers, can't be in on the decision and are powerless, save after disasters, to unseat a CEO—is a rational, independent appraisal of the value of the services purchased. The outside shareholders, in Davenport's metaphor, are buying a pig in a poke.

To forge a link between CEO compensation and company performance, one that complements Weitzman's proposal for compensating rank-and-file production workers, fixed salaries should in large part be replaced with targeted bonuses that vary with profits or are contingent on achieving predesignated profit levels. If significant portions of those bonuses were payable in book-value stock—shares that the company wouldn't buy back until retirement or separation—CEOs would tend to function more like equity-owning entrepreneurs than like hired hands. Under present practices, as Graef S. Crystal, the dean of U.S. corporate compensation consultants, points out, "What is called an annual bonus is nothing more than base salary in drag." Crystal is equally critical of boards that liberally grant stock options—some with provisions that compensate CEOs for market price declines after they exercise their options—the costs of which, under current accounting rules, never affect the income statement, but—by increasing the number of shares outstanding—dilute shareholders' equity when they are exercised.[37]

Thus far I've concentrated on *changes* in executive pay, ways to link it to performance so that success is rewarded and failure is severely punished. Now I want to consider *levels* of pay, not only of CEOs but of the whole upper managerial echelon.

If managerial pay levels are linked to sales growth and head counts, if the company is pursuing a strategy of maximizing "corporate wealth"—seeking among other goals the highest possible sales and the biggest work force—high costs and low profits are bound to ensue. And the tendency will be strongly reinforced if middle managers are rewarded by promotions and permanently higher pay rather than by targeted bonuses. Yet that's just what's happening in far too many corporations according to recent research.[38] At Citibank in the early 1970s, pay and promotion were closely tied to the number of people supervised, a system formalized by Hay Associates—the Philadelphia-based consultants who bear blame for the current troubles of Sears, Roebuck.[39] After a great deal of log rolling and bargaining among Citicorp's banking divisions, there was attached to each and every official position a specific number of "Hay points" and a corresponding salary range. It was a system of salary administration—since sharply altered at Citibank and I hope elsewhere—that encouraged overstaffing.

Thus far we've been dealing with monetary compensation—salaries, bonuses, and stock options. What remains are the perquisites—benefits or real income in kind, most of which are tax free. I've already alluded to executive dining rooms and large, posh offices.

But there's much more to the good life at the corporate summit than such mundane, though costly, amenities.

T. Boone Pickens relates with malicious pleasure how in 1982 his archenemy Fred L. Hartley, so boundlessly indignant in his moralizing attacks on corporate raiders, flew Unocal's company jet to Spain at a cost of about $30,000 to join Texaco's former CEO, John McKinley, in a red-legged-partridge-shooting party. McKinley, of course, also flew his company's plane, and the travels of both great hunters were a legitimate "business expense." Before he was deposed as CEO of Revlon, Michel Bergerac "traveled in a Boeing 727 that was lavishly decorated with a separate bedroom, a kitchen, and a gun rack"[40]—an airborne palace for a corporate prince.

According to the Federal Aviation Administration, there were nearly 12,000 "executive aircraft" in 1987—planes registered to corporations other than commercial airlines and piloted by professionals. The fleet is considerably smaller than it might be had the 10 percent corporate tax credit on new planes not been repealed in 1986.

It's doubtful that more than a few hundred of those aircraft can be justified by a balancing of the benefits against the costs: that the convenience and the time saved by maintaining an in-house alternative to scheduled airlines or special charters are really commensurate with the costs in this age of instant voice communication and fax machines. In addition to large investments in aircraft that are grossly underutilized by commercial standards, the benefits should also exceed the salaries of pilots and other personnel. They don't, but then rationality isn't to be expected in the acquisition of status symbols.[41]

In 1981, at a time when the federal government was guaranteeing Chrysler's large loans, *The Wall Street Journal* reported that the automaker's corporate jet landed near a spring baseball training camp in Florida. The U.S. Treasury forced Chrysler to sell the jet over the chairman's objections. It's a tale Lee Iacocca didn't tell in his last book where he opines that, "The real problem is not the existence of perks; it's the abuse of them. . . . When you see guys traveling to golfing matches in company planes, you really have to wonder if the company is keeping records and billing everybody, as it ought to.''[42]

If anything can be said in defense of corporate air fleets, it is that they're highly visible and monitoring their improper use isn't very difficult. Other perquisites for which shareholders also pay dearly are surreptitious: the prerogatives of founding families, nepotism, and abuses that border on larceny.

In publicly owned corporations that are controlled by founding entrepreneurs or their families, there's a temptation, not always resisted, to regard the shareholders' property—company cars, company planes, company residences, and highly paid company positions—as personal property.

The Mobil-Tavoulareas case—which got wide media coverage because of a libel suit against *The Washington Post*—turned on a charge of nepotism that was obscured by a more pressing concern about First Amendment press protection. In November 1979 the *Post* carried a prominent story about how, in 1974, Mobil's president, William P. Tavoulareas, "set up his son," Peter, then in his mid-twenties, as a partner in a London maritime company which in turn was awarded a lucrative contract to operate some of Mobil's ships. The Tavoulareases, charging that the piece defamed them, held them up to ridicule, and embarrassed them, sued for $50 million. In 1982, a U.S. District Court jury awarded the elder Tavoulareas $2,050,000 in damages, but a year later a District Court judge overturned the jury decision, holding that the story contained no lies or statements "made in reckless disregard of the truth." Then, in the spring of 1985—with trials of the suits brought by General William C. Westmoreland against CBS and General Ariel Sharon against *Time* under way and widespread antipathy toward news media—a U.S. District Appeals Court, in a 2–1 decision, concurred in by Judge Antonin Scalia, who now sits on the Supreme Court, reinstated the jury verdict, branding the allegations of nepotism false and suggesting gratuitously that the real problem was the *Post*'s brand of journalism, the desire by editor Robert Woodward, of Watergate fame, for "high-impact investigative stories of wrongdoing."

The *Post* won on a rehearing in 1987. Yet the news media failed to consider the substance and significance of the story or raise questions about Mobil's reaction, which was to pull advertisements out of newspapers that gave the story space. The general indifference to what goes on inside corporations was epitomized by Anthony Lewis in *The New York Times,* who deplored the U.S. Court of Appeals decision but opined that he "personally thought the Tavoulareas story was an overblown and unconvincing tale not worth the play or space."[43] He was wrong.

In 1975, Robert J. Buckley—a lawyer whose first success came as manager of labor relations in General Electric's big Schenectady, New York, plant—became CEO of Allegheny Ludlum Industries, a Pittsburgh-based specialty steel producer that sought new blood. Buckley chose to shunt Allegheny down the primrose conglomerate path. By selling off the lackluster steel business and acquiring consumer-product companies—Sunbeam, the Wilkinson Sword Group Ltd., Oster, Rowenta, and Northern Electric—and making what proved disastrously bad investments in real estate, oil, and gas, the rechristened Allegheny International Inc. (AI) had $2.6 billion of revenues in 1982. They were confidently predicted to hit $5 billion in 1986, but it never happened.

AI's profits began a steep decline in 1982 and in 1985 the company reported a loss of $109 million. The price of its stock fell from a peak of $55 in 1981 to $15 by the summer of 1986, and it was during that painful descent that word of exorbitant perks enjoyed by Buckley and his minions leaked out to restive shareholders. One of them, Horace J. De Podwin of Rutgers University's Graduate School of Management, told its unresponsive directors that AI was "out of control." With his help *Business Week*, after a three-month investigation, ran a cover story that led to Buckley's downfall in August 1986.[44]

Here are some of the perks to which Buckley and his fellow AI executives helped themselves:

- An elegant $450,000 Tudor mansion in Pittsburgh and a bill for furniture, draperies, and crystal that almost matched the purchase price.

- A fleet of five jets, dubbed the "Allegheny Air Force," heavily used by families of executives.
- More than $30 million in personal loans available to AI executives at 2 percent interest.
- A job for Buckley's son, Christopher, as manager of the Dover Hotel in midtown Manhattan—purchased by AI for $5.7 million—who also occupied its penthouse, which was refurbished at a cost of more than $1 million.
- The $500,000 purchase of a Ligonier, Pennsylvania, resort condominium, frequently used as a vacation retreat by Robert Buckley and family.
- A $16 million AI investment in a poorly built Vero Beach, Florida, condominium project in which Buckley and other AI executives owned units.

Since he was fired "for cause" in August 1986—and subsequently sued by the SEC, along with AI, for failure to disclose perks—Buckley was denied the three years of severance salary paid his lieutenants who "voluntarily" resigned. But weep not: in addition to a one-time payment of $106,944, Buckley's monthly pension runs to about $12,900. AI's shareholders were treated less kindly. Bankruptcy was declared in February 1988 and under a reorganization plan proposed by AI's board, which fended off dissidents in a June proxy fight, the common stockholders' interest was reduced by 75 percent.[45]

If you're wondering how all of the above could have escaped the attention of AI's board of directors, especially the stellar outside members, there are some answers in the next chapter.

In his *Laws,* Plato wrote that: "In a state which is desirous of being saved from the greatest of all plagues—not faction but rather distraction—there should exist among the citizens neither extreme poverty nor, again, excess of wealth, for both are productive of both these evils." He took Athens' standard city lot as the unit of wealth and proposed that no man be permitted to accumulate more than the equivalent of four of them. Early in this century J. P. Morgan is said to have set a ratio of about twenty to one for the highest- to the lowest-paid person in companies that he controlled. In 1987, according to a *Fortune* survey, U.S. corporations with revenues of more than $1 billion paid their CEOs an average of $983,000, thus boosting the ratio to about fifty to one.[46]

What's more, those U.S. CEOs were paid far more than heads of comparable companies in other countries: in second-place France the average was only $577,000, followed by Switzerland at $468,000, West Germany at $403,000, Britain at $342,000, and Japan at just $330,000. The major element of the disparity was stock options in the United States. In Europe, a CEO's pay was, in general, six to eight times that of an entry-level professional; in the United States, it was fourteen times. Even more glaring is the contrast between the treatment of ordinary employees and CEOs who are dismissed as a result of mergers and buyouts. In 1987, the ten largest golden parachutes—the lump-sum severance payments that boards of directors mandated for CEOs when control changed—ranged between $5.8 million and $25 million, and averaged out to more than $10.8 million.[47]

Graef Crystal writes that: "No society is going to tolerate awesome after-tax pay differentials for long unless there is good reason for them to exist. And performance is about the only good reason that comes to mind." I thought his thinking wishful when he warned that "if some companies can't get their acts together to discipline executive pay abusers, then we may have legislation to curb executive pay." Shortly after the appearance of his article, the United States Senate by a 98–1 vote approved legislation that would have banned golden parachutes, except where authorized by a majority of the shareholders, a straw in what could become the winds of restraint.[48]

# 5

# DIMENSIONS OF POWER:

## Boardrooms, Markets, Ideas, and Politics

The great question which, in all ages, has disturbed mankind, and brought on the greatest part of those mischiefs which have ruined cities, depopulated countries, and disordered the peace of the world, has been, not whether there be power in the world, nor whence it came, but who should have it.

—John Locke, 1690.[1]

The control of corporations by autonomous managers with broad discretion to ignore the interests of shareholder-owners is breaking down. That's the clear implication of the wave of makeovers that began in 1975 and continues to batter the foundations of the established corporate order. But what is likely to emerge? If the old-line, autonomous managers are losing power, who is gaining it?

The answer, in a word, is that the gainers are the institutions—pension plans, insurance companies, brokerage houses, and specialists in corporate restructuring. Let's look at some recent developments that may be waves of the future.

At the zenith of their influence in 1986, efforts were made to fit Michael Milken and Drexel Burnham Lambert into a fittingly exalted context by historical analogies. Samuel L. Hayes, III, a professor of investment banking at the Harvard Business School, opined in *Business Week* that: "The only figure comparable to Milken who comes to mind is J. P. Morgan, Sr." In that same issue, Drexel's chief, Frederick H. Joseph, saw his firm's equity holdings in more than one hundred companies as a revival of nineteenth-century merchant banking. "We're," he said, "going back to our roots." But in point of fact, neither Hayes nor Joseph was on the mark. There's no evidence that Milken or Drexel ever exercised direct control over major corporations as J. P. Morgan did, first in railroads and then in steel. Their role—a major accomplishment which should in no way be denigrated—was financing changes of corporate control, not effecting them. Leon Black, one of Drexel Burnham's more thoughtful partners, understood it well when in a 1979 planning session he said that their goal was to finance the "robber barons who would become the owners of the major companies of the future."[2]

Kohlberg Kravis Roberts & Company (KKR) comes closer to the spirit and substance of J. P. Morgan, Sr. It has been the leader of leveraged buyouts (LBOs) since its founding in 1976, and its preeminence continues despite the 1987 departure of Jerome Kohlberg, Jr., to establish a new firm, Kohlberg & Co. As I explained earlier, KKR sets up partnerships with financial institutions, principally pension funds and other large investors, and then identifies, negotiates, and consummates LBOs; prominent among them have been Beatrice, Safeway, Duracell, and Owens-Illinois. More recently, it was the winner of a spirited competition to take RJR Nabisco private, beating out Shearson Lehman Hutton as well as other LBO partnerships.

In the spring of 1988, KKR had more than $40 billion available for LBOs: $5.6 billion in cash equity committed to partnerships by institutional investors, a base on which at least $35 billion could be borrowed from commercial banks or by issuing junk bonds.[3]

Profits are turned—or losses may be suffered—when the businesses acquired by the partnerships are then sold to other operating corporations or taken public again through public offerings of stock. But deals such as KKR's aren't instantly unwound: some years elapse between the buyout of companies and their disposition. Investors in LBO partnerships typically pledge their capital for five or six years. In the interim, the businesses not only have to be operated, but must be run very well—better than ever before—if they're to be sold at profitable prices. To ensure profitability KKR—surely one of Wall

Street's more reclusive organizations—maintains a staff of some two dozen people to monitor the performance of its companies. In friendly buyouts, the incumbent CEO might remain in place—as in the case of Safeway, where KKR played white knight to prevent its takeover by Herbert and Robert Haft—but there is no hesitation to replace underachievers with new, hired guns.

The shroud of secrecy that covers KKR's operations was lifted a bit by Donald P. Kelly, one of the more ebullient of the big-time players in the makeover game. As CEO of Esmark—a conglomerate assembled around the old Swift meat-packing business—he unloaded the company's energy subsidiary in 1980, just before oil prices peaked. Four years later, he sold Esmark to Beatrice, a huge, lackluster conglomerate, for $2.7 billion, and then in 1986 he teamed up with KKR to take over Beatrice in what was then the biggest LBO on record. As CEO of E-II, a Beatrice spinoff, the indefatigable Kelly launched a 1987 raid on American Brands which ended when he agreed to be quite profitably acquired by the big tobacco company.

Here's how Donald Kelly, a man whose net worth is said to exceed $100 million, looked upon his relationship with KKR:

> Sure, if I wanted to go it alone, I could probably raise a lot of money without KKR. But I believe that Don Kelly always needs someone of equal or greater power than he. I can be very convincing and very hard to change when I get going on something. I get going like a freight train, and I can dominate the conversation, dominate the thinking. It's terribly difficult for people who work for me to walk into this room and say, "Kelly, you're wrong. You're basically, fundamentally wrong." I need somebody objectively looking at what I'm doing, monitoring me. We had no inside directors on the Esmark board until two years before we sold it. They were not going to be dominated by Don Kelly. The same is true of KKR. If Henry Kravis thinks we should go a particular way, I damn well better understand where he's coming from before I reject it out of hand. Hopefully, he says the same thing before rejecting my ideas.[4]

Donald Kelly's message was that he was comfortable as a member of the KKR team, that he was treated with greater deference than accorded the chief of a subsidiary in a large conglomerate. But just what sort of a business organization is KKR? Carol J. Loomis of *Fortune* writes that it is "the second largest U.S. conglomerate, just a touch behind General Electric in annual revenues."[5] The numbers are right, but the "conglomerate" tag is wrong. First, all of KKR's holdings are on the block, for sale, and the faster they're sold, the faster the LBO partnerships are dissolved. GE isn't seeking to sell off Kidder Peabody or RCA any more than ITT in its heyday was in the business of restructuring and disposing of its operating companies. Second, there is an important distinction between KKR's partners and GE's shareholders. Since there are far fewer investors in each of the limited KKR partnerships than there are GE shareholders, the relationships between owners and agents differ significantly. KKR's limited partners can define and defend their interests more readily than even GE's larger institutional shareholders. In a 1984 deal for which information is available, thirty-nine limited partners, only two with as much as 10 percent of the total, invested $189 million of equity with KKR to buy $1.6 billion of properties, subsequently called Pace Industries.[6] There are good reasons to believe that each of those limited partners had much greater access to KKR, the general partner, than the largest of GE's institutional shareholders had to its top management.

KKR is not a conglomerate but a vehicle—both a financial and a managerial intermediary—that affords institutions such as pension plans effective control over the companies in which they invest. What I mean by that emerges from a look at Carl C. Icahn's failure to take over Texaco in the spring of 1988, one of the great proxy battles of this century in which KKR, for reasons of self-interest, voted its huge block in support of management.

Icahn lost for two reasons. First, the pension funds, which in proxy fights usually vote against incumbents, were split, not out of any regard for Texaco's sorry management but because they dismissed Icahn—wrongly, I think—as an opportunistic greenmailer. The second, and probably crucial, development was Texaco president James W. Kinnear's commitment to give the pension plans board representation, an understanding that Icahn denounced as "boardmail." Edward V. Regan, the New York State comptroller, rationalized his support of management with the comment that the institutional directors would "exert continuing pressure on Texaco's management to improve performance." But Abbott Lebans, general counsel to the Pennsylvania Public School Employees Retirement System, another management supporter, was doubtful that the promise would ever be kept. He correctly pointed to "a conceptual and legal problem" with fund officials as company directors. "A plan's representative," he said, "has a fiduciary responsibility solely to the funds. A director's responsibility is to all holders. Those two interests usually are, but may not always be in sync." Texaco averted Lebans's problem and satisfied the demand of the pension plans when it nominated John Brademas—president of New York University and a former Indiana congressman—for a seat on its board.[7]

At the time of the June 1988 shareholders' meeting, Texaco's management had firm agreements to sell the equivalent of about 60 million barrels of its gas and oil reserves and announced plans to sell Saudi Arabia's Aramco Services Company an interest in three U.S. refineries and access to service stations in the eastern and gulf states. Pension-plan managers—smarting from huge losses of dividend income and the depression of the share price as a result of Texaco's bankruptcy and $3-billion-plus settlement with Pennzoil—were still very uncertain about ever seeing a reasonable return on their investments. Even with the promised board representation—a concession that if made would more likely than not prove hollow—they would still be at the mercy of Texaco's management. The contrast between such powerlessness and the strong control exercised by KKR and other partnerships is striking.

Through partnerships the pension plans—which by the end of this century are expected to own about half of all the common shares outstanding—can secure a degree of control comparable to that exercised earlier in this century by J. P. Morgan, Sr., in this country, Walther Rathenau in Germany, and the Japanese *zaibatsu,* family-based money cliques that controlled such groups as Mitsui, Mitsubishi, Sumitomo, and Yasuda.[8] By contrast, the new control is exercised on behalf of very large numbers of pensioners rather than members of a family and their close associates.

The essential change—the one that may ultimately make a significant difference in the management and conduct of U.S. corporations—is a new trend toward greater concentration of share ownership. Control could not have been vested in autonomous managers—creating a regime of what Adolf Berle came to call "power without property"—without the great dispersion of stock ownership so that no single investor in the largest companies of the late 1920s owned more than a fraction of 1 percent of the outstanding shares. With the bulk of personal savings in the U.S. economy being channeled through pension plans—the current value of the deferred income invested on behalf of some 60 million American workers is now more than $1.7 trillion—the stage was set for a reversal of the trend, the reconcentration of shareholding.

But taken alone, share concentration in pension plans and other institutions posed no threat to managerial control. The managers of pension plans and other fiduciary institutions were, and in large part still are, passive players. What made the crucial difference was the predicament in which institutions were placed by America's fall from world dominance, the great inflation of 1965–80, the markets' undervaluation of securities, and the consequent need to "restructure" companies—a euphemism for the changes required to transform them from organizations serving the interests of their autonomous managers to those serving the interests of their owner-shareholders. Or in terms of agency theory, the new developments tie the agents, the managers, more tightly to the interests of their principals, the shareholders.

KKR, with $5.6 billion of available equity, was by far and away the largest buyout fund in 1988, but it was by no means alone. Sarah Bartlett, then of *Business Week,* reported that Morgan Stanley, Prudential-Bache, Merrill Lynch, Shearson Lehman Hutton, and four smaller houses among them raised $9.4 billion of equity,[9] a base on which as much as $50 billion might be borrowed. In the autumn of 1988, my rough estimate was that there was at least $25 billion of equity available for LBOs, against which (depending on how much leverage is assumed) $125 billion to $225 billion could borrowed for a total buyout fund ranging from $150 billion to $250 billion.[10]

If you're wondering what could have been accomplished with $250 billion in 1988, bear in mind that the market value of the top five U.S. corporations, ranked in order—IBM, Exxon, General Electric, American Telephone & Telegraph, and General Motors—came to less than $229 billion.[11] So, assuming $40 billion in premiums over market values, four of the big five might have been bought out or, as an alternative, many more of the lower-ranking companies.

## Outside Directors: Myths and Realities

There is a widely held but naive belief—recently bolstered by developments in the leveraged buyout of RJR Nabisco—that the interests of shareholders are protected by outside directors—people who are not employees of the companies on whose boards they sit.

It's true that outside directors—especially the board chairman, Charles E. Hugel, the chief executive officer of Combustion Engineering, Inc., and David Mahoney, formerly head of Norton Simon—prevented RJR Nabisco's F. Ross Johnson and a handful of his top managers from pullling off a deal with Shearson Lehman Hutton that might have netted them $2.5 billion on a total personal investment of only $20 million. But the RJR Nabisco case was unique. Johnson's high-handed cupidity angered not only the outside directors but some of the insiders as well, all of whom were keenly aware of the danger of shareholders' suits and ruinous personal liability judgments had they accepted the initial offer.[12] The sad truth about typical outside directors in less dramatic circumstances is that they rarely challenge the insiders.

After the Texaco proxy fight, Harrison J. Goldin, comptroller of the City of New York and co-chairman of the Council of Institutional Investors, a group of sixty pension plans with more than $250 billion in assets, said that "companies will find it in their interest to invite us on the board." Goldin is right. Other companies may follow Texaco's lead in considering seats on their boards for pension plans, but doing so will be in *their,* management's, interests, not those of the pensioner-shareholders. There is no good reason to suppose that the presence of pension-plan representatives on boards is going to make one whit of difference in company policy. Richard H. Koppes, chief counsel to the $46 billion California Public Employees Retirement System, who supported Texaco's management, said, "We want to be viewed as partners."[13] But a seat on the board doth not a partner make.

For Goldin and Koppes to achieve protection for their pensioners, they need a measure of truly effective control, the power to effect rapid changes of management. They themselves couldn't and wouldn't want to manage companies in which they have big stakes. What they need, whether or not they realize it, is a mechanism for ensuring that managers and company policies, for better or worse, can be changed quickly. KKR's and other partnerships are one means of achieving that end; doubtless other forms will emerge.

Most outside directors are high officers of other corporations or well-known figures from politics or academia; and until late in this makeover wave such appointments were a convenient way of maintaining useful contacts within the establishment, the old-boy network of movers and shakers. Now, with shareholders ever ready to sue in ever friendlier courts and sky-high personal liability insurance rates, outside directorships have lost much of their charm.

With a few honorable exceptions, outside directors tend obediently to endorse whatever the insiders on a board propose. They are highly paid boardroom appurtenances, whose presence is sometimes exploited as a cover for insider mischief, rather than independent guardians of shareholders' interests. The term "independent outside director" is more often than not an oxymoron. There are, in addition to RJR Nabisco, instances in which outside directors have courageously discharged their fiducial responsibilities but they are too few to justify the extra expense that is borne by the shareholders.

Anyone who believes that outside directors provide protection against managerial misconduct and dereliction of fiduciary responsibility had better consider the cautionary tale of Allegheny International (AI) told in the last chapter. In September 1987 its directors consented to a Securities and Exchange Commission injunction that bars them from such future violations of the security laws as failing to maintain adequate internal accounting controls and neglecting to "disclose third party transactions between officers and others"—legal boilerplate for conceding that they countenanced practices that violated the law.[14]

Robert J. Buckley, the AI CEO who was sacked "for cause" in 1986, was as extravagant in assembling a celebrity cast of outside directors as he was in providing perks for corporate managers and their families. Among the nine outside directors on the fourteen-man board were: Alexander M. Haig, Jr., former secretary of state; Richard M. Cyert, president of Carnegie-Mellon University; Jean-Jacques Servan-Schreiber, the French writer; Anthony J.F. O'Reilly, CEO of H.J. Heinz Co.; and Mark H. McCormack, agent and investment adviser to major athletes.

The first problem was that some of those outsiders weren't all that independent. When Haig joined the board in 1983, there was an agreement—a copy of which was duly filed with the SEC but not disclosed to the shareholders—under which Buckley agreed to pay him, in addition to his director's fee, $10,000 per day or $50,000 a year for no more than five days' worth of advice "in the area of safety and protection devices."[15] Two consulting firms with which director McCormack was associated were paid $160,000 for work done for AI in 1985. Still a third outside director received money from AI over and above his director's fee.

Hicks B. Waldron, chairman of Avon Products, Inc., quit the AI board in late July 1986 and later explained: "I had knowledge of what was cooking . . . I had to limit the number of boards I was on, and that's the one I decided to get off."[16]

The question, then, is why the other outside directors—those whose independence cannot be called into question by their dual role as vendors—seemed so oblivious to what was going on. One of them, George T. Farrell—then president of the Mellon Bank, which was a big lender to AI—surely had a parochial interest in putting a stop to the managerial mischief. Richard Cyert, an economist who specialized in U.S. business behavior and policy, can't be very happy about what happened in a local company on his watch. My answer is that they saw and heard no evil because outside directorships are at the very least comfortable sinecures—upward of $25,000 in larger companies for about ten days' work a year—and at most attractive opportunities for selling high-priced consultative and other services. Because they were protected against shareholders' suits—or at least thought they were—by personal liability insurance, there was little need for AI's directors to be overly inquisitive or unduly critical. Mavericks and inquisitors who displease CEOs and the other insiders are eliminated by the simple expedient of withdrawing their names from the management slates in shareholder elections.

In the absence of conflicts of interest or lassitude most outside directors would still be ineffectual, because it's very difficult as part-timers to get a firm grasp on the intricacies—to say nothing of the internal factional rivalries—of a particular business. Although auditing committees of many U.S. corporations are headed by outside directors, their presence is no guarantee against unpleasant surprises, even when every honest effort is made by management to arrive at balance-sheet truth. Outside directors, and most insiders, don't really know the extent to which a manufacturing company's assets may be inflated by carrying obsolete inventories at their original cost. Being burned by a big retroactive inventory write-off, which in a restatement of a company's earnings can turn quarterly profits into losses, makes an outside director wary but not really any more knowledgeable.

Even in the highly regulated commercial banking industry, outside directors can find themselves very much in the dark. When the Mellon Bank of Pittsburgh posted a nearly $60 million first quarter loss in 1987, its first ever in one hundred and eighteen years, Nathan Pearson, an outside director and financial adviser to Paul Mellon, said that he was "shocked and surprised" by the size of the "problem loans," bankspeak for loans unlikely to be repaid. Pearson, who temporarily took over as chairman, told the annual meeting of shareholders that his first inkling of trouble came when the departed CEO, J. David Barnes, made a public announcement. If that excuse strained the credulity of his listeners, it wasn't noted in the news accounts.[17]

Outside directorships would be an expensive though relatively harmless way of providing incomes that can exceed $300,000 a year to retired executives and former holders of high federal offices[18] if their appointment weren't a disingenuous attempt to deflect blame from the insiders who wield the power and make the critical decisions. Corporate managers can be made more responsive and shareholders' money can be saved by abandoning pretense and dispensing with boardroom supernumeraries.

## Shareholders' Property: Alienable or Inalienable?

One of the distinguishing features of a prosperous, market-oriented economy is that property and property rights are transferrable, freely bought and sold, what lawyers call "alienable." Recent historical analysis argues powerfully for the proposition that the economic rise of the Western world was in an important part due to an efficient system of property rights, one that encourages individuals to engage in activities that are both privately and socially desirable.[19] In that light, recent attacks on corporate makeovers pose a danger that cannot be ignored by a country seeking to maintain a rising standard of living.

The alienability of real property, land in particular, gradually evolved with the erosion of feudal institutions. In England, it wasn't until the Law of Property Act of 1925 that primogeniture was finally abolished—laws under which the eldest child, especially the eldest son, inherited the entire estate of both parents—and "the freehold tenants in possession" gained "unrestricted power of alienating in fee simple"—which meant, in effect, that owners were free to sell their land to buyers who in turn could exercise the same power.[20]

In the United States feudal impediments to the alienation of real property were few,[21] and more recent efforts to limit alienability through restrictive covenants against sales to blacks, Asians, Hispanics, Jews, and other targets of discrimination are no longer enforceable. It's probably for those reasons as well as because of the scant attention paid corporate governance in general that so little has been said about the implications of the 1985 decisions of the Delaware courts in the Household International case.[22] In holding that Household's poison-pill provisions were legal, the Court of Chancery, with the affirmation of the State Supreme Court, in effect ruled that an owner of Household International stock was free to sell shares only at a 200 percent premium above the market price at the time the poison pill was adopted. In other words, a buyer who swallowed the pill with its punitive provisions would pay about three times the preraid market price for the shares. So what the Delaware courts countenanced was tantamount to a restrictive covenant in a deed to real property, though instead of an outright proscription of sales to certain classes of buyers, the same end was achieved by arbitrarily setting a very high price.

The immediate effect of adopting poison pills was predictable: share prices of those companies fell, because investors knew that they were no longer objects of bidding contests. But no one loudly objected that a fundamental tenet of private property, alienability, was breached, that the Delaware courts were depriving owner-shareholders of additional wealth in order to protect their agent-managers. Searching questions about whose ox was gored and whose divine right was preserved were never raised about the Household decision, or about the antitakeover laws passed by twenty-nine states.

Since hostile takeovers are more often than not followed by layoffs in efforts to achieve greater efficiency, the response by blue-collar workers and middle-level managers is one of highly emotional, re-flexive hostility. But what protestors fail to realize (recall, though, that Phillips Petroleum's people in Bartlesville, Oklahoma, did finally get the message) is that true job security is provided by lean, highly profitable companies. Moreover, most employees of medium and large companies, although usually oblivious of the fact, are them-selves share-owning members of pension plans whose retirement benefits hinge critically on the health of the companies in which they own shares.

But the failure to identify and act upon self-interest is only part of the difficulty. Much of the animosity toward takeovers stems from an old dogma according to which business corporations, especially large ones, are not private property.

Irving Kristol, the neoconservative writer and editor, holds that view. In 1978, he wrote in *Two Cheers for Capitalism* that:

> when . . . the Committee for Economic Development drew up a kind of official declaration of the responsibilities of management a few years ago, it conceived of the professional manager as a "trustee balancing the interests of many participants and constituents in the enterprise," and then enumerated these participants and constituents: employees, customers, suppliers, stockholders, government—practically everyone. Such a declaration serves only to ratify an accomplished fact: the large corporation has ceased being a species of private property, and is now a "quasi-public" institution. But if it is a "quasi-public" institution, some novel questions may be properly addressed to it: By what right does the self-perpetuating oligarchy that constitutes "management" exercise its powers? On what principle does it do so? To these essentially political questions management can only respond with the weak economic answer that its legitimacy derives from the superior efficiency with which it responds to signals from the free market. But such an argument for efficiency is not compelling when offered by a "quasi-public" institution. In a democratic republic such as ours, public and quasi-public institutions are not supposed simply to be efficient at responding to people's transient desires, are not supposed to be simply *pandering* institutions, but are rather supposed to help shape the people's wishes, and ultimately, the people's character, according to some version, accepted by the people itself, of the "public good" and "public interest". . . .[23]

How does the claim of a multiple constituency by the Committee for Economic Development—a carbon copy of hundreds of other utterances by self-serving corporate managers that divert attention from their failure to maximize company values—"ratify an accomplished fact"? Just what is a "quasi-public institution," and how does it differ from its presumed opposite, the "private" institution? Kristol doesn't tell us, although he makes a giant leap by assuming that his never defined "quasi-public" entity is endowed with the mystical power of shaping peoples' "wishes" and "character."

Kristol might profitably have expatiated on his apposite remark about the illegitimacy of corporate management's power—an issue raised by Peter Drucker in 1942 but not revisited by him until 1986. Instead, he's content to warn that corporations need to have outside directors if they are to avoid having government domination of their boards as well as a constituency of shareholders "which will candidly intervene in the 'political game' of interest group politics . . ."[24] But little, save Kristol's service as a Mobil director, came of that notion.

By the late 1980s, Kristol, the theoretician of neoconservativism, was at one with the paleo-corporate establishment. He proposed—after the example of the Potlatch Corporation, a San Francisco-based paper producer—that shareholders who haven't held their shares for a year shouldn't be able to vote for directors. His reason is that hostile takeovers and "coerced" leveraged buyouts are harbingers not only of corporate "dismemberment" but of economic and social "convulsion." He writes,

The "economic point of view" is so powerful these days that it is easy for analysts and commentators to forget that a corporation is a sociological institution as well as an aggregation of economic assets. It is an institution capable of adjusting to gradual change, and people who make up that institution often understand and appreciate that corporate change is synonymous with corporate survival. But abrupt, radical change, imposed from without for reasons having nothing to do with current business conditions— that they cannot and will not accept.[25]

Not a word about U.S. unemployment falling during the wave of makeovers—a development surely at odds with talk of "convulsion," a term not often heard since the 1930s.

For some of the more persistently vocal opponents of corporate makeovers, there are conflicts between sentiment and self-interest. One of them, Felix Rohatyn, opened an essay entitled "The Blight on Wall Street" with: "A cancer is spreading in our industry. . . .

The cancer is called greed."[26] But greed, it seems, can be a matter of whose pockets are being lined. What his readers didn't know was that Rohatyn, a very senior partner at Lazard Frères, was—at about the time his article appeared—secretly counseling two of his major clients, Lee Iacocca of Chrysler and Edward L. Hennessy, Jr., of Allied-Signal, on a joint $40 billion takeover of General Motors, a transaction that couldn't have been anything but hostile. Allied-Signal was to acquire the auto-parts businesses and Chrysler the five auto divisions. Rohatyn's contribution—according to Iaccoca who broke the story—was the suggestion that they enlist the help of the data-processing billionaire H. Ross Perot, founder of EDS, now a GM subsidiary, who in December 1986 was removed from GM's board and paid $700 million for his stock, twice its market value, after publicly feuding with CEO Roger Smith. Although he protested weakly that he's "against hostile takeovers," it wasn't out of principle that Iacocca abandoned the GM raid. He writes that a "check with a takeover lawyer on the sly" and concerns over financing led to the conclusion "that it might be easier to buy Greece."[27]

## One Share, One Vote: The Corporate Class Struggle

On another battleground of the corporate war, there is what an inspired headline writer on *The Wall Street Journal* calls "class struggle," disputes over classes and categories of stock, particularly voting and non-voting stock.[28] The slogan "one share, one vote," raised by T. Boone Pickens's United Shareholders Association, conjures an image of "corporate democracy" that is analogous to political democracy, and that is misleading. In elections for corporate directors, unlike those for political offices, the investor with the most shares has the most votes and therefore the most power. The fight is not over whether all shareholders can vote, but over whether all shares have equal weight or voting power in the election of directors.

There's nothing at all egalitarian or democratic about corporate governance, any more than there is about the governance of football teams, theatrical productions, magazines, and symphony orchestras. Power must be vested—by owners or their agents—in a coach, a director, an editor, or a conductor if any of those ventures are to succeed. So the dispute over voting and non-voting stock, the baby talk notwithstanding, is not about something called shareholders' democracy but about power, power to appoint managers and power to shape company policies.

Classes of stock with unequal voting rights are issued to ensure the control of a founding family or some other group of insiders. In mid-1988 there were 359 companies with shares of disparate voting rights (up from only 119 in 1985)—60 that traded on the New York Stock Exchange, 117 on the American Stock Exchange, and 182 on the National Association of Securities Dealers' automated quotation system, or NASD.

The largest corporation with stocks of unequal voting power, the Ford Motor Company, went public in November 1955 when the Ford Foundation, originally set up as a family tax shelter, offered more than 7 million shares to the public, which were quickly snapped up. In order to retain family control the Fords reached a unique agreement with the New York Stock Exchange, then eager for the big chunk of new business but which wouldn't list other companies with dual classes of stock until the end of 1986. Common shares were sold to the public while the Ford family retained the B, or super voting power, shares. Both carry voting rights, but 40 percent of the voting power is vested in the relatively small number of B shares, thus assuring the family effective control. The Fords' holdings in 1988 accounted for less than 7.5 percent of the total shares, common and B, outstanding. Under the company's current certificate of incorporation, the super voting power of the B stock is reduced to 30 percent if the Ford family holdings fall below 22.5 million shares from the present level of 37.7 million, and it vanishes altogether when the number is less than 15.1 million shares. Ford B shares aren't publicly traded; but since their voting power is more than eight times that of the common shares, the upper-boundary value of the Ford family's holdings in July of 1988—assuming a raider to pay top dollar for them—was more than $6 billion.[29]

A similar arrangement in Dow Jones & Company, Inc., the publisher of *The Wall Street Journal*, enables members of the Bancroft family—legatees of Clarence W. Barron, the legendary editor and publisher—to exercise control so long as they continue to invest their wealth in a minimal number of super voting power shares. But family control of The Washington Post and The New York Times companies is preserved without the maintenance of minimal equity positions. Power to accept or reject an offer to take over The Washington Post Company is vested solely in the Graham family by virtue of its holdings of an unspecified number of supershares. All that's necessary to preserve the Sulzberger family's control of The New York Times Company is their ownership of a relatively small number of supershares, less than 1 percent of the authorized total of common stock.[30]

In a crucial test in the spring of 1988, Media General, another communications company, won a suit that prevented a hostile takeover by Burt Sugarman, a Hollywood film producer, who offered $70 for each of the outstanding shares when they were trading in the market at less than $46. The court, in effect, said that the founding Bryan family can retain 70 percent of the voting power even if they sell most of their supershares.[31]

The economic consequences of dual classes of stocks are not difficult to fathom. Potential wealth—unless it's assumed that control will never be sold—is denied the outsiders as the present value of the company grows and the gap widens between the value of the ordinary shares and the supershares. Vesting unchallengeable control in a single family or other insider group also compels the outsiders to bear greater risks and suffer larger losses if unwise policies are pursued for longer than they would be by managers who are more easily removed.

Nonetheless, investors do buy company shares that carry little or no voting power. Jeffrey Coors, president of Adolph Coors Co., Colorado brewers, told a Senate committee, "We're selling investment, not control."[32] Why, then, shouldn't investors be free to enter into any sort of contractual relationship they deem in their interests? The answer is that there are conflicts between private interests and the public interest, which is a consensual view of what is good. That is why contracts for surrogate motherhood are being invalidated in many states and chattel slavery is illegal. By rendering autonomous managers even more impervious to criticism, dual classes of stock diminish corporate efficiency.

There's a distinction between Ford and the newspaper publishers, which have for long reserved control for the insiders, and companies that issue new shares of non-voting stock as a defense against unfriendly takeovers, sometimes by actions of the directors alone. It's a tactic that the SEC moved to outlaw in July 1988 when it adopted a narrowly drawn one-share, one-vote rule. What the rule says is that shares of companies that in the future abolish or reduce voting rights can't be traded on the organized exchanges or in the major over-the-counter markets. Most existing shares with unequal voting rights were exempted as well as issues of companies going public and those authorized under state antitakeover laws.[33]

In obliquely attacking the problem of unequal voting rights through its power to regulate the securities markets, the SEC, which debated for years before making the rule, avoided the controversial question of federal intrusion into internal corporate governance, historically the province of the chartering states. Critics of corporate takeovers, notably former Senator William Proxmire of Wisconsin, then chairman of the Banking Committee, assailed the SEC action as "legally unauthorized," and it may well be subjected to challenges in the courts. Weighing in on the other side, Proxmire's House Commerce Committee counterpart, Representative John Dingell of Michigan, expressed regrets that the SEC came up with a rule seriously weakened by exemptions.

Although generally skeptical of government regulation, I cheer the SEC for belatedly though courageously taking a step in the right direction.[34] Giving entrenched managers a free hand to disenfranchise shareholders would have been a travesty—the ultimate separation of power from property that Adolf Berle predicted and feared.

International economic pressures may ultimately force Congress to reconsider the federal government's role in corporate governance. The Constitution, Article I, section 8 (3), gives Congress explicit authority to regulate interstate commerce, in which almost every business corporation of any consequence is engaged. There are solid grounds for legislation mandating the federal chartering of corporations; but short of such a radical and unlikely resolution of the governance problem, Congress could selectively preempt the states on issues such as takeovers that clearly impinge on the national interest.

## Japan, Inc.: Can Corporate America Compete?

Despite Western technological and cultural influences, Japan retains its uniqueness. Ethnic homogeneity, feudal and dynastic traditions, xenophobia, and a one-party political system are the elements of a highly disciplined society. Japanese corporate managers are far more amenable than their Western counterparts to the whims and wishes of government ministries, but they benefit from the stronger loyalty of their employees.[35]

Whatever weight given cultural differences, there's no denying Japan's place as the world's most successful exporter, a spectacular accomplishment despite rather than because of heavy-handed government intervention. MITI—Japan's Ministry of International Trade and Industry, once the war production agency—initially opposed the export of automobiles. It is the excellence of Japan's products—innovative designs, high quality, and, most important, effectively competitive pricing—not Tokyo's protectionist policies that accounts for a large, bilateral trade surplus with the United States.

What is especially noteworthy is the speed with which Japanese corporations made the painful adjustment to the *endaka* (sky-high yen), the more-than-doubling of the value of the yen against the dollar from the beginning of 1985 through mid-1988. When the yen rose to Y150 = $1, up from the low of Y263.65 = $1 on February 25, 1985, it became cheaper for Japanese companies to manufacture in the United States—or such newly industrialized countries (NICs) as South Korea and Taiwan—and they were quick to move overseas, leaving smaller subcontractors in the lurch, a process called "industrial hollowing-out." The United States had faced the same problem earlier, during the sharp appreciation of the dollar against the yen, from 1980 to 1985. Losses of employment in U.S. manufacturing, especially in the mid-western "rust belt," were gradually offset by new, often lower-paid jobs in the rapidly growing services sector—among others, in retail establishments and finance. But the process was very painful in the United States, and it was feared that Japan, with its smaller domestic market, would find itself in the same predicament of high unemployment. Thus far, it hasn't happened and isn't likely to do so as long as Japan produces attractively priced, innovative products of high quality. What's more, Japan did not increase its import protection as the United States did when it twisted arms in Tokyo for a "voluntary" restraint—a quota in all but name—on exports of autos to the U.S. market.[36]

The automobile is a metaphor for what's right with corporate Japan and wrong with corporate America. In 1980, Japan, with an output of 7 million units, supplanted the United States as the world's largest auto producer and has, narrowly, maintained its dominance.[37] Despite trade barriers—first import quotas and then "voluntary" exports restraints—and after 1984 a sharply appreciating yen, Japan's share of the U.S. market rose from 22.7 percent in 1980 to 23.2 percent in 1987, a figure that doesn't include Japanese units that are assembled here. That rise of market share reflects two hard facts of automotive life. The first is that the Japanese turn out vehicles, over most of the price-size range, that are clearly superior to ours, both in design and in the quality of workmanship. Ford, with a 1987 domestic market share of 20.2 percent, scored a great success with its stylish Taurus, but along with big sales came big headaches for customers: among others, steering flaws that threatened a loss of control.[38] Fact two is that protection weakens rather than strengthens the competitive position of the U.S. auto industry. Restraints on Japanese imports notwithstanding, the U.S. auto makers lost market share because of high prices and their utter failure to come up with any innovative products. Under protection there's no real need to innovate. Opening the U.S. market to the full force of Japanese competition would benefit U.S. consumers through lower prices, force General Motors and Chrysler to shape up, shrink their operations, or get out of business. And with the still sky-high yen, that competitive shock could be absorbed with little adverse impact on employment because the U.S.-based operations of Japanese auto manufacturers would expand.

U.S. industries, such as steel and autos, that are in trouble because of a failure to innovate or maintain efficiency typically seek import protection from Congress. But the U.S. semiconductor industry—the makers of chips, silicon, and other wafers of microcircuitry for computers and other sophisticated electronic products—hardly fits that description, not in early 1986, when a few companies charged the Japanese with "unfair dumping," and not now. In 1988 the United States was the only significant player in the exciting market for reduced instruction set computers (RISCs)—microprocessors that run at speeds four to ten times those of conventional models. Along with genetic engineering, in which the United States has a wide lead, our pioneering semiconductor industry continues to be an innovating adornment to world science and technology.

The call for "saving" an industry that really needed no help came in 1986 from a handful of companies that specialized in the 64-kilobyte DRAMs—dynamic random access memory chips that stored 64,000 bits of information—then used in personal computers. Already obsolescent, the 64-k DRAMs were a glut on the market, and some U.S. companies couldn't match the lower costs of their larger Japanese rivals. The "dumping" of which they complained was little more than plain-vanilla price cutting. It was Charles E. Sporck, president of National Semiconductor of San Jose—a big company with a penchant for missing out on expanding product markets and a costly failure to shrink its 64-k DRAM—who most loudly raised the specter of a Japanese chip invasion and a threat to the national security. To paraphrase Samuel Johnson, national security is the last refuge of a corporate scoundrel.

Protectionist bureaucrats and advisers to the Reagan Defense and Commerce departments duly responded by pushing for a cartel agreement with their obliging counterparts in MITI—under which the two governments would impose production and export restraints in an effort to maintain higher prices in the United States and other export markets. Consummated at the end of July 1986, it permitted U.S. chipmakers to expand their share of the Japanese market from 8.5

percent to more than 20 percent by 1991. Within one month of the agreement, spot chip prices doubled and there were complaints of a "shortage." But, predictably, the cartel accord broke down because of a failure to control output. There was a thriving gray market for chips in Japan, in which prices were falling, a development that caused Washington to cry "cheating." So in March 1987, President Reagan, anxious to appease Congress by some well-staged Japan bashing, imposed tariff surcharges of as high as 100 percent on some $300 million of Japanese imports. MITI resolved the conflict when it dragged its feet on issuing export licenses, thereby forcing a reduction of Japanese chip production. A glut gave way to still another chip shortage, since neither the MITI–Commerce Department bureaucrats nor the big U.S. producers on whose behalf they were acting had the wit or foresight to predict the turns of the sophisticated, rapidly changing product markets. No one does, which is why the temptation to tamper with markets should be resisted.

The chip war may soon become history. Changing technology and new products are altering the market. With the rising demand for more highly integrated chips, U.S. computer firms shifted to bigger and more integrated chips, 256-kilobyte and 1-megabyte DRAMs, which they design in substantial part for manufacture in Pacific rim countries. Complaints of a chip shortage early in 1988 gave way to ample supplies and falling prices by midyear. But an expensive and potentially mischievous memento of that episode survives: Sematech, an industry research-and-development consortium, established at the behest of the Semiconductor Industry Association and supported in part by a five-year, $500 million matching commitment from the Defense Department. Sematech drew plaudits from proponents of an "American industrial policy"—what they think of as MITI-style central planning. Started up in April 1988 and headed by Robert N. Noyce, a chip pioneer and co-founder of Intel, Sematech drew criticism from the outset for concentrating on the manufacturing skills of the big merchant chipmakers, such as National Semiconductor and Intel, and ignoring the small, entrepreneurial companies that often come up with the most important innovations. Aside from the waste of lavishing tax dollars on large chipmakers, there is the danger that Sematech will play a pivotal role in perpetuating the chip cartel.[39]

Are the automobile and semiconductor cartels the norms for future trading relationships between the United States and Japan? In Louis Galambos and Joseph Pratt's history of U.S. corporate policy in this century, *The Rise of the Corporate Commonwealth,* that question is answered in the affirmative.[40] Galambos and Pratt believe that the "flexibility of the American business system," in evidence since the beginning of this century, will assure its survival. By "flexibility" they mean the resourcefulness of corporate leaders in the "control of external environments," and they offer J. P. Morgan, Sr., and Lee Iacocca as archetypes. Morgan controlled his external environment by assembling the United States Steel Corporation in 1901. He sharply reduced competition by bringing Andrew Carnegie's more efficient plants under his oligopolistic tent and saw to it that a collusive floor was built under steel prices through the notorious industry dinners hosted by Judge Elbert H. Gary, U.S. Steel's chief. Iacocca, the contemporary system builder, solved Chrysler's external problem by pushing for a federal loan guarantee in 1980 and, more importantly, by continually lobbying for quotas and other restraints on Japanese auto imports. Galambos and Pratt warmly endorse such protectionist policies because they believe that they will "persuade American business and labor to make needed adjustments in the adversarial system."

Are Galambos and Pratt right in thinking that the future will be modeled on Iacocca's "system"? I think not.

Today the U.S. economy is far more open to foreign competition than it was in Morgan's time. Foreign trade and foreign investment— from and to the United States—now comprise much larger shares of the gross national product than they did in 1900. In a world of increasingly mobile capital, the Japanese responded to protectionist auto-import policies by setting up plants here, a trend that was greatly accelerated by the *endaka,* or sky-high yen. Direct Japanese investment in U.S. manufacturing (the total was about $50 billion in 1988) diminishes fears about losses of blue-collar jobs. And such investment, both direct and portfolio or financial, is a two-way street. There is a high degree of interpenetration, both industrial and financial, of the U.S. and Japanese economies, a scrambling of eggs that isn't going to be undone. Honda and Sony aren't going to pull their operations out of the United States any more than IBM and Citibank will leave Japan.

Because of double-digit unemployment early in the decade and the shocks suffered by manufacturing industries, especially in the Middle West, a lamentably protectionist trade bill was enacted in 1988. But there is small comfort in the defeat of the egregious amendment sponsored by Missouri's Representative Richard Gephardt that mandated punitive action against any country running a persistently large bilateral trade surplus with the United States. And it's my hope that the balance of economic and political forces will be tipped against protectionism.

In a future certain to be marked by increasing international competition, one in which it will be more difficult to maintain or advance living standards, Americans will become more aware than ever before of the costs of protective subsidies, whether they benefit farmers or domestic producers of automobiles, steel, or textiles. In 1980 Lee Iacocca was the hero who saved Chrysler from bankruptcy, but in 1986 he was the bum who closed down the American Motors plant in Kenosha, Wisconsin.

The import restraints for which Iaccoca lobbied add an average of about $2,500 to the price of every car sold in this country. With the slower growth of U.S. family income, there will, I think, be an ever heightening awareness of whose pockets get picked and whose get stuffed in the political process. Important tests will come as the European Economic Community (EEC) moves toward its 1992 goal of closer economic integration. In the process, the EEC will doubtless attempt to protect Western Europe from external competition by highly protectionist policies. The problem then will be to dissuade America from shooting itself in the foot by counterproductive retaliation.

But whatever the difficulties with the EEC, the United States can continue to engage in a mutually beneficial, competitive relationship with Japan. Of all pairs of industrially advanced economies, they are among the most complementary. Save for fish, densely populated

CORPORATE MAKEOVER

Japan is a woefully inefficient food producer while the United States ranks among the world's most efficient. Greater imports of food, especially rice, would ultimately free up land for housing in Japan.

Japan produces superb automobiles and its production could well surpass the combined output of both the United States and Europe by 1990.[41] It can serve the huge U.S. market well, either through exports or factory migration. And if you think that any country is divinely ordained to be the leader of auto production for eternity, bear in mind that the original technology was invented in France during the 1890s and quickly transferred to other countries. "Automobile," "garage," "transmission," "magneto," and "chauffeur" are French words.

The United States excels in pure science and high technolgy while Japan's forte—as demonstrated by its complete dominance of the video recorder market—is product development and mass production. Both economies are highly productive, together accounting for about 40 percent of the world gross product. What's more, Japan's spectacular success as an exporter and its great advance in accumulated wealth have ushered in domestic economic changes that should benefit U.S. industry. Japanese living standards are on a rising trend as people there seek greater amenities, such as better telecommunications and more commodious housing—demands that U.S. industry is in a good position to fill.

In the year after the resolution of the chip war, progress was made in opening the Japanese market to imports, especially for citrus fruits and other U.S. agricultural products. At the same time the high yen opened Japan to an experience familiar to American business, a flood of cheap imports from the newly industrialized countries of Asia.[42] So Japan, for once, will be losing some trade battles with countries other than the United States as its trade surplus shrinks.

## The MBA Syndrome, or What's Wrong with Managers

The ideas of economists and political philosophers, both when they are right and when they are wrong, are more powerful than is commonly understood. Indeed the world is ruled by little else.

Practical men, who believe themselves to be quite exempt from any intellectual influences, are usually the slaves of some defunct economist. Madmen in authority, who hear voices in the air, are distilling their frenzy from some academic scribbler of a few years back. I am sure that the power of vested interests is vastly exaggerated compared with the gradual encroachment of ideas. Not, indeed, immediately, but after a certain interval; for in the field of economic and political philosophy there are not many who are influenced by new theories after they are twenty-five or thirty years of age, so that the ideas which civil servants and politicians and even agitators apply to current events are not likely to be the newest. But, soon or late, it is ideas, not vested interests, which are dangerous for good or evil.

—John Maynard Keynes[43]

The ideas that are weakening corporate America are symbolized by an academic degree, the MBA or Master of Business Administration. According to the U.S. Department of Education, more than 70,000 MBAs were awarded in 1987–88, up from a little more than 4,600 in 1958–59. In 1987–88, the peak of the market crash, there were nearly 270,000 registrants for the Graduate Management Admissions Test, the screen for business school applicants. But such numbers only begin to tell the story of what has happened in American corporate life over the past thirty years. In *The Big Store,* his splendid account of the troubles of Sears, Donald R. Katz writes of Howard Lasky, the "terrier-like" chief of the big Los Angeles group of stores, who "tended to keep the fact of his rare 1950s MBA from Stanford to himself."[44] Lasky's diffidence was shared by my better students at Rutgers University in the early 1950s, bright, well-trained mechanical, chemical, and electrical engineers—then earning about $9,000 a year—who couldn't have cared less about an MBA but wanted to learn anything that would help them move into better-paying sales, administrative, and finance jobs. Today the MBA, far from being a rarity or a credential that anyone would want to conceal, is far too often an essential requirement, a sine qua non, for being hired and placed in the fast-track executive training programs of most large corporations.

Licensing—whether of a barber who may never earn more than

$25,000 a year, or a board-certified ophthalmologist, who may realize as much as $250,000—is a time-honored means of limiting entry into crafts and professions, thereby bolstering the income levels of those who are "in" and protecting them from those who are "out."[45] The ostensible purpose of licensing is to save the public from incompetents, and for that dubious protection we are compelled to pay considerably more for services than we would if entry into crafts and professions were free and the increased number of practitioners heightened competition and lowered prices. Happily, governments and quasi-governmental authorities—which certify accountants as well as peddlers of securities, insurance policies, and real estate—haven't instituted the formal licensing of corporate managers, and they may never. But much the same effect is achieved by limiting executive-track jobs to graduates of prestigious business schools.[46]

Although meritocratic, accepting only MBAs from good schools with high class rankings is a practice that shuts out equally bright young people with diverse educational backgrounds. The best young manager in my time at Citicorp had a Ph.D. in biophysics, and he probably wouldn't have gotten a foot in the trainee door had he been confronted by today's MBA-oriented personnel people and managers. Limiting the field to graduates of one sort of school fosters standardized thinking, deepens the bureaucratic lassitude that afflicts corporations, and perpetuates a thoroughly pernicious myth that was recently underscored by John P. Kotter, a fresh voice from the Harvard Business School, when he wrote :

> It would help greatly if we could take the concept of the professional manager who can manage anything and drive a stake through its ever so resilient heart. That concept is still very influential. . . . It haunts MBA education. It influences how managers think about their careers. . . . It is used to justify tragic staffing decisions, some of the more outrageous acquisitions by raiders, and many of the least successful diversification efforts in the last two decades.[47]

If the harm done by business schools were confined only to the belief that professional managers can "manage anything," there wouldn't be as great a cause for concern. That myth, a truly delusive conceit, persists because it is part of an ethos that the business schools, Harvard in particular, do much to perpetuate. It is the ethos of managerial control in which corporations serve the interests of their employees, white and blue collar, rather than those of the shareholder-owners. Management's objective, as defined in an authoritative research monograph by Gordon Donaldson of the Harvard Business School, is the maximization of "corporate wealth," that is, "cash, credit and other purchasing power by which management commands goods and services"—rather than profits or the present value of the company.[48] Donaldson's findings are based on interviews with the managers of some very large corporations, and it's my surmise that what the interrogators were told was critically shaped by what the respondents learned as Harvard Business School students or as readers of its publications. There is an incestuous relationship between the faculty of the B School and those of its graduates who hold high corporate posts, a relationship that spawns conflicts of interest. Some of the professors whose putatively objective Harvard "case studies" are used in the classroom serve as directors or consultants to those same companies being studied.[49] But whatever the precise relationship between the alma mater and her children, it's clear that the B School is an ideological fountainhead of managerial control.

That said, the dangers posed by Harvard and other business schools shouldn't be exaggerated. Since the 1987 stock market crash, they've lost much of their pecuniary attraction; total enrollment is declining.[50] Moreover, as the breakdown of managerial control proceeds, the doctrines espoused by the better business schools will, with a lag, change. Courses on entrepreneurship are now offered by schools with curricula that are still essentially geared to the needs of large, bureaucratic organizations. So it's possible that the academic likes of Michael Jensen and John Kotter will play a constructive role in creating a new regime of corporate control.

## On Corporate Responsibility and Corporations in Politics

I have never known much good done by those who affected to trade for the publick good.

—Adam Smith

Directors who refuse to *maximise* profits because, for example, they pay attention to competing social interests such as those of employees, cannot be legally penalised: indeed they are likely to be popular.

—Robin Marris[51]

Business corporations as creatures of the state enjoy many privileges and immunities, in fact, too many. But it does not follow—as many critics seem to assume—that they must therefore shoulder reciprocal responsibilities that transcend the imperative of profitability. There are two reasons why corporations shouldn't be "socially responsible"—shorthand for obligations to employees, communitities, industries, and even direct competitors. The first is that business organizations aren't particularly good at doing things outside of their main line of work. Second, good corporate deeds or social responsibility may well conflict with the interests of shareholders.

This is illustrated by a dispute that raged in the late 1960s over building a large department store on Manhattan's Upper West Side. The proposal, which called for locating the store on the lower floors of a tall apartment building, came up for zoning clearance before a then very militant community board, and a bitter fight ensued. In return for its approval, the board demanded that the corporation provide on-site facilities for young children and old people. But when it became apparent that the price of those public amenities was going to be very steep, the project was abandoned. Several hundred good new jobs were thereby lost, and to add insult to injury, a poorly designed building was erected on the site which provided only a few new jobs in ground-floor stores.

While the neighborhood militants were widely blamed for pressing extravagant demands that resulted in a loss both of employment and the convenience of an attractive store, fundamental issues weren't raised. Aside from having what were perceived as deep pockets, the corporation in question was hardly qualified to provide facilities for children or elderly people. If such facilities were in fact needed, a much more efficient way to establish them would have been by specialized public or private welfare agencies. Another issue that was glossed over was the question of who was going to bear the burden of those facilities. The assumption was that "it," the corporation that operated a small group of department stores, would ante up. But the "it" was really they, the owners; and what happened was that the dominant shareholders, members of the founding family, decided that the return on the projected investment, net of the costs of the amenities, wasn't sufficiently attractive.

Other, much larger corporations take a more liberal view and bestow such public benefactions as large cash contributions to the arts, a practice aptly characterized by Michael Kinsley, editor of *The New Republic*, as "executives playing Medici with other people's money." Philip Morris—the sixth-ranking U.S. corporation by market value in the spring of 1988, even before it added Kraft to its collection of food, drink, and tobacco jewels, is surely the art world's favorite corporation. Among the beneficiaries of its tax-deductible generosity are the Metropolitan and Whitney art museums in New York, the Brooklyn Academy of Music, the National and Corcoran galleries of art and the Kennedy Center in Washington, the Joffrey Ballet, and the Alvin Ailey American Dance Theater. All are admirable institutions that enrich American cultural life, mine included: but there's a boorish, unanswered question of principle. Is Hamish Maxwell, Philip Morris's cultivated chairman, making good use of the shareholders' money? Perhaps those contributions can be justified as acts of goodwill that win the public's approbation and offset the criticisms of Philip Morris's tobacco business.[52] Texaco's management attempted to tap a reservoir of public goodwill when it warned that an Icahn victory in the great 1988 proxy battle would end its decades-long sponsorship of Saturday-afternoon radio broadcasts of Metropolitan Opera performances. Whatever the answer, the issue of shareholders' benefits hasn't been seriously addressed.

There's a much more important dimension of the social-responsibility issue: whether corporations should deliberately pursue employment and other operating policies that diminish profits. It's a demand made by communities that oppose the closing of obsolete or otherwise uneconomic manufacturing facilities. And what they are saying is that the shareholders of the corporation should absorb the losses that would ensue. But does it really make sense to postpone job losses for one set of workers by diminishing the pension benefits of another set of workers? That's what's going to happen to an increasing degree as the share of corporate stocks and bonds owned by pension plans increases.

Robert Kuttner, the economics editor of *The New Republic,* plays a variation on that same basic theme. Rightly concerned about the passive role to which employee stock ownership plans (ESOPs) are usually relegated, he writes that: "Congress might pass a chartering law creating a new corporate form, which would enjoy certain tax advantages and regulatory protections against hostile takeovers, but in turn would be structured institutionally to give workers coequal power with shareholders."[53]

I strongly support Kuttner's view that all shares held by ESOPs should carry voting rights, rights that now are withheld in the vast majority of cases. If that were done, there would be no problem of workers having coequal power, since everything would depend on the size of an ESOP's share holding. But I disagree with Kuttner when he assumes that a worker-controlled company could somehow ignore the profit imperative and still survive. Surely the evidence thus far isn't encouraging. An ESOP-owned and controlled Hyatt Clark plant in New Jersey closed in July 1987. It was losing money, and the worker-owners were as disdainful of their own managers as they were of those whom they had replaced. And an ESOP that took control of the old General Dynamics shipyard in Quincy, Massachusetts, is struggling to escape the same fate.[54] The problem is that of lemon socialism: an obsolete plant or other installation doesn't cease being a lemon just because it's owned and operated by its workers.

State-owned or -controlled enterprises in Mexico and Brazil, such as Pemex and Petrobras, their nationalized oil companies, illustrate the dangers of unbounded "social responsibility" and the failure to separate economic from political power. In both instances, chronic losses or deficits resulting from swollen labor forces and politically determined wage levels are financed by central bank credit, and that creation of new money adds to inflation pressures.

By passing legislation that inhibits corporate takeovers and subjecting plant closings to long and very costly delays, the federal and state governments may so impair the incomes of private pension plans, and those of the parent companies, that they're unable to pay the benefits due retirees. Under the pension insurance provisions of the Employee Retirement Income Security Act (ERISA), the federal government would be duty bound to provide those benefits. But if the ERISA insurance fund were to be exhausted, the government would then have to borrow, plausibly on a scale that would result in more rapid inflation.

Preserving the autonomy of the business corporation guarantees a separation of political from economic power, a goal toward which reformers in communist and some Third World countries are striving. That separation is essential on grounds other than economic efficiency, because an intrusive government that controls hundreds of millions of business transactions—activities that can only be automatically coordinated by free markets—is also very likely to deny elemental liberties to its subjects.

But even with the cleanest separation of powers, the business corporation cannot be divorced from the political process. Shareholders have an interest in government as regulator not only of their company but as a large customer as well. It's a relationship that creates knotty problems. Take, for example, the quotas on Japanese automobiles that were imposed in 1980 at the behest of the domestic auto manufacturers. It was, as I've already argued, a bad policy which hurt American consumers by raising all auto prices, thus relieving pressures that might have compelled the domestic manufacturers to become more competitive. That's my view when I wear my consumer's or economist's hat. But as a big Chrysler shareholder, I would have been in a dilemma. My short-run interests would have been served by going along with Lee Iacocca's Japan bashing, even though my personal gains from protectionism were likely to be wiped out over the longer run.

Another problem arises out of corporate efforts to alter the general political evironment as opposed to lobbying on issues directly affecting specific industries or companies, usually through contributions to tax-exempt foundations with strong conservative biases. Shareholders of an opposite persuasion can legitimately complain that their money is being spent in loathsome causes. As agents of the shareholder-owners, managers have a fiduciary responsibility to maximize the value of the company; playing ideological public-relations games diverts resources from that task.

# 6

## PEERING INTO THE CORPORATE FUTURE:

### Forces, Directions, and Conjectures

Nations stumble upon establishments which are indeed the result of human action, but not the execution of any human design.
—Adam Ferguson, 1767[1]

The control of large corporations by autonomous managers was not readily predictable but the same cannot be said of its decline and ultimate demise. Ineluctable forces are arrayed against managerial control that will ultimately destroy it. The only uncertainty is the timing—whether the decline and fall of managerial control will be measured in years or decades—and the interrelated question of what kind of regime will replace it.

Far from being the creature of conscious planning, the rise of managerial control was largely accidental. It grew out of the trusts of the 1880s and 1890s, arrangements under which companies in the same industry exchanged their stock for interests in a new corporate entity established for the purpose of raising or at least stabilizing product prices in a time of deflation. Effective industry trusts required a transfer of broad discretionary power from owners—founding entrepreneurs or small groups of investors who owned a majority of company shares, such as that led by J. P. Morgan, Sr.—to trustees, professional managers with unquestioned authority to make crucial decisions. Trusts were eventually dismantled after the passage of the Sherman Act of 1890, but the discretionary powers conferred on the managers were retained and expanded, not only in state legislation that facilitated corporate mergers through the device of holding companies but in court-made law as well.

Another prime mover in the evolution of managerial control was the rise of a thriving middle class early in this century. Increasingly affluent farmers, lawyers, doctors, storekeepers, and salesmen were saving money and needed to invest it. In an era of very little and often no borrowing by the state and federal governments, the safest investments were high-grade corporate securities, stocks and bonds. And when the growing needs of savers were complemented by an efficient network of brokerage houses and banks that underwrote and marketed securities, the ownership in large corporations became widely dispersed, especially as founding owners saw very large profits to be made by selling off portions of their share holdings. With an ever broader dispersion of stock ownership, control of those companies became firmly vested in their professional managers.

Managerial control survived the depression of the 1930s and faced few challenges before 1975, largely because the dominance of the U.S. economy in a world devastated by the Second World War masked the failure of managers to pursue value-maximizing policies. That grace period came to an end with the worldwide inflation of 1965–80 and the equally disruptive disinflation that ensued. Wide disparities were created between the valuation of corporations by the stock market and the much larger sums that could be realized by buying control of a company and dismantling it, selling off plants or entire lines of business. That fundamental disparity elicited an unprecedented wave of hostile takeovers, defensive restructuring, and buyouts that take once publicly held companies private. It's a burst of activity that is largely fueled by financial institutions—pension plans, insurance companies, and mutual funds—which together now own more than half of all corporate shares. This new concentration of ownership has reversed the dispersion of shareholdings that was crucial to the preservation of managerial power.

## Will Washington Stall the Makeover?

Unlike *perestroika*—efforts to restructure Soviet-bloc economies from the top down by political fiat—the corporate makeover in the United States is driven by market forces. It affects single companies rather than entire industries or economic sectors, and thus far efforts by state legislatures—and a half-hearted thrust by the Federal Reserve Board—to slow the momentum have been largely ineffectual. But will the picture be changed by the intrusion of the federal government?

The great surge of leveraged buyouts in 1988, especially RJR Nabisco, began troubling Washington's lawmakers, and their concern might have been heightened by a Christmas message from Fred L. Hartley, the irrepressible chairman of Unocal whose expensive war on Spain's red-legged partridges was earlier noted. He wrote: "If Christmas in the year 2000 is to be as joyful as those you and I have shared, this country must curtail LBOs and other destructive business activities."[2]

Nor did the issue escape the attention of President Bush. In the course of a press conference held shortly before his inauguration, there was this exchange:

> Q. Mr. President [sic], last year there were over 3,000 leveraged buyouts and mergers and acquisitions, both friendly and unfriendly. There are very few publicly owned corporations left. What are you going to do to stop this alarming trend?
>
> BUSH: In the first place, you're talking to one who would, as much as possible, rely on market forces. Secondly if there are abuses of tax laws, they will be seriously reviewed . . . to see how they can be eliminated. For example, if people say that equity is debt . . . and indeed it is really equity, there are things you can do in the tax laws to correct that. . . .[3]

The President's alert reply neatly reflected current thinking, both on Capitol Hill and in the Treasury headed by his friend Nicholas F. Brady. Critics of corporate makeovers assert that junk bonds are not debentures—loans to be repaid with interest—but are really equities or stocks. Once that dubious premise is granted it follows, according to the corporate income-tax code, that interest paid by issuers of junk bonds should be no more deductible as a corporate expense than the dividends paid on shares of stock.

An anonymous investment banker struck at the heart of the tax deductibility of junk bonds when he remarked that Bush's statement implies that "there is some metaphysical definition of debt and equity that exists outside the [legal] rights of securities holders."[4] The functional distinction between the two classes of investments and investors is clear: bondholders are creditors with prior claims on interest and principal, and equity holders own the residual. Those who argue to the contrary are either genuinely bewitched by the corporate substitution of junk bonds for common stocks—they really believe that a junk bond is a share of stock, much as they would confuse a chicken with a turkey because they can eat either bird—or they're looking for any reason, however implausible, to halt corporate makeovers.

An assault on the tax deductibility of junk bonds is not a venture to be taken lightly. It would mean a radical, ex post facto change in the rules of the game and a body blow to a $185 billion financial market. Enemies of the corporate makeover on Capitol Hill—or a Commissioner of Internal Revenue who dreams of striking a blow by ukase—must be prepared for bloody political combat. All the more so when it becomes apparent that the bulk of junk bonds are issued to raise working capital and finance business expansion, purposes unrelated to makeovers.

My clearly biased view is that the Bush administration, after testing the political waters, will either back off or settle for an anemic, easily circumvented restraint such as that so foolishly imposed by the Federal Reserve Board. The early Bush record confirms that judgment. In hearings before the Senate Finance Committee, Nicholas Brady, the Treasury secretary, was unhappy about debt-financed makeovers, but said: "We really don't have a solution." The Federal Reserve's chairman, Alan Greenspan, didn't believe that the issue of makeovers could be addressed through the tax system. And Lloyd Bentsen, the Finance Committee chairman, said: "Whatever we do will not, in my estimate, be particularly dramatic."[5] Even if that caution gives way to recklessly resolute action, the corporate makeover will only be stalled, not stopped. In a market system, economic forces have a way of working their will.

## Control Wars: Weapons and Strategies

While Washington girds for what could be a great battle, the war for corporate control continues in other theaters of combat.

At the end of October 1988, Martin Lipton, dean of takeover defense lawyers and originator of the once formidable poison pill, wrote a widely circulated memorandum, "Is This the End of Takeovers." It opens on a note of alarm:

> The state takeover laws did not stop them. Litigation—antitrust and other—did not stop them. The reaction to the Pac Man defense of Martin Marietta against Bendix did not stop them. Shark re-pellents and poison pills did not stop them. And jawboning by the Fed and the failure of the Federated Department Stores junk bond offering will not stop them.
>
> Our Nation is blindly rushing to the precipice. As with tulip bulbs, South Sea bubbles, pyramid investment trusts, Florida land, REITs, LDC loans, Texas banks and all other financial market frenzies of the past, the denouement will be a crash. We and our children will pay a gigantic price for allowing boot-strap, junk-bond takeovers. . . .
>
> The only remedy is effective legislation. Perhaps it is already too late. The institutional investors—who have gained control of vir-tually every major company—show no restraint and no regard for the public good. They must be policed . . . public institutions like banks, insurance companies, pension funds and mutual funds should be prohibited from loading up on junk bonds.

After that lamentation, there is the suggestion of a new defense strategy, the sort of thinking for which Wachtell, Lipton, Rosen & Katz are handsomely compensated:

> At the moment, the courts are our only hope. The poison pill is an effective defense against abusive takeovers. The courts are now

199

recognizing this. Hopefully, they will make it clear that a board of directors does not have to redeem a pill and either auction the company to the highest bidder or restructure by turning equity into debt. In other words, the courts should affirm that a board of directors, acting in good faith and on reasonable grounds, has the *absolute right to reject any takeover bid*.[6]

Had it been accepted by the courts, Lipton's dogma of directorial infallibility—dubbed by critics, with apologies to Nancy Reagan, the "just say no" defense—would have dealt a devastating blow to shareholders. Happily, it wasn't. Just after the memorandum was written, the Delaware Court of Chancery—which earlier had invalidated Macmillan's poison-pill defense in its unsuccessful effort to avert a takeover by Robert Maxwell—ruled against Interco, a Wachtell, Lipton client. A St. Louis-based shoe and furniture manufacturer, Interco, was under hostile attack by the Cardinal Acquisition Corporation, an investment company owned by the Rales brothers of Washington, D.C., who were represented by Skadden, Arps, Slate, Meagher & Flom, the raiders' most successful legal strategists. After making a counterproposal to restructure the company that approximated the value of the Rales's tender offer, Interco's managers then attempted to nullify it by interposing a poison pill, an action that would have denied the shareholders a choice. What Interco wanted to avoid by invoking Lipton's doctrine of an absolute right was a bidding auction that would have benefited the shareholders but surely resulted in the ouster of its manager-directors. The Court of Chancery upheld the Rales brothers, who soon afterward withdrew their tender offer, an action that mooted Wachtell, Lipton's appeal to the Delaware Supreme Court.[7]

Prior to that development, Lipton circulated a second memorandum, "The Interco Case," in which he advised clients that they should consider giving up their Delaware charters if the Court of Chancery were upheld. He pointed out that the Ohio and Pennsylvania statutes permit directors to reject hostile offers solely because they believe them to be against the long-term interests of the shareholders. About 45 percent of all companies listed on the New York

Stock Exchange and more than half of the *Fortune* 500 are incorporated in Delaware but there is little if any evidence of an exodus from Wilmington, and with good reason. Businessmen are not about to abandon the experienced chancellors of the Delaware court, despite the pain that their decisions inflict, for untried and perhaps uninformed jurists in other states.[8]

The U.S. Congress has ample authority under the commerce clause of the Constitution to preempt the states and enact a uniform code for changes of corporate control that would eliminate charter shopping and other really pressing problems. But it's very doubtful that the Bush White House or the Congress, preoccupied with intractible fiscal, trade, and exchange-rate problems, will open a can of political worms by clashing head on with the states on the issue of their long-exercised power to charter and regulate corporations. A first rule of Potomac pragmatism is that you don't fix what isn't so badly broken that it can't work at all.

Martin Lipton was wrong about "the failure" of the Federated junk-bond offering. That deal—stuck for a week or so when lenders demanded that the borrowers put up more equity—was consummated within days after the appearance of Lipton's first memo. But what of his concern about "financial market frenzies" that end with "a crash"? Will takeovers, buyouts, and recaps be added to the procession of manias that have gripped markets from time to time?

Risk is an often neglected reminder that while big money can be quickly made in financial deals, it can also be quickly lost. The leveraged buyout of Revco, the country's largest drugstore chain, ended in bankruptcy, and there will no doubt be much bigger failures as the profits from makeovers decline and investors, forever overreaching, are enticed into increasingly riskier deals. All of which is to say that the breakdown of managerial control is an untidy drama— marred by both greed and fraud—that will continue to inflict pain.

But those failures aren't going to paralyze the financial system any more than it was paralyzed by the stock market's plummet of 1987 or that it will be paralyzed by insolvent savings and loan associations. Nor is it at all likely that takeovers and buyouts, like the seventeenth-century Dutch tulip mania, will suddenly cease and be forgotten.

There is, to be sure, a limit to the number of makeovers that can be done within any short period. Bear in mind, however, that new opportunities are constantly born, that today's megamergers—Philip Morris's union with Kraft or General Electric's conglomerate embrace of Kidder, Peabody and RCA—are fodder for tomorrow's makeovers. Despite confident assurances to the contrary, the diseconomies of large scale are still very much with us. Business organizations cannot grow very large very quickly without encountering the bureaucratic problems of coordination and communication that result in inefficiencies, higher costs, and lower profits.

Makeovers aren't going to continue at their torrid 1985–88 pace, but they won't cease. And there may well be some stunning surprises. If RJR Nabisco can be spun apart to make the separate businesses more profitable than the glued-together whole, is there really good reason to believe that the same won't happen to General Motors or IBM or Citicorp before they succumb to the disabilities of giantism that afflict Sears?

## What's to Replace Managerial Control?

My final objection is to Mr. Lipton's sweeping assertion that "institutional investors . . . have gained control of virtually every major company." Would that it were true.

Lipton equates the heavy ownership of shares by institutions, which is a fact, with their effective control of corporations, which isn't a fact at all. Despite the participation of some very large pension plans as partners in leveraged buyouts, most institutions are still passive investors. Until recently, the Fidelity High Income Fund, which holds more than $1.5 billion of junk bonds and other securities, epitomized that passivity. One of the more sophisticated of the mutual funds, it moved only in October 1988 to eliminate "fundamental limitations" on "investing in companies for the purpose of exercising control or management." While eschewing any intention of "directing . . . the day-to-day operations of any portfolio company" the Fund included among the activities in which it might now engage "seeking changes in the portfolio company's directors or management, seeking changes in a company's direction, seeking the sale of a company or a portion of its assets or participation in a takeover effort or in opposition to a takeover effort."[9]

What the Fidelity managers didn't make explicit in their proxy statement is that authority to press for changes of control is essential in the event that one of the companies whose bonds they hold can't meet its interest payments. Rather than force it into bankruptcy—an often counterproductive option, as commercial banks discovered long ago—Fidelity can now join with other creditors and shareholders to effect a "work out" that might include radical changes in management or the direction of the business.

But while appropriate for a mutual fund, Fidelity's decision doesn't address the broader question of who will control corporations. What's required is not a financial intermediary—be it a mutual fund or a bank or pension plan—with a troubleshooter's license to intervene but the kind of authority that J. P. Morgan, Sr., and his partners continuously exercised when they had absolute control of major steel and railroad corporations.

Kohlberg Kravis Roberts and perhaps other leveraged-buyout partnerships are at the moment playing Morgan-like roles. But the ultimate purpose of an LBO partnership—a creature of the corporate transformation that is unlikely to endure—is not the management of businesses but their recapitalization, radical reorganization and eventual sale. It is not KKR or Clayton & Dubilier or Forstmann Little that are foreshadowing the future but the kind of corporations that they and other LBO partnerships are creating through buyouts.

## From Agent-Managers to Owner-Managers

What, as they say in the fashion business, is the new corporate look? It will be that of a very tightly run company, focused on a single line, or closely related lines, of business with a heavy component of debt and closely held stock, upward of a third of the total shares in the hands of a few top *owner-managers.*

The restructured Safeway Stores, Inc., once the nation's largest food retailer, is beginning to fit that description[10]—a company that's in transition from managerial control to control by owner-managers. Stagnating and under attack by the Haft family's Dart group, Safeway was acquired in 1986 and taken private by KKR in a $4.25 billion LBO deal that burdened it with about $5.75 billion of debt. To pare it down and meet the interest charges, more than half of Safeway's 2,326 stores were sold and stern measures were taken to reduce labor costs, which brought it into sharp conflict with its unions. The end of that restructuring ordeal was a smaller but much more profitable and innovative company.

KKR gave Safeway's top managers rights to buy up to 10 percent of the equity in the restructured company—the shares of which are called stubs—and George Roberts of KKR says that they and Safeway's managers will retain a controlling interest if the company is taken public again. If that happens, there would be a closely held company with a high ratio of debt to equity; sizable share holdings by outsiders would conflict with the determination of KKR and the managers to maintain control.

But the virtues of corporate debt aren't limited to the preservation of control. "Look what happens," writes *Business Week*'s Christopher Farrell, "when debt triggers restructuring. Under outside pressure managers borrow to squeeze 'hidden value' from assets. Then they must streamline operations, slash bureaucracies and labor costs, shut down inefficient plants, and redirect their energies. Debt is a strict disciplinarian."[11]

The downside of heavy debt is bankruptcy, a specter on which the disapproving Cassandras of the old managerial establishment never cease to dwell. Bankruptcies, to be sure, are on the rise: 51 large companies defaulted on $11 billion of debt in 1984, and in 1987, 87 companies defaulted on $21.4 billion.[12] But recourse to bankruptcy and its attendant hardships will diminish as the use of strip financing grows. As explained in chapter 3 (pages 117–118) strip financing is an arrangement under which equities and debentures, various types of stocks and bonds, instead of being offered separately are bundled together for buyers, whose rights and remedies are carefully spelled out. By exercising them, institutional investors, such as Fidelity, can forestall bankruptcy through managerial changes.

## Corporate Makeover and the New Bottom Line

Between 1890 and 1930, as managers became increasingly autonomous, corporate control and corporate ownership were separated. But now the pieces are coming back together again. Tomorrow's corporations—the typical company by the year 2010—will be controlled by a new breed of owner-managers. They will personally hold blocks of stock sufficiently large to elicit the unceasing efforts that are required to maximize present values. The bottom line will be a new corporate regime that's far more conducive to the efficiency of the American economy and the welfare of consumers.

# NOTES

## 1. WITH NEITHER A BODY TO KICK NOR A SOUL TO DAMN:
### The Publicly Held Corporation

**1.** It is surprisingly difficult to get a good statistical fix on just when corporations outstripped partnerships and proprietorships in the private production of goods and services. Good data on corporate income begin only in 1916 with federal income tax returns.

By the turn of the century corporations accounted for some 70 percent of manufactured goods, about the same share of the output of mines, and for virtually all of the services provided by railroads, banks, electrical utilities, and telephone, telegraph, and insurance companies. But together corporations—still rare in agriculture, retail trade, and the independent professions—would not have produced more than half of the GNP. In an address to the Chattanooga, Tennessee, meeting of the American Bar Association in 1910, Woodrow Wilson said: "The corporations now overshadow partnerships altogether. Still more do they overshadow all individuals engaged in business on their own capital and separate responsibility." (William Z. Ripley, *Main Street and Wall Street* [Boston: Little, Brown, and Company, 1927], p. 5.) I think that Wilson was probably right and that corporate dominance of the privately produced GNP—more than half—came sometime before 1910 as the share of the farm sector continued to fall while those of the manufacturing and financial-service sectors rose.

**2.** Heinz Martin Lubasz, "The Body Politic of the Kingdom. A Study of the Sovereignty of the King-in-Parliament" (doctoral dissertation, Yale University, 1959), chaps. 2–3.

**3.** The first joint-stock corporation—one in which a number of investors were permitted to buy shares of limited duration—was chartered in 1555, according to W. R. Scott, *The Constitution and Finance of English, Scottish and Irish Joint Stock Companies to 1720* (Cambridge: Cambridge University Press, 1910–12), vol. 2, p. 37.

**4.** Virginia Cowles, *The Great Swindle. The Story of the South Sea Bubble* (New York: Harper & Brothers, 1960). On John Law and the Mississippi Bubble: Harvey H. Segal, "Money Markets Against Governments: Two Centuries of a Spectacular Game," *Contemporary Policy Issues,* Fall 1985, pp. 36–37. Dutch speculation in the Mississippi Company is noted in Simon Schama, *The Embarrassment of Riches: An Interpretation of Dutch Culture in the Golden Age* (New York: Alfred A. Knopf, 1987), pp. 214–215, 365–67.

For the Bubble Act of 1720: Edward S. Mason, "Corporations," *International Encyclopedia of the Social Sciences* (New York: Macmillan Company & The Free Press, 1968), vol. 3, p. 397. Armand B. DuBois, *The English Business Company After the Bubble Act, 1720–1800* (New York: Oxford University Press, 1938).

**5.** Joseph Stancliffe Davis, *Essays in the Earlier History of American Corporations* (Cambridge: Harvard University Press, 1917), vol. 2, pp. 22–31. Of the 337 charters, two were granted by the U.S. Congress: for the Bank of North America in 1781 and for the Bank of the United States in 1791.

On waves or cycles of incorporation: George Heberton Evans, Jr., *Business Incorporations in the United States, 1800–1943* (New York: National Bureau of Economic Research, 1948). It is the single most comprehensive statistical source on chartering.

**6.** Adam Smith, *An Inquiry into the Nature and Causes of the Wealth of Nations,* ed. R. H. Campbell and A. S. Skinner (Indianapolis: Liberty Press, 1981), vol. 2, p. 741.

**7.** *Minneapolis Railway Company* v. *Beckwith,* 129 U.S. 26 (1889).

**8.** One of the first pools, dating back to 1868, was the Michigan Salt Association. See William Z. Ripley, ed., *Trusts, Pools and Corporations,* rev. ed. (Boston: Ginn and Company, 1916), chap. 1.

**9.** Benjamin Graham and David L. Dodd, *Security Analysis. Principles and Techniques.* 1st ed. (New York: McGraw-Hill Book Company, 1934), p. 332. That "water," which was written off the balance sheet—deducted from earnings—by 1929, was not shown as a goodwill item but concealed by an overvaluation of the fixed assets in the "Property and Investment Accounts."

For a contemporary, detailed analysis of U.S. Steel's stock watering, see the U.S. Commissioner of Corporations, *Report on the Steel Industry,* vol. 1, July 1, 1911, reprinted in Ripley, ed., *Trusts, Pools and Corporations,* chap. 6.

10. For a readable account, see L. J. Davis, "Delaware Inc.," *The New York Times Magazine,* June 5, 1988.

11. Ripley, *Main Street and Wall Street,* pp. 37–38.

12. See Robert Lacey, *Ford. The Men and the Machine* (New York: Ballantine Books, 1987), chaps. 5, 10; and Allen Nevins and Frank Ernest Hill, *Ford: Expansion and Challenge, 1915–1933* (New York: Charles Scribner's Sons, 1957), chap. 4.

The outside investors sold their 41.5 percent stock interest back to the Fords for a little more than $105.8 million, but only a few years later Henry and Edsel were offered $1 billion for their stock. See Keith Sward, *The Legend of Henry Ford* (New York: Rinehart & Company, 1948), p. 73.

13. Smith, *The Wealth of Nations,* p. 741.

14. Thorstein Veblen, *The Theory of Business Enterprise* (New York: Charles Scribner's Sons, 1904), pp. 174–175.

15. Rudolf Hilferding, *Finance Capital. A Study of the Latest Phase of Capitalist Development* (London: Routledge & Kegan Paul, 1985; a translation of *Das Finanzkapital,* first published in Vienna, 1910), p. 127.

16. *Report of the Committee Appointed . . . to Investigate the Concentration of Control of Money and Credit,* House Report No. 1593, 62nd Cong., 3rd sess. (Washington: U.S. Government Printing Office, 1913), pp. 146–47. Italics added. The committee's chairman was Representative Arsene P. Pujo of Louisiana, and the chief counsel, who is credited for the excellence of the hearings, was Samuel Untermeyer, a distinguished New York lawyer.

"Mutual" insurance companies and savings institutions are owned by their policyholders or depositors who receive profits as dividends. The Prudential—among other insurers—switched from a stockholder-owned to a mutual company early in this century in order to forestall a hostile takeover, the reasoning being that the management could rely on the support of the numerous and, for the most part, financially unsophisticated policyholders. The irony is that Prudential and several other mutuals now want to become stock companies again so that they can raise capital in the stock and bond markets, but the New York regulatory authorities, who set national standards, would make that conversion extremely unattractive by insisting—rightly, in my view—that the entire equity of the mutual companies first be distributed to their policyholders, the de jure owners of the companies.

**17.** Walther Rathenau, *In Days to Come,* trans.by Eden and Cedar Paul (New York: Alfred A. Knopf, 1921), pp. 121, 123. The original, *Von kommenden Dingen*, was published in 1916; sixty-five thousand copies had been printed by 1921. Rathenau, a Jew, was murdered by rightist anti-Semites while serving as foreign minister of the Weimar Republic.

**18.** In *Die neue Wirtschaft* [*The New Economy*] (Berlin: S. Fischer, 1919), Rathenau proposed the standardization, rationalization, and unification of German industry and commerce in one great trust that would operate under a state charter that armed the authorities with extensive power over prices, production, and the exploitation of science and technology. Some of Rathenau's closest collaborators later became members of the Hitler brain trust; and so it was the Nazis, ironically, who put his totalitarian economic principles into practice. In the United States, ideas akin to those of Rathenau's surfaced in Bernard Baruch's coordination of U.S. armaments production in the First World War; Herbert Hoover's direction of the Commerce Department in the Coolidge adminstration, and, especially, Franklin D. Roosevelt's National Recovery Adminstration (NRA), which sought to control wages, prices, and output through the imposition of industry-wide cartel codes.

**19.** Adolf A. Berle, Jr., and Gardiner C. Means, *The Modern Corporation and Private Property* (New York: The Macmillan Company, 1932). The book was first published by the Corporation Clearing House, which was controlled by the Corporation Trust Company. Berle's Clearing House editor, one Darr, told him that General Motors, through pressure on the CTC, was responsible for his withdrawing the book. See Berle's account, as related to the Oral History Project at Columbia University, in Beatrice Bishop Berle and Travis Beal Jacobs, eds., *Navigating the Rapids, 1918–1971: From the Papers of Adolf A. Berle* (New York: Harcourt Brace Jovanovich, 1973), pp. 21–22. Some thirty years later, General Motors once again displayed an unerring instinct for brilliant public relations when it hired detectives to delve into the private life of a young lawyer who wrote that its Corvair, a Chevrolet compact, was "unsafe at any speed." The result of the exposure of that snooping was the overnight celebrity of Ralph Nader.

Charles Beard, then arguably the country's most distinguished historian, compared the importance of *The Modern Corporation* with that of *The Federalist Papers* in a front-page review in *The New York Herald Tribune*'s Sunday book-review section (February 19, 1933).

Berle was hardly lacking in resources and overweening ambition to promote the book on his own. A prodigy who graduated from Harvard College at eighteen and from Harvard Law School at twenty-one, he was personally acquainted with Supreme Court justices Louis D. Brandeis and Harlan Fiske Stone, both of whom cited *The Modern Corporation* in decisions within months after its appearance. See Jordan A. Schwarz, *Liberal: Adolf A. Berle and the Vision of an American Era* (New York: Free Press, 1987), pp. 16, 51.

**20.** It was through Ripley that Berle, in 1927, got a Rockefeller Foundation grant for research on *The Modern Corporation*. See Schwarz, *Liberal,* p. 51.

For Berle's "brains trust" role as a strong advocate of federal intervention in markets, an opponent of antitrust and other procompetitive policies, and a proponent of state planning, see his papers in Berle and Jacobs, *Navigating,* pp. 31–109.

**21.** For a highly critical, but in my view accurate assessment of Means's thesis, see George J. Stigler, *Memoirs of an Unregulated Economist* (New York: Basic Books, 1988), pp. 55–57, 108–112.

**22.** Berle and Means, *The Modern Corporation,* pp. 32, 94 and chap. 4.

**23.** Berle and Means, *The Modern Corporation,* p. 122. Chapter 6 of Book 1, "The Divergence of Interest Between Ownership and Control"—from which the quote is taken—is Berle and Means's weakest.

**24.** The authoritative study is Edward S. Herman's *Corporate Control, Corporate Power* (Cambridge: Cambridge University Press, 1981), pp. 5–9, 53–79.

**25.** Berle and Means, *The Modern Corporation,* pp. 40–41.

**26.** Herman, *Corporate Control,* p. 191. Also, Leonard W. Weiss, "The Extent and Effects of Aggregate Concentration," *Journal of Law & Economics,* June 1983, pp. 429–55.

**27.** Berle and Means, *The Modern Corporation,* pp. 45–46.

**28.** Berle and Means, *The Modern Corporation,* appendix F, pp. 365–66.

**29.** Berle and Means, *The Modern Corporation,* p. viii. "The future may see the economic organism, now typified by the corporation, not only on an equal plane with the state, but possibly even superseding it as the dominant form of social organization" (p. 357).

**30.** Berle and Means, *The Modern Corporation,* bk. 4, chap. 2, esp. pp. 343–44.

**31.** Adolf A. Berle, Jr., *Power Without Property: A New Development in American Political Economy* (New York: Harcourt, Brace & Co., 1959), pp. 68, 73.

**32.** Peter F. Drucker, *The Future of Industrial Man: A Conservative Approach* (New York: New American Library, 1965), pp. 75–76.

**33.** Peter F. Drucker, "A Crisis of Capitalism," *The Wall Street Journal,* September 30, 1986.

**34.** Thomas C. Cochran, "Business in Veblen's America" in Carlton C. Qualey, ed., *Thorstein Veblen: The Carleton College Veblen Seminar Essays* (New York: Columbia University Press, 1968), p. 63. See also Cochran, *Railroad Leaders: The Business Mind in Action* (Cambridge: Harvard University Press, 1953).

**35.** Berle, *Power Without Property,* pp. 70–75.
On delineating the categories of control: In 1959, when Berle wrote, Henry Ford II controlled the Ford Motor Company by virtue of the family's ownership of the voting B stock, which entitles them to 40 percent of the voting power, even though their holdings account for less than 8 percent of the total shares outstanding—that is, the B plus the nonvoting A stock. So the company was then under absolute shareholder control, because each share of B stock carried about eight times as much voting power as an ordinary share of A stock. But with the appointment—for the first time in the company's history—of a chief executive from outside the family, there is a question of where Ford fits into the control schema. If the family passively grants chairman Donald E. Petersen and his team a free hand in the company's affairs, Ford will be managerially controlled, despite the family holdings of voting stock.
At the end of 1988, it was reported that two family members, Edsel Ford, II, and William Clay Ford, Jr., were pressing for seats on the company's powerful executive and finance committees, moves resisted by Petersen. That suggests a managerial control that can still be overturned by a determined Ford clan effort. See Alex Taylor, III, "Fords for the Future," *Fortune,* January 16, 1989; Doron P. Levin, "Two Fords Flex Their Muscles," *The New York Times,* December 31, 1988; Melinda Grenier Guiles, "Edsel Ford II Airs His Dissatisfaction, Worrying Officials. Criticism of Firm's Chairman Recalls Company Turmoil During Father's Tenure," *The Wall Street Journal,* January 5, 1989.

**36.** Berle and Means, *The Modern Corporation,* p. 108. There were then 196,119 Pennsylvania Railroad shareholders.

**37.** In "Corporate Takeovers—What Is to Be Done?" *The Public Interest,* Winter 1986, Drucker—in a section called "Corporate capitalism—the rule of autonomous managers as the 'philosopher kings' "— writes (pp. 19–20) that: "From the beginning, anyone with any knowledge of political theory or political history would have predicted that this would not work." And he adds in a footnote, "As I did indeed predict in my 1942 book, *The Future of Industrial Man.*"

In point of fact, Drucker did not predict that it "would not work" but as quoted above, confined himself to characterizing managerial control as "illegitimate." Perhaps the reader in 1942 was to infer that what is illegitimate cannot long endure. But if that was what Drucker meant, he should have returned to the issue before 1986. So far as I can determine, he did not. There is not a word about the illegitimacy of managerial power in either *The Concept of the Corporation* (New York: New American Library, 1946), the book—written at the invitation of General Motors—that made Drucker's reputation, or his *Management: Tasks, Responsibilities, Practices* (New York: Harper & Row, 1974), the conclusion of which is entitled, "The Legitimacy of Management," pp. 807–11.

In 1959, Berle, after dancing around the issue, concluded in *Power Without Property* that "the real legitimacy of power-holding at base depends on its acceptance by the public consensus" (p. 110). There is an implication that there was such a consensus.

**38.** Niccolò Machiavelli, *The Prince,* trans. Peter Bondanella and Mark Musa, in the *The Portable Machiavelli* (New York: Viking Portable Library, 1979), p. 144.

**39.** Berle, *Power Without Property,* p. 74, and *The American Economc Republic* (New York: Harcourt, Brace & Co., 1963), p. 29.

**40.** For the assertion, really a non sequitur, that shareholders are not owners but risk takers, see Nicholas Wolfson, *The Modern Corporation: Free Markets Versus Regulation* (New York: Free Press, 1984), p. 40. For a recent Drucker statement on the subordination of shareholder rights to higher community interests: "Corporate takeovers," p. 23.

**41.** For an old but excellent treatment by a distinguished legal scholar with a strong bent toward economics, see Karl N. Llewellyn, "Agency," *Encyclopedia of the Social Sciences* (New York: Macmillan Company, 1930), vol. 1, pp. 483–85.

**42.** Ronald H. Coase, "The Nature of the Firm," *Economica,* 1937, reprinted in George J. Stigler and Kenneth E. Boulding, eds., *Readings in Price Theory* (Chicago: Richard D. Irwin, 1952), pp. 331–51. Although Coase's insights into transaction costs were regarded as an important explanation of the emergence of the firm and the determination of its size when I was a graduate student in the later 1940s, it was not until the late 1960s that they were developed and applied to the analysis of the corporation.

**43.** Coase, "The Nature," p. 350.

**44.** Michael C. Jensen, "Agency Costs of Free Cash Flow, Corporate Finance and Takeovers," *American Economic Review,* May 1986, p. 323.

Much of what follows in the text is freely based on Michael C. Jensen and William H. Meckling, "Theory of the Firm: Managerial Behavior, Agency Costs and Ownership Structure," *Journal of Financial Economics,* 1976, pp. 305–60, reprinted in Michael C. Jensen and Clifford W. Smith, Jr., eds., *The Modern Theory of Corporate Finance* (New York: McGraw-Hill Book Company, 1984), pp. 78–133. The Jensen-Meckling article is essential reading for anyone who wants a firm understanding of agency theory. Understanding it requires a familiarity with microeconomic theory. The Jensen-Smith anthology contains a number of other valuable articles on agency theory and corporate takeovers.

**45.** Assume that our hypothetical company will on the average earn $10 million a year for the next ten years and that the return on capital is 9 percent. To determine its present value, the net income stream must be discounted. Let $V^*$ = discounted present value; $r$ = rate of discount; $y$ = net earnings; and there are 1, 2, 3 . . . $n$ years. It then follows that: $V^* = y_1/(1 + r) + y_2/(1 + r)^2. \ldots y_n/(1 + r)^n$. The answer is that the present discounted value of the company is $23,674,242. The discount factor for ten years at 9 percent is 0.4224 and is taken from the widely reproduced present value table.

**46.** Jensen and Meckling, "Theory," pp 88–90.

**47.** Gordon Donaldson, *Managing Corporate Wealth: The Operation of a Comprehensive Financial Goals System* (New York: Praeger Publishers, 1984).

**48.** Donaldson, *Managing,* pp. 10–11.

**49.** Donaldson, *Managing,* pp. 21–22.

**50.** Donaldson, *Managing,* pp. 22–23. Italics in the original. Donaldson's B School colleague, the business historian Alfred D. Chandler, Jr., made pretty much the same point—though without directly supporting evidence—in his highly praised book, *The Visible Hand: The Managerial Revolution in American Business* (Cambridge: Harvard University Press,

1977): "In making administrative decisions, career managers preferred policies that favored the long-term stability and growth of their enterprises to those that maximize current profits. . . . If profits were high, they preferred to reinvest them in the enterprise rather than pay them out in dividends" (p. 10).

Since there is a symbiotic relationship between top corporate management and the B School, the question of whether Donaldson's research findings are tainted by prior classroom indoctrination will be addressed in chapter 5.

**51.** Using the same symbols as in note 45, let $V^*$ = discounted present value; $y$ = net earnings; $i$ = growth rate of net earnings; $r$ = rate of discount; and there are 1, 2, 3 . . . $n$ years.
Then: $V^* = y_1(1 + i)/(1 + r) + y_2(1 + i)^2/(1 + r)^2 \ldots + y_n(1 + i)^n/(1 + r)^n$.

At a 20 percent rate, the $1.5 millon of net earnings grows to $7.36 million at the end of the sixth year. And when the nets for each of the six years are discounted at 12 percent and cumulated, we get the present value or the capital required today—$23.89 million—to generate that rising stream of income.

**52.** The reciprocal of the E/P or the EPS is the rate at which the market is discounting the earnings per share. In the case of Xyzco, the rate is about 6.3 percent.

**53.** Eugene F. Fama and Michael C. Jensen, "Separation of Ownership and Control," *Journal of Law & Economics,* June 1983, esp. pp. 313, 304.

**54.** See, among others, Robin Marris, *The Economic Theory of "Managerial" Capitalism* (London: Macmillan, 1964), and William J. Baumol, *Business Behavior, Value and Growth* (New York: Macmillan, 1959).

**55.** Marris, *Managerial Capitalism,* especially chaps. 1, 2; Chandler, *The Visible Hand,* p. 10.

## 2. ON DINOSAURS AND HARES:
### Corporate Size, Profitability, and Survival

**1.** I've chosen ten—though the number could well be higher—to exclude those intimate work situations in which the ambience is poisoned by a single person in authority.

For larger organizations: If $I$ = an index of incivility and $n$ = the number of people involved, I'm saying that $I = n^{1.05}$. That suggests that an organization of one hundred is slightly more than twice as uncivil as one of fifty, that a one-thousand-person organization is more than eleven times as incivil as one with only one hundred and that the increase in incivility when you move from one thousand to ten thousand is nearly sixteen times.

Note that I said "people involved." It's possible to be part of an organization and yet minimally involved, otherwise engaged. But such a posture is neither commonplace nor easily managed.

**2.** I say "business organizations" rather than "firms" because the latter is particularly British and now refers principally to partnerships, such as law or accounting firms, even though many of them in this country are now incorporated.

**3.** Dennis H. Robertson, *The Control of Industry* (London: Nisbet & Co., 1947), pp. 85–86.

**4.** Ronald H. Coase, "The Nature of the Firm," *Economica,* 1937, reprinted in George J. Stigler and Kenneth E. Boulding, eds., *Readings in Price Theory* (Chicago: Richard D. Irwin, 1952), pp. 331–51.

**5.** This account is largely based on Alfred D. Chandler, Jr., *Strategy and Structure: Chapters in the History of Industrial Enterprise* (Garden City: Doubleday & Company, 1966), pp. 138–54, though the inferences I draw are different.

**6.** Alfred P. Sloan, Jr., *My Years with General Motors* (New York: Doubleday & Company, 1964), p. 161.

**7.** Benjamin Klein, Robert G. Crawford, and Armen A. Alchian, "Vertical Integration, Appropriable Rents, and the Competitive Contracting Process," *Journal of Law & Economics,* 1978, reprinted in Michael C. Jensen and Clifford W. Smith, Jr., eds., *The Modern Theory of Corporate Finance* (McGraw-Hill Book Company, 1984), see esp. pp. 266–69. The government was attempting to demonstrate—*United States* v. *Du Pont & Co.,* 366 U.S. 316 (1961)—that the purpose of the merger was to compel Fisher to purchase its glass from Du Pont, which then controlled GM. In depositions Sloan and others provided the above explanation which—in terms of the potentially enormous costs to GM—is much more plausible.

**8.** Sloan, *My Years,* p. 282.

**9.** Allen Nevins, *Ford: The Times, the Man, the Company* (New York: Charles Scribner's Sons, 1954), pp. 139–40. This is the first of a three-volume, authorized company history. The authors (Frank Ernest Hill coauthored the second and third volumes) were not equipped—even had they been so inclined—to pass judgment on the efficiency of the Ford organization.

**10.** On backward integration: Allen Nevins and Frank Ernest Hill, *Ford: Expansion and Challenge, 1915–1933* (New York: Charles Scribner's Sons, 1957), pp. 218, 220, 223, 225, 236, 231. On accountants: Robert Lacey, *Ford. The Men and the Machine* (New York: Ballantine Books, 1986), pp. 278–79, 284.

**11.** Keith Sward, *The Legend of Henry Ford* (New York: Rinehart & Company, 1948), p. 136.

**12.** Adam Smith, *An Inquiry into the Nature and Causes of the Wealth of Nations* (Indianapolis: Liberty Classics, 1981), vol. 1, bk. 1, chap. 3. For a brilliant contemporary analysis of Smith's theorem, see chap. 12 of George J. Stigler's *The Organization of Industry* (Chicago: University of Chicago Press, 1983).

**13.** Stigler, *The Organization,* chap. 9, "The Dominant Firm and the Inverted Umbrella"; the quote is from p. 112.

**14.** See the excellent article by Rick Wartzman and Carol Hymowitz, "Uneasy Revival: Big Steel Is Back, but Upturn Is Costly and May Not Last," *The Wall Street Journal,* November 4, 1988, and Rick Wartzman, "Bethlehem Steel Profit Tripled in Third Period," *The Wall Street Journal,* October 27, 1988.

**15.** For a good technical account, see Jack Robert Miller, "Steel Minimills," *Scientific American,* May 1984, pp. 33–39. See also J. Ernest Beazley, "Big Steel's Push to Extend Import Quotas Draws Debate," *The Wall Street Journal,* December 30, 1987; and George Melloan, "Making Money Making Steel in Texas," *The Wall Street Journal,* January 26, 1988.

**16.** For an account of the operations of SCI, Inc., a major supplier of IBM's circuit boards, see Hank Gilman, "The Parts Maker," *The Wall Street Journal,* August 14, 1987.

IBM is reported (*The New York Times,* January 3, 1988) to have shifted from a reliance on outside suppliers with the introduction of its PS/2 line in 1987. The object is to make those models more difficult to clone by developing unique, IBM-produced parts. Jack D. Keuhler, the senior IBM vice-president in charge of PS/2 manufacturing, said: "What we've discovered is that if you are the leader in technology, whether it's bits per chip or megabytes per disk, you are the low cost leader too. That's what IBM is all about." His statement is a non sequitur, even if the new models succeed and are cloned. There's no reason to believe that Asian suppliers would be unable to match IBM's unit costs; and if the PS/2 line fails and is thus not widely cloned, IBM's integrative strategy could prove very costly. Compaq, once the most successful of the clones, is betting that it will fail.

17. See the informative piece by Gary Lamphier, "Magna Hopes Sum of Parts Tops Whole," *The Wall Street Journal,* July 10, 1987. Magna International Inc. of Markham, Ontario, is an auto-parts maker with more than $1 billion (Canadian) of sales. Modules accounted for less than 10 percent of its 1986 volume but the company expects that share to rise to 30 percent between 1988 and 1992. On GM's downsizing, vertical integration, and profitability in the U.S. auto industry, see Jacob M. Schlesinger and Joseph B. White, "Shrinking Giant: The New GM Will Be More Compact but More Profitable," *The Wall Street Journal,* June 6, 1988.

18. Stigler, *The Organization,* p. 87.

19. Schumpeter's thinking on innovation is contained in three of his books: *The Theory of Economic Development: An Inquiry into Profits, Capital, Credit, Interest and the Business Cycle* (Cambridge: Harvard University Press, 1934); *Business Cycles: A Theoretical, Historical and Statistical Analysis of the Capitalist Process* (New York: McGraw-Hill Book Company, 1939; 2 vols.); and *Capitalism, Socialism and Democracy* (New York: Harper & Brothers, 1942).

20. Sloan, *My Years,* pp. 162–63.

21. My account of Sears, Roebuck is based on the following: Boris Emmet and John E. Jeuck, *Catalogues and Counters: A History of Sears, Roebuck and Company* (Chicago: University of Chicago Press, 1950), not a pleasure to read but a treasure house of information, especially statistical data; Alfred D. Chandler, Jr., *Strategy and Structure. Chapters in the History of American Industrial Enterprise* (Garden City: Doubleday & Company, 1966), chaps. 5, 6; and for the most recent years, Donald R. Katz, *The Big Store. Inside the Crisis and Revolution at Sears* (New York: Viking, 1987). As a journalist and quintessential outsider, Katz was given an unprecedented opportunity to look inside with none of the restraints that inhibit authorized historians.

22. With a larger number of women working full time and more two-income families, the mail-order business has enjoyed a revival in the l980s. Catalog circulation was estimated at more than one billion in late 1987, but the new business differs from the old with a large number of small, highly specialized vendors of such items as down quiltings, sophisticated electronic products, and job lots of all sorts of discontinued

models of products that are offered at low prices. Sears still is the biggest catalog seller, but its growth has been lagging behind that of the industry (*The Wall Street Journal,* December 7, 1987). Montgomery Ward is out of the catalog business.

**23.** Francine Schwadel, "Humbled Giant: Its Expansion Lagging, Sears Now Struggles to Stay Independent," *The Wall Street Journal,* November 2, 1988.

**24.** Stigler, *The Organization,* chap. 7, "The Economies of Scale," p. 73.

**25.** Stigler, *The Organization,* pp. 77–78.

**26.** Calculated from data reprinted in Emmet and Jeuck, *Catalogues and Counters,* p. 204. Ward's share rose from 27.5 percent in 1913 to 37 percent in 1925, a 34.5 precent increase. The National Bellas Hess share was up 9.8 percent over the same period.

**27.** *The Wall Street Journal,* December 1, 1987, and Schlesinger and White, "Shrinking Giant."

**28.** The paragraphs that follow draw on Robert J. Schoenberg, *Geneen* (New York: Warner Books, 1985), an unauthorized, readable, and insightful biography of a remarkable, though hardly admirable figure.

**29.** It was the argument I advanced at the time in editorials for *The Washington Post,* though I do not now think it very weighty.

**30.** The passages that follow draw on my article, "The Time of the Conglomerates," *The New York Times Magazine,* October 27, 1968. Its great weakness was my failure to foresee that the boom would end quickly and rather unhappily. But I did take a duly skeptical view of conglomerates.

**31.** Cary Reich, *The Financier: The Biography of André Meyer* (New York: William Morrow and Company, 1983), p. 298.

**32.** Most of the conglomerate merger exchanges were tax free, ITT-Hartford being a notable exception because Rohatyn, at André Meyer's suggestion, "sold" a big block of Hartford shares to Mediobanca of Italy in order to get a favorable tax ruling from the Internal Revenue Service. But the Securities and Exchange Commission later held, with very good reason, that it wasn't at all an arms-length sale but that Rohatyn had "parked" the shares. The SEC charged Lazard, ITT, and Mediobanca with violations of the Securities Act, and two senior ITT executives with insider trading. The suit was settled out of court. Schoenberg, *Geneen,* p. 301; Reich, *The Financier,* chap. 24, esp. pp. 303–7.

**33.** Abraham J. Briloff, the Distinguished Emmanuel Saxe Professor of Accounting Emeritus at Baruch College, the City University of New York, exposed the evasions and distortions of conglomerate accounting with the zeal of an Old Testament prophet. Neither a lawsuit nor a shabby effort at intimidation by one of the country's largest accounting firms, Peat Marwick, silenced him. His three books, essential reading on conglomerates in particular and the state of corporate accounting in general, are: *Unaccountable Accounting* (New York: Harper & Row, 1972); *More Debits than Credits* (New York: Harper & Row, 1976); and *The Truth about Corporate Accounting* (New York: Harper & Row, 1981).

**34.** George Soros, *The Alchemy of Finance: Reading the Mind of the Market* (New York: Simon and Schuster, 1987), in an incisive appraisal of conglomerates, makes the point (p. 57) that the "climactic event" came in 1969 when Saul Steinberg of Reliance Insurance tried to acquire Chemical Bank of New York, an attempt that was "fought and defeated by the establishment." I think that there was already a lot more going against conglomerates than that defeat. But I can testify to Soros's point about the establishment.

In the spring of 1969, when a member of the editorial board of *The New York Times,* I was visited by Charls E. Walker, then an under-secretary of the treasury in the Nixon administration, who importuned me to write an editorial opposing the Chemical acquisition. I had encountered Walker, a Texan and a pale clone of John Connolly, in my years on *The Washington Post* as the louche lobbyist for the American Bankers Association. So—with tongue in cheek—I asked him just why the administration was so interested in stopping the merger. When he solemnly and disingenuously replied that the confidentiality of information about Chemical's corporate customers would be compromised under Steinberg, I brushed him off by remarking that he ought to take off his ABA hat now that he was sitting in the Treasury. The *Times* editorial page was silent on the Chemical matter.

On leaving government, Walker became a leading corporate lobbyist on Capitol Hill. In 1976, he got Bechtel—the big international construction company, with billions at stake in Saudi Arabia—off the hook by persuading then Senator John Tower of Texas, later President Bush's unsuccessful nominee for secretary of defense, to block a bill that would have effectively countered the Arab boycott of Jews in general and Israel in particular. See Laton McCartney, *Friends in High Places: The Bechtel Story* (New York: Simon and Schuster, 1988), pp. 194–96.

**35.** Quoted by Janet Guyon, "GE Chairman Welch, Though Much Praised, Starts to Draw Critics. Some Accuse Him of Creating a Muddled Conglomerate and Destroying Morale," *The Wall Street Journal,* August 4, 1988.

**36.** Corporate profit estimates cited here are those of the Bureau of Economic Analysis of the U.S. Department of Commerce. They appear in the department's monthly *Survey of Current Business* as well as the tables appended to the Economic Report of the President. The figures are adjusted to eliminate gains or losses on inventory valuations and to take account of the capital consumed—the wear and tear on equipment, the aging of structures, and so forth—in each year. I computed the dividend payout ratios and in estimating real retained earnings used the implicit price deflators for the gross national product where 1982 = 100.

**37.** Benjamin Graham and David L. Dodd, *Security Analysis. Principles and Technique,* 1st ed.(New York: McGraw-Hill Book Company, 1934), chap. 29 and appendix, note 41.

**38.** Graham and Dodd, *Security Analysis,* p. 339. Italics in the original.
 The fifth, 1988 edition of Graham and Dodd, written by other hands, takes a different, typically managerial view. The logic of their analysis suggests that "all really successful companies should follow a program of substantial reinvestment of profits, and that cash dividends should be paid only to the extent that opportunities for profitable expansion or diversification are not present."
 But they note the difficulty of calculating future returns on retained capital and conclude that "this very real uncertainty will make it more difficult for stockholders in general—and their alter ego, 'the stock market'—to abandon their ingrained preference for cash dividends in favor of the theoretical advantages of retained profits." Sidney Cottle, Roger F. Murray, and Frank E. Block, *Graham and Dodd's Security Analysis,* 5th ed. (New York: McGraw-Hill Book Company, 1988), p. 564. Better a bird in the hand . . .

**39.** Michael C. Jensen, "Takeovers: Their Causes and Consequences," *The Journal of Economic Perspectives,* Winter 1988, pp. 28–29.

**40.** In the jargon of financial analysis, free cash flow is in excess of what's required to fund all projects that have positive net values when discounted by a rate of return that is equivalent to the cost of capital. See chapter 1, notes 45 and 51.

**41.** Jeff Bailey, "Plastic Pitfall," *The Wall Street Journal,* February 10, 1988. In addition to the more than $400 million of direct losses on Discover, there are indirect losses suffered by the profitable Sears credit card. Both cards are accepted at Sears, Roebuck retail stores.
 The credit card industry can be difficult even for managers who are

a lot more sophisticated than the Sears people. In the early 1970s Citibank, in one mailing, sent more than 26 million credit cards to households west of the Mississippi. The promotion, based on purchased mailing lists, really "worked." Card volume soared—and so too did the loss rate, as deadbeats made full use of their newly acquired credit. But that problem, unlike Sears', was easily, if not cheaply, solved.

**42.** *The Wall Street Journal,* March 8, 1988. It's not clear how much of Mobil's subsequent investment in Montgomery Ward—more than $1 billion—was included in the $2.3 billion of debt that was assumed by the new company. I've assumed that all of it was included.

**43.** John P. Kotter, *The Leadership Factor* (New York: The Free Press, 1988), p. 7. See also Joseph B. White, "Rebate Sought on Price Paid for Hughes," *The Wall Street Journal,* December 5, 1988.

**44.** John Markoff, "IBM to Sell Rolm to Siemens," *The New York Times,* December 14, 1988; Paul B. Carroll, "IBM Is Selling Much of Rolm to Siemens AG," *The Wall Street Journal,* December 14, 1988.

**45.** L. J. Davis, "Trailblazers of the New High Finance. Sophisticated, Resourceful, a Nimble Global Player—That's Today's C.F.O. The Ford Challenge: $10 Billion in Cash," *The New York Times Magazine,* December 4, 1988; Paulette Thomas and Bradley A. Sterz, "Ford Unit Buys 2 Sick Michigan Thrifts, Raising Total Rescued This Year to 155," *The Wall Street Journal,* December 19, 1988; *Business Week,* December 21, 1987, pp. 79, 82; Nathaniel C. Nash, "Ford Motor to Buy Weak Savings Units With Federal Help," *The New York Times,* December 31, 1988.

**46.** Jonathan P. Hicks, "Quantum Announces $50 Payout," *The New York Times,* December 29, 1988. The total payout came to about $1.28 billion. John Hoyt Stookey, Quantum's CEO, said: "The primary thrust is to deliver value to the shareholders. . . . Most chemical companies are selling at about half of the the price-earnings ratio of the Standard & Poor's 500. We hope that it sets a new standard for how the tools of leverage can be used in a responsible way." At the time of the announcement, Quantum was carrying out a $3 billion capital spending program.

**47.** $80 \times .45 = $36.

**48.** Alfred Marshall, *Principles of Economics,* 9th (variorum) ed. (London: Macmillan and Co., 1961), vol. 1, pp. 315–16. Italics added.

**49.** James E. Meade, "Is the New Industrial State Inevitable," *Economic Journal,* June 1968, p. 387. This is a review of John Kenneth

Galbraith's *The New Industrial State,* and I'm grateful to Roger E. Alcaly for calling it to my attention.

## 3. THEY'RE SYMPTOMS, NOT THE DISEASE:
Hostile Takeovers, Leveraged Buyouts, and Recaps

**1.** Peter F. Drucker, *The Frontiers of Management* (New York: E. P. Dutton, 1986), pp. 243, 185.

**2.** Alison Leigh Cowan, "The Resurgence of Takeovers," *The New York Times,* February 6, 1988.

**3.** For elegant and insightful accounts of Giannini and Young (basically pieces that originally appeared in *The Saturday Evening Post* and *The New Yorker*), see Matthew Josephson, *The Money Lords: The Great Finance Capitalists, 1925–1950* (New York: Weybright and Talley, 1972), pp. 141–44, 238–44.

**4.** Some earlier hostile takeovers were consummated without public tenders. In 1935, for example, J. Paul Getty got control of the large Tidewater Associated Oil Company by purchasing, with foreknowledge of its imminent availability, a big block of stock from its owner. Tidewater was the foundation of Getty's oil empire. See Thomas Petzinger, Jr., *Oil and Honor: The Texaco-Pennzoil Wars* (New York: G.P. Putnam's Sons, 1987), pp. 53–54.

**5.** Robin Marris, *The Economic Theory of "Managerial" Capitalism* (New York: Basic Books, 1968, originally published in 1964); see especially "A Theory of Take-over," pp. 29–42.

**6.** Alison Leigh Cowan, "The Trench Warriors: Boardroom Battles Are Breaking Out All Over," *The New York Times,* May 29, 1988; Christopher Power, "Why the Proxy Fight Is Back," *Business Week,* March 7, 1988.

In 1984 there were only thirteen instances in which dissidents satisfied the Securities and Exchange Commission requirement for alternative slates of directors, and elections actually took place in only eight. See Edward Jay Epstein, *Who Owns the Corporation? Management vs. Shareholders* (New York: Priority Press Publications, 1986), appendix A.

But in 1985, Carl C. Icahn won a major victory against Phillips Petroleum when the shareholders voted down management's financial restructuring plan and forced the adoption of one similar to that which he—and earlier on Boone Pickens—had proposed. T. Boone Pickens, Jr., *Boone* (Boston: Houghton Mifflin, 1987), pp. 234–35, and Jeff Madrick, *Taking America: How We Got from the First Hostile Takeover to Megamergers, Corporate Raiding, and Scandal* (New York: Bantam Books, 1987), pp. 278–82.

**7.** Based on the excellent account in Madrick, *Taking America,* chaps. 1–4.

**8.** John Brooks, *The Takeover Game* (New York: E. P. Dutton, 1987), pp. 238–39, 253. Italics added.

**9.** Brooks, *The Takeover Game,* pp. 237, 253. Rifkind was not only a Revlon director at the time of the hostile bid but also sat on the board of Perelman's MacAndrews and Forbes Holdings, a position he occupied through his association with the family of Perelman's former wife. When he was unable to dissuade Perelman from his assault on Revlon, Rifkind resigned from the MacAndrews and Forbes board. See Connie Bruck, *The Predators' Ball: The Junk-Bond Raiders and the Man Who Staked Them* (New York: The American Lawyer/Simon and Schuster, 1988), pp. 196–206.

**10.** Madrick, *Taking America,* pp. 269–70.

**11.** Philip Cagan and Robert E. Lipsey, *The Financial Effects of Inflation* (Cambridge: Ballinger for the National Bureau of Economic Research, 1978), p. 24. I have cited their estimates of the "Market Value of Equity per Dollar of Net Worth," version C, which treats financial assets and short-term liabilities at face value, long-term liabilities at market value, and tangible assets at current cost. The ratios are for nonfarm, nonfinancial corporations. The decline of the ratio from 1970 through 1977 was from 1.155 to 0.498.

The Cagan-Lipsey measures, which unfortunately haven't been calculated beyond 1977, are far superior to the "Q ratios" of replacement costs to market values of stocks and bonds which used to appear in the reports of the President's Council of Economic Advisers.

**12.** The average market price to average book-value ratio for the Standard & Poor's 400 hit 1.14 for 1982, a 25-year low. The high for the period 1961–1985 was 2.23 in 1965. Sidney Cottle, Roger F. Murray, and Frank E. Block, *Graham and Dodd's Security Analysis*, 5th ed. (New York: McGraw-Hill Book Company, 1988), p. 562.

**13.** Pickens, *Boone,* pp.140–42.

For a good explanation of vertical integration and other structural features of the petroleum industry, see David Glasner, *Politics, Prices and Petroleum: The Political Economy of Energy* (Cambridge: Ballinger Publishing Company, 1985), esp. chap. 4.

**14.** Drucker, *The Frontiers*, p. 235, declares, in original italics, that *"in any inflation the cost of capital goods tends to rise much faster than the prices of the goods they produce. It thus becomes economical to buy existing capital assets rather than to invest in new facilities and new machines."*
It sounds authoritative, but it just isn't so. Prices of capital goods, in fact, rise no faster, and if anything somewhat more slowly, than others during inflation. The salient point—which Drucker misses—is that in the disinflation phase of the cycle, the prices of producers' equipment, as well as the prices of other finished goods used in industry, fall little, if at all, while commodity prices plummet.

**15.** Michael C. Jensen, "Takeovers: Their Causes and Consequences," *The Journal of Economic Perspectives,* Winter 1988, pp. 28–36. For an extended version, see Jensen, "The Free Cash Theory of Takeovers: A Financial Perspective on Mergers and Acquisitions and the Economy," in Lynn E. Browne and Eric S. Rosengren, eds., *The Merger Boom* (proceedings of a conference held in October 1987) (Boston: Federal Reserve Bank of Boston, n.d.), pp. 102–43.

**16.** Michael Kinsley, *The Wall Street Journal,* July 18, 1985. For an insightful analysis of why some companies are raided and broken up, see Dean LeBaron and Lawrence Speidell, "Why Are the Parts Worth More Than the Sum? 'Chop Chop,' a Corporate Valuation Model," in Browne and Rosengren, eds., *Merger Boom*, pp. 78–95. LeBaron owns Batterymarch Financial Management, which oversees billions in investments for pension plans and other institutions.

**17.** Steve Coll, *The Deal of the Century: The Breakup of AT&T* (New York: Atheneum, 1986), chap. 35.

**18.** I am indebted to Arnold Hoffman of the Pension and Welfare Benefit Administration, U.S. Department of Labor, for help in getting a fix on the number of people covered by one pension plan or more in 1988. It's a rough estimate.
Frederick Yohn of the flow-of-funds unit, Board of Governors of the Federal Reserve System, kindly provided the pension-plan asset numbers. The equities are valued at market prices and the bonds are valued at book, or par prices.
The total market value of listed equities as of the end of September 1988 was as follows: by the New York Stock Exchange, $2.4 trillion; by the American Stock Exchange, $0.11 trillion; and by the National Association of Securities Dealers, $0.38 trillion; total: $2.89 trillion.

**19.** On TIAA-CREF, L. J. Davis, "$60 Billion in the Balance," *The New York Times Magazine,* March 27, 1988.

Harrison J. Goldin was a friend of Ivan Boesky's and a personal investor in two Boesky companies. He got campaign contributions from Boesky, Carl C. Icahn, and Drexel Burnham Lambert. See Richard J. Meislen, "Goldin Solicited Friends to Invest With Boesky"; "Goldin Discloses He Had Interests in Two Other Boesky Companies"; and "Inquiry Grows in Goldin Link With Boesky"; *The New York Times,* January 31, 1987, February 11, 1987, and February 20, 1987, respectively.

**20.** See the full-page displays, paid for by Koppers, in both *The New York Times* and *The Wall Street Journal,* March 25, 1988. Greene's letter is dated March 21, 1988. On the agreement to maintain Koppers's headquarters in Pittsburgh for three years, see *The New York Times,* June 4, 1988. For a thoughtful account of the implications of the fight, see Bryan Burrough, "Wall Street Winces at Shearson Victory: Few Will Emulate Its Role in Koppers Fight," *The Wall Street Journal,* June 3, 1988.

**21.** Hope Lampert, *Till Death Do Us Part. Bendix vs. Martin Marietta* (New York: New American Library, 1984), chap. 1 and pp. 43, 90–106.

**22.** Hilary Rosenberg, "The Revolt of the Institutional Shareholders," *Institutional Investor,* May 1987, p. 139.

**23.** The letter to Avon Products dated February 23, 1988, is signed by Alan D. Lebowitz, deputy assistant secretary of labor in the Pension and Welfare Benefits Administration. For general news media commentary, which was slow in coming, see Judith H. Dobrzynski, "Whose Company Is It, Anyway?," *Business Week,* April 25, 1988, pp. 60–61; and Edward V. Regan (New York state comptroller), "Private Pension Funds Discover Their Proxies," *The Wall Street Journal,* May 3, 1988.

**24.** Unless otherwise indicated, this account of Milken draws on Edward Jay Epstein, "How Mike Milken Made a Billion Dollars and Changed the Face of American Capitalism," *Manhattan, Inc,* September 1987, pp. 113–33; and Bruck, *The Predators' Ball.* Both are based on rarely granted interviews with Milken and other Drexel Burnham officials. Connie Bruck's book is the most comphrehensive single source of information on Milken and Drexel Burnham.

**25.** W. Braddock Hickman, *Corporate Bond Quality and Investor Experience* (Princeton: Princeton University Press for the National Bureau of Economic Research, 1958). Thomas R. Atkinson, *Trends in Cor-*

*porate Bond Quality* (New York: Columbia University Press for the National Bureau of Economic Research, 1967).

A bond yield is the rate of interest that brings the actual market price and the face, or par, value of a bond into equality. Suppose that a perpetuity, a bond without a redemption date, is issued at par, 100 or a price of $1,000, with a 5 percent, or $50 annual coupon. If its price then falls to $80, its yield rises to 6.25 percent—$50/$800. The arithmetic is more complicated for bonds of specified maturities, but their yields are easily calculated from widely available tables.

The lower the price of a bond, the higher its yield, and vice versa.

**26.** Douglas Hallett, "Life Insurance Industry Needs Junk Bonds," *The Wall Street Journal,* July 29, 1987. Hallett is a Los Angeles attorney specializing in insurance. Corcoran's action was aimed at Fred Carr's First Executive Corporation, a California life insurer that heavily invested in junk bonds. His action, as might have been expected, was supported by the Life Insurance Council of New York.

**27.** Bruck, *The Predators' Ball,* p. 276.

**28.** Bruck, *The Predators' Ball,* p. 359.

**29.** Based on the details in James B. Stewart and Daniel Hertzberg, "Drexel and Milken Are Focus of Federal Probe That Is Growing Wider," *The Wall Street Journal,* September 11, 1987. Confirmed by Epstein, "How Mike Milken Made a Billion"; also Madrick, *Taking America,* pp. 258–59.

**30.** Steve Swartz and Laurie P. Cohen, "Executive Anguish: Drexel's Chief Faces Decision That Offers Little Solace for Firm," *The Wall Street Journal,* December 19, 1988.

**31.** Robert E. Taylor and Thomas E. Ricks, "Drexel Lobbies Congress to Keep Banks out of Junk-Bond Underwriting Business," *The Wall Street Journal,* July 1, 1988.

**32.** Prior to 1987, the largest default was on LTV bonds. In 1987, $9 billion of junk bonds went into default, but mostly from Texaco, reduced to junk status when it filed for voluntary bankruptcy. See *Business Week,* March 28, 1987, p. 102.

**33.** *Securities and Exchange Commission* v. *Drexel Burnham Lambert Incorporated, Drexel Burnham Lambert Group Incorporated, Michael Milken, Lowell Milken, Cary Maultasch, Pamela Monzert, Victor Posner, Stephen Posner and Pennsylvania Engineering Corporation,* United States District Court for the Southern District of New York. Securities and Exchange Commission, Litigation Release No. 11859, September

7, 1988. For a news summary, *The Wall Street Journal,* September, 8, 1988.

For a summary of the SEC charges to which Drexel Burnham would plead guilty, see *The New York Times,* January 25, 1989.

**34.** Bruck, *The Predators' Ball,* p. 332.

**35.** For abundant documentation of the managerial control of large corporations, see Edward S. Herman, *Corporate Control, Corporate Power* (New York: Cambridge University Press, 1983).

**36.** The "lock-up" bid came from Forstmann Little & Company, a house specializing in leveraged buyouts. For the court decisions, see *MacAndrews & Forbes Holdings Inc.* v. *Revlon, Inc.,* No. 8126, Delaware Chancery, New Castle County (October 23, 1985), and *Revlon Inc.* v. *MacAndrews & Forbes Holdings Inc.* 506 A2d 173 (Delaware 1986). The latter citation was the Delaware Supreme Court ruling of November 1985 upholding the chancery court. MacAndrews & Forbes is a Perelman-held company.

For a thoughtful commentary, see Robert J. Cole, "For Sale or Not? The Courts' View," *The New York Times,* March 31, 1988.

**37.** Steinberg's take was only moderately large. For a selective list of greenmail payments, see Epstein, *Who Owns the Corporation?,* appendix B. For more on Steinberg as wunderkind, see chap. 2, note 34.

**38.** Stephen J. Adler and Laurie P.Cohen, "Even Lawyers Gasp Over Stiff Fees of Wachtell Lipton," *The Wall Street Journal,* November 2, 1988. Wachtell, Lipton's fees are based on a percentage of the deal, not on hours worked. Herbert Wachtell declined to confirm the $20 million figure but did say, "We got $2 billion more for the stockholders."

**39.** The decision upholding the poison pill, which was affirmed by the Supreme Court of Delaware, is *Moran* v. *Household Internatl, Inc.* 490 A.2d 1059 (Del. Ch. 1985), affirmed 500 A.2d 1346 (Del. Ch 1985). For empirical evidence of the depressing effect of poison pills on share prices and shareholders' wealth, see Michael Ryngaert, "The Effect of Poison Pill Securities on Shareholder Wealth," *Journal of Financial Economics,* no. 1–2, 1988.

**40.** Felix Rohatyn, "Restoring American Independence," *The New York Review of Books,* February 18, 1988, p. 9. Iacocca also cited the threat from foreign investors for loading Chrysler up with takeover repellents. See Cowan, "The Resurgence of Takeovers."

**41.** See Bevis Longstreth, *Management Buyouts: Are Public Shareholders Getting a Fair Deal?* (Washington: Securities and Exchange Commission, 1983); Benjamin J. Stein, "Leveraged Buyouts: On the Level?" *The New York Times Magazine,* January 17, 1988. Stein, a writer and lawyer, blocked a leveraged buyout of the Narragansett Capital Corporation—an investment company with holdings in cable TV and other closely held enterprises—on the grounds that the insiders refused to provide publicly available information on companies in their portfolio. He was thwarted when Narragansett's directors then sold out for $276 million to Monarch Capital, an insurance holding company. The terms included $32 million in consultants' fees for Narragansett's former managers, payments that Stein rightly describes as "a thinly disguised management buyout." See also Richard B. Schmitt, "If an Investment Bank Says a Deal Is Fair, It May or May Not Be," *The Wall Street Journal,* March 10, 1988; and Robert J. Cole, "GAF Backs $1.47 Billion Heyman Proposal," *The New York Times,* October 21, 1988. *Business Week,* March 28, 1988, reports on three disputed leveraged buyouts, Farm Fresh, Colt, and Days Inn Corporation, in which the outside shareholders were pressing for higher prices (pp.30–31).

**42.** Judith H. Dobrzynski, "Was RJR's Ross Johnson Too Greedy for His Own Good?" *Business Week,* November 21, 1988, p. 95; Benjamin J. Stein, "A New Low? The RJR LBO Makes a Travesty of Fiduciary Responsibility," *Barron's,* November 14, 1988; John Helyar and Bryan Burrough, "Buyout Bluff: How Underdog KKR Won RJR Nabisco with Highest Bid," *The Wall Street Journal,* December 2, 1988; and James Sterngold, "Nabisco Battle Redefines Directors' Role," *The New York Times,* December 5, 1988.

**43.** Assume that there are two companies, A and B, which are identical in every way except for their capital structures. Each has 5 million shares of common stock outstanding. A, which has no debt at all, has earnings per share (EPS) of $2. But, because of a debt serviced at an annual cost of $5 million, B's EPS are only $1. Now suppose that the sales revenues of each company grow by 18 percent in a single year and that all their costs change proportionally. A's EPS rise to $2.36, or by the same 18 percent. But B's EPS rise to $1.36, or by 36 percent, twice as fast. If sales then fall back to their original level in the third year, A's EPS drop by only 15.3 percent, but B's drop by 26.5 percent. Positive leveraging works only so long as the after-tax cost of borrowing is less than the return on total capital, an assumption implicit in the foregoing model.

**44.** Based on the estimates of W. T. Grimm & Company, which were kindly provided by Alex Ladias.

**45.** James P. Miller, "Joining the Game: Some Workers Set Up LBOs of Their Own and Benefit Greatly. ESOP Buy-Outs Are Helped by Federal Tax Breaks; Productivity Often Soars," *The Wall Street Journal,* December 12, 1988. Some sixteen hundred companies are controlled by ESOPs. Early in 1989, the Polaroid ESOP, with 14 percent of the outstanding shares, blocked a hostile takeover by Shamrock Holdings, and Procter & Gamble, encouraged by a favorable Delaware Court of Chancery ruling in Polaroid, moved to increase the shares held by its ESOP to 20 percent. Timothy D. Shellhardt, "P&G to Boost Its Employees' Stake to 20%," *The Wall Street Journal,* January 12, 1989.

**46.** For a lucid explanation and review of this option, see Alison Leigh Cowan, "Recapitalizations: The New Way to Halt Raiders," *The New York Times,* May 29, 1987.

**47.** For a careful analysis and excellent graph of merger and other activity, see Mack Ott and G.J. Santoni, "Mergers and Takeovers— The Value of Predators' Information," *Review of the Federal Reserve Bank of St. Louis,* December 1985, pp. 16–28.

**48.** Based on W. T. Grimm & Co. estimates.

**49.** Michael C. Jensen, "A Helping Hand for Entrenched Managers," *The Wall Street Journal,* November 4, 1987. Jensen's estimates are based on data compiled by W.T. Grimm & Co. See Jensen, "Takeovers: Their Causes and Consequences," p. 21.

The $120 billion of benefits for 1988 is my own rough estimate, based on W. T. Grimm's dollar total of 1988 deals and the percentage premium—the average percentage difference between the price paid in a consummated deal and the price five days before its announcement.

**50.** Quoted in Epstein, "How Mike Milken Made a Billion." The Lipton memo is quoted in Bruck, *The Predators' Ball,* p. 204.

**51.** This passage draws on my op-ed page piece, "The Fed's New Junk Bond Rule," in *The Washington Post,* January 27, 1986, and the documents—statements pro and con submitted to the Fed—on which it's based.

Some Federal Reserve System insiders believed that Volcker supported the Reg G extension because it was urged on him by E. Gerald Corrigan, his protégé and president of the Federal Reserve Bank of New York. But on reflection, I think it likely that Volcker, already outnumbered by Reagan appointees to the Fed, wanted, if only by a symbolic gesture, to curry favor with the congressional critics of takeovers, Democrats and Republicans who might have strongly urged his reappointment by the President. See also, Harvey H. Segal, "Einde van de Volcker Saga," *NRC Handelsblad* (Rotterdam), June 10, 1987.

**52.** Rick Wartzman, "Judge Says He'll Halt Bid for Koppers If He Finds Suitor Broke Margin Rules," *The Wall Street Journal,* May 20, 1988.

**53.** For a clear review of the provisions of the Delaware law and an insider's apologia, see E. Norman Veasey, "A Statute Was Needed to Stop Abuses," *The New York Times,* February 7, 1988. Veasey is a past president of the Delaware State Bar and former chairman of its corporation law committee.

**54.** Susan E. Woodward, an economist and assistant secretary of housing and urban development in the Reagan administration, estimated that the Indiana antitakeover law cost shareholders $2.65 billion in lower share prices. See her piece, "How Much Indiana's Anti-Takeover Law Cost Shareholders," *The Wall Street Journal,* May 5, 1988, and a letter from Brendan E. Quirin, an Amoco Corporation economist, disputing that claim, *The Wall Street Journal,* May 24, 1988. Woodward's conclusions are based on a regression analysis in J. Gregory Sidak and Susan E. Woodward, "Corporate Takeovers, the Commerce Clause and the Efficient Anonymity of Shareholders," unpublished ms., March 17, 1988; I'm grateful to her for a copy.

Information on opt-outs from the antitakeover law was provided from the office of Delaware's state secretary.

**55.** Based on Epstein, *Who Owns the Corporation?,* pp. 20–21; *Panter v. Marshall Field & Company,* 646 F.2d 271 (7th Cir. 1981).

**56.** Footnote 35, above. For an analysis, see Jensen, "Takeovers: Their Causes and Consequences," p. 42.

**57.** For a readable account of Gutfreund, his lifestyle and Salomon, see John Taylor, "Hard to Be Rich. The Rise and Wobble of the Gutfreunds," *New York,* January 11, 1988.

**58.** One of the scandalous conflicts of interest revealed in depositions, documents that Pennzoil attempted to conceal from the press, was that it had offered the Texaco directors protection from personal liability as an inducement to reach a settlement. See Matthew L. Wald, "Promises by Texaco's Creditors," *The New York Times,* March 12, 1988; also, Allana Sullivan, "Pennzoil-Texaco Case Is Producing Zany Depositions," *The Wall Street Journal,* March 14, 1988. The latter curiously plays down the conflict of interest, touching on it only toward the end of the story. On the capitulation of the shareholders, see Matthew L.

Wald, "Texaco Appears Close to Ending Bankruptcy," *The New York Times*, March 19, 1988.

**59.** 213 U.S. 419 (1909).

**60.** The misappropriation theory first surfaced as court-made law in 1982 in the insider trading conviction of Adrian Antoniu, a former Morgan Stanley investment banker. It was upheld by the U.S. Supreme Court in November 1987 when it affirmed the lower court conviction of R. Foster Winans for mail and wire fraud. Winans wrote the "Heard on the Street" column for *The Wall Street Journal*. In 1983, in advance of publication, he revealed what he was going to say about particular stocks to two brokers and a lawyer who traded on the information, sharing the profits with him. In upholding the mail and wire fraud convictions—there was a 4-4 tie on the the securities fraud conviction—the Court broadened the scope to embrace the misuse not only of such tangible assets as money or property but information as well. For good accounts and analyses, see the lead stories in *The New York Times* and *The Wall Street Journal*, November 17, 1987.

**61.** Henry G. Manne, *Insider Trading and the Stock Market* (New York: Free Press, 1966), chap. 9.

**62.** As Manne's analysis implies (chaps 7–8), if there are no leaks and there is no insider trading on price-raising news, there won't be any transfer of wealth from outsiders to insiders. The price of the stock will rise to its new high within hours, if not minutes, of the announcement and all shareholders will gain. But if there is insider trading and leaking, the price of the stock will rise gradually over days, weeks, or months, and in that interregnum there will be wealth transfers from outsiders to insiders. Their magnitude will depend on the proneness of the outsiders to sell on the basis of short-term price movements. In other words, outsiders who for whatever reason tend to ignore short-term price changes and market rumors will fare better than those who are sensitive to price swings.

**63.** James Sterngold, "Arbitrager Said to Have Helped Boesky," *The New York Times*, February 25, 1988. Gulf pulled out of a bid for Cities Service—later acquired by Occidental Petroleum—causing a collapse of the price of its stock in which Boesky had invested more than $100 million.

Boesky was rescued from bankruptcy through the efforts of his friend John A. Mulheren, Jr., partner in Jamie Securities, an extraordinarily gifted trading strategist and arbitrager who is much admired on Wall Street. Boesky, as is his wont, repaid that kindness by fingering Mulheren for what might have been no more than a minor infraction of SEC regulations. A manic depressive whose psychic balance is maintained by lithium, Mulheren cracked under the strain of the investigation and threatened the lives of Boesky and Michael Davidoff, once Boesky's chief trader. Since both were important federal witnesses, Mulheren was briefly imprisoned for that offense.

**64.** James H. Stewart and Daniel Hertzberg, "The Wall Street Career of Martin Siegel Was a Dream Gone Wrong," *The Wall Street Journal,* February 17, 1987.

**65.** "Out on a Limb: Drexel's Milken Finds Himself More Isolated as Indictment Nears," *The Wall Street Journal,* December 23, 1988.

**66.** Thomas E. Ricks, "Dingell Opposes Bill Defining Insider Trading," *The Wall Street Journal,* March 9, 1987. In an appearance before the Securities Industry Association, Representative John D. Dingell (D-Mich.), chairman of the House Energy and Commerce Committee, which oversees the SEC, said flatly that "there will be no definition of insider trading." Dingell opposes defintive legislation for fear that it would open up exploitable loopholes.

**67.** Jensen, "A Helping Hand," points out that the Williams Act compels the raider to give up most of the profits—an estimated 86 percent—to free-riding investors who spend nothing on the research and reorganization planning that are essential to a successful takeover.

**68.** George Anders, "Drexel Criticized for Giving Clients Data on Prospective Takeovers to Raise Funds," *The Wall Street Journal,* December 9, 1986.

**69.** Kurt Eichenwald, "Court Eases Firm's Securities Bond" and "Prosecutor Cites Drexel Role in Princeton/Newport Case," *The New York Times,* October 18 and 20, 1988. Ann Hagedorn, "Princeton/Newport Sets Liquidation; Officials Faced Racketeering Charges," *The Wall Street Journal,* December 8, 1988.

**70.** Matthew Josephson, *The Money Lords,* pp. 9–10, 87–88.

**71.** Henry G. Manne, "The Real Boesky-Case Issue," *The New York Times,* November 25, 1986.

**72.** Stein, "Leveraged Buyouts"; See also footnote 41 above.

**73.** Quoted by Adam Smith, "How Private Deals Clean Out Public Business," *Esquire,* February 1988.

**74.** For a readable review of the literature on takeovers, pro and con, but which fails to draw the distinction that I deem crucial, see "Do Mergers Work?" *The Economist,* December 17, 1988, pp. 76–78. The very title is wrong.

Also see: David J. Ravenscraft and F. M. Scherer, *Mergers, Sell-Offs and Economic Efficiency* (Washington: The Brookings Institution, 1987), and Louis Lowenstein and Susan Rose-Ackerman, eds., *Knights, Raiders, and Targets: The Impact of the Hostile Takeover* (New York: Oxford University Press, 1987).

Ravenscraft and Scherer analyzed statistical data on some six thousand mergers between 1950 and 1976. It was a period dominated by conglomerates, and the findings—chaps. 4 and 5—support my view, as set forth in the previous chapter, that the acquirers didn't do "very well" (p. 122), that returns on their acquisitions were below industry averages. Ravenscraft and Scherer are inconclusive (chap. 6) on the impact of subsequent divestitures, again dominated by conglomerates. But, contrary to some fears, they found no evidence of post-divestiture reductions of spending for research and development or advertising (pp. 190–191).

**75.** Ennius Bergsma, "Do-It-Yourself Takeover Curbs," *The Wall Street Journal,* February 12, 1988.

**76.** Frank R. Lichtenberg, "What Makes Plant Productivity Grow?" *The Wall Street Journal,* December 24, 1987. There is a full, technical account of the findings in Frank R. Lichtenberg and Donald Siegel, "Productivity and Changes of Ownership in Manufacturing Plants," unpublished paper, January 1988, which Professor Lichtenberg kindly made available.

Steven Kaplan of the University of Chicago analyzed seventy-six large management buyouts between 1979 and 1984 and found that they resulted in solid efficiency gains. See his "Management Buyouts: Efficiency Gains or Value Transfers?," paper presented at the Salomon Brothers Conference Center, New York University, December 8–9, 1988.

**77.** Irving Fisher, *Booms and Depressions* (New York: Adelphi Co., 1932); "The Debt-Deflation Theory of Great Depressions," *Econometrica,* October 1933; and *100% Money* (New Haven: The City Printing Company, 1945), chap. 7.

**78.** For a calm account of those concerns, see Lindley H. Clark, Jr., and Alfred L. Malabre, Jr., "Borrowing Binge: Takeover Trend Helps Push Corporate Debt and Defaults Upward," *The Wall Street Journal,* March 15, 1988.

**79.** Jensen, "Takeovers," pp. 31–32.

**80.** F. M. Scherer, "Corporate Takeovers: The Efficiency Arguments," *Journal of Economic Perspectives,* Winter 1988, p. 77. For a critical account of General Electric as a conglomerate, see Janet Guyon, "GE Chairman Welch, Though Much Praised, Starts to Draw Critics. Some Accuse Him of Creating a Muddled Conglomerate and Destroying Morale," *The Wall Street Journal,* August 4, 1988.

## 4. WORKERS AND SHIRKERS:
### Corporate Salvation by Carrots and Sticks

**1.** There is an overall balance-of-payments deficit when U.S. expenditures on the goods and services of other countries—for imports, investments, and such "transfers" as immigrants' remittances and government outlays for military and economic assistance—exceed the rest of the world's expenditures on U.S. goods, services, investments, and transfers.

U.S. balance-of-payments deficits were then financed through sales from the U.S. gold stock to foreign governments or their central banks. Until the breakdown of the Bretton Woods international monetary system in 1971, the dollar was convertible to gold, first at the official price of $35 an ounce and then at prices in the $40 range, but still far below the free market level. Ownership of gold—coins or bullion—by private U.S. citizens was illegal between 1934 and 1975.

In the 1960s, the United States ran a "current account" surplus—our exports of goods and services exceeded our imports—but that surplus was more than offset by outflows of U.S. capital. Today we are running a large current account deficit which is financed by capital inflows from abroad—that is, purchases by foreign investors of U.S. securities and real assets.

I joined *The Washington Post* as an editorial writer and columnist in the summer of 1962 and for the next six years followed our balance-of-payments problems in proximity to the policymakers.

**2.** Robert E. Lipsey and Irving B. Kravis, "The Competitiveness and Comparative Advantage of U.S. Multinationals, 1957–1984," *Banca Nazionale del Lavoro Quarterly Review,* June 1987. The *Left Business Observer,* January 1988, compares the recent rise (1985–87) of the ratio of U.S. export prices to labor costs and the fall of the same ratio for Japan and concluded that "it is clear that U.S. firms are not pricing their goods aggressively, and that Japanese firms are."

**3.** Ernest Campbell Mossner and Ian Simpson Ross, eds., *The Correspondence of Adam Smith* (Oxford: Oxford University Press, 1977), p. 262. Italics in the original.

**4.** Paul Kennedy, *The Rise and Fall of the Great Powers. Economic Change and Military Conflict from 1500 to 2000.* (New York: Random House, 1988), p. 226.

**5.** Robert E. Lipsey and Irving B. Kravis, *Saving and Economic Growth: Is the United States Really Falling Behind?* (New York: The Conference Board, 1987), p. 14.

**6.** According to the principle of purchasing power parity (PPP), $100 worth of yen should buy as much in Japan as $100 buys in the United States. In practice, the dollar-yen exchange rate may be above or below PPP, which is calculated by comparing price levels in the two countries. An overvalued dollar—its converse or mirror image is an undervalued yen—means $100 worth of yen buys more in Japan than $100 does in the United States. In 1984, the dollar was very much overvalued in relation to the dollar/yen PPP, and that was taken into account by a higher estimate of Japan's real output per head than would have been derived from converting yen to dollars at the then current exchange rate of about $1 = Y250.

*The Economist,* April 2, 1988, compared PPP measures based on prices of Big Mac hamburgers around the world. On March 28, 1988, a Big Mac cost Y370 in Japan and $2.39 in the United States. The PPP ratio or exchange rate was 370/2.39 = 155 or $1 = Y155. But the actual exchange rate on that day was $1 = Y124. So by the Big Mac standard, the dollar was undervalued by 20 percent, 124/155 = .80—a dollar bought more junk food in the United States than a dollar's worth of yen bought in Japan. But the U.S. dollar was overvalued by 66 percent against the Australian dollar and by 145 percent against the Hong Kong dollar—it had higher junk-food purchasing power in those countries than at home. Hong Kong, unlike Japan, doesn't restrict imports and keep beef prices sky high, and Australia is a major cattle producer with low domestic beef prices.

A survey as of June 30, 1988, indicated that the Big Mac was still selling for 370 yen in Japan, which were then equivalent to $2.78. So the yen was overvalued by 27 percent. George Anders, "What Price Lunch?" *The Wall Street Journal,* supplement, September 23, 1988.

**7.** Calculated from tables B-1 and B-2 in the Economic Report of the President, February 1988 (Washington, U.S. Government Printing Office, 1988), pp. 248–51. The 1950 total was barely under 5 percent of the GNP.

There is good reason to believe that the official totals of "National Defense Expenditures" understate the actual outlays for military purposes. Some of the foreign-assistance grants that are categorized as civilian are actually for military programs. Then there are the "black," off-budget, secret expenditures by the Pentagon, the Central Intelligence Agency, and the office of the national security adviser. But even if such outlays come to several billions annually—as they well might—and are misclassified as "civilian," the percentages of GNP aren't very far off.

Military expenditures account for about 6 percent of the world gross product. See R. P. Smith, "Military Expenditures" in *The New Palgrave: A Dictionary of Economics* (New York: Stockton Press, 1987), vol. 3, p. 463.

**8.** Paul Baran and Paul M. Sweezy, *Monopoly Capitalism* (New York: Monthly Review, 1965), argue that military spending prevents economic stagnation, but U.S. experience hardly bears out that thesis. James Cypher, "Capitalist Planning and Military Expenditures," *Review of Radical Political Economics* no. 3, 1974, p. 6, contends that military spending has been used as an anticyclical device in the postwar period. The evidence he adduces, however, suggests that even when its timing is correct, military spending isn't a very effective contracyclical force.

Tom Riddell, "U.S. Military Power, the Terms of Trade, and the Profit Rate," *American Economic Review,* May 1988, pp. 62–64, presents a model of a positive relationship between military power and the U.S after-tax profit rate. Military power is defined—in my view, dubiously—as the number of incidents annually from 1948 through 1981 in which the United States used its military forces without actual conflict. What Riddell claims, in essence, is that a one-point increase in the index of military power is associated, a year later, with a 0.14 percent increase in the rate of profit. To me, that finding is intuitively implausible, a spurious relationship reflecting the effect of influences that Riddell failed to take into account.

**9.** Seymour Melman, "The Economics of the Arms Race: The Second-Rate Economy," *American Economic Review,* May 1988, p. 56, and *Profits Without Production* (New York: Alfred A. Knopf, 1983), pp. 170–71.

**10.** Dwight D. Eisenhower, farewell address, January 17, 1961, quoted in George Seldes, *The Great Thoughts* (New York: Ballantine Books, 1985), p. 121. It's not clear which of the President's speech writers, Bryce N. Harlow or Malcolm Moos, was responsible for the "military-industrial complex."

**11.** U.S. Bureau of Labor Statistics data appearing in Economic Report of the President, February 1988 (Washington: U.S. Government Printing Office, 1988), tables B-45–47.

**12.** On May 2, 1987, the U.S. Supreme Court by a 6-2 vote upheld the defendant in *Business Electronics* v. *Sharp Electronics,* (85–1910). Business Electronics, a Houston retailer, won an antitrust suit against Sharp, an electronics manufacturer, for terminating its dealership at the behest of a competitor who complained about its price cutting. In overturning the lower court verdict, Justice Antonin Scalia suggested that it is sometimes "legitimate and competitively useful" for manufacturers to curb discounting by retailers. Scalia, a member of the sometimes perverse and wrong-headed Chicago school of economic jurisprudence, enraged a sizable number of both Republicans and Democrats in Congress, and it's likely that his judicial activism will be countered by new legislation.

**13.** For two excellent accounts, see Paul Ingrassia and Amal Kumar Naj, "Revving Up: U.S. Auto Makers Get Chance to Regain Sales from Foreign Rivals," *The Wall Street Journal,* April 16, 1987, and John Bussey, "Fateful Choice: Did U.S. Auto Makers Err by Raising Prices When the Yen Rose?," *The Wall Street Journal,* April 18, 1988.

**14.** This account draws in part on Harvey H. Segal, "The Gold Standard," *The New York Times Encyclopedic Almanac 1970* (New York: New York Times Book, 1969), pp. 645–46.

**15.** For a shrewd analysis—from a political and defense burden-sharing perspective—of the very rapid buildup of dollar holdings by foreign central banks in 1987–88, see Dale Hale, "Accounting for the Dollar Glut," *The Wall Street Journal,* April 18, 1988.

**16.** Each of the dollar exchange rates—for example, the dollar/DM and the dollar/yen—are weighted by the volume of U.S. trade with that country, and averages of the weighted rates are then computed.

**17.** Economic Report of the President, February 1988, tables B-45–47, 24. The 1974 business situation was very confusing, what with high inflation and a frantic scramble to accumulate inventories in anticipation of shortages and further price hikes. Although the business cycle peak came in 1973, even in early 1974 many managers didn't believe that the economy was in recession.

The corporate profit figures cited are before adjustments for changes in the valuation of inventories or capital consumption charges. Both those adjustments are conceptually sound but subject to errors of estimation, especially in periods of disinflation. In any case, my remark about the dismal profit picture still holds.

**18.** The price elasticity of demand for "natural" bread in the above example is 2.24. In computing it, I used an arc formula to cover the segment of the demand function:

$$e = (q_0-q_1/q_0+q_1)(p_0+p_1/p_0-p_1) = .32 \times 7 = 2.24$$

where $q_0$ and $q_1$, $p_0$ and $p_1$ are the initial and terminal quantities and prices, respectively.

Elasticity at a point on a demand curve is: $e = dq/dp(p/q)$, where $dq$ is the change in quantity sold, $dp$ the change in price, $p$ and $q$ are the initial prices and quantities. The first term on the right-hand side of the equation is the slope.

When the price elasticity of demand is finite, as it is for any except a horizontal, or zero-slope, demand function that price takers, such as farmers face, the change in the marginal revenue from the sale of an additional unit is below the average revenue or price. For more, see a price theory text.

The marginal revenue, $mr = p(1-1/e)$, where $p$ is the price or average revenue and $e$ is the elasticity.

**19.** Melvin W. Reder, "The Rise and Fall of Unions: The Public Sector and the Private," *Journal of Economic Perspectives,* Spring 1988, p. 106. There was, by contrast, a large gain in the much smaller public sector, which includes teachers, where the organized share of the labor force rose from 10.8 to 33.1 percent over those same twenty-five years.

**20.** H. Gregg Lewis, *Union Relative Wage Effects* (Chicago: University of Chicago Press, 1986), p. 9 and chap. 9. Lewis's estimates are based on a survey of the best quantitative research for the years 1967–79. The average union-nonunion gap for those thirteen years was 15 percent.

The average gap for the 1980s may well be higher because of the rapid growth of low-paying, nonunion jobs in service industries.

**21.** Justin Kaplan, ed., *Great Short Works of Mark Twain* (New York: Harper & Row, 1967), esp. "Official Rank and Dignity of a Pilot. The Rise and Decadence of the Pilots' Association," pp. 52–67. These wonderful pieces originally appeared in *The Atlantic Monthly* for 1875, and I'm indebted to Harry G. Segal for calling them to my attention. For the classic analysis of the impact of the American Medical Association and state licensure, see Milton Friedman and Simon Kuznets, *Income from Independent Professional Practice* (New York: National Bureau of Economic Research, 1945), esp. chaps. 4 and 6. Both Friedman and Kuznets won Nobel Prizes.

**22.** After federal authorities moved against the mobsters in the early 1940s, the late Professor Salomon J. Flink, my colleague at Rutgers University's Graduate School of Management in Newark, was the court-appointed trustee of the local. Because of death threats, he and his family at one point had around-the-clock police protection.

**23.** Roy Rowan, "The Mafia's Bite of the Big Apple," *Fortune,* June 6, 1988. Because of the prevalence of crime, Governor Mario Cuomo appointed a special construction industry strike force of some one hundred prosecutors and investigators.

The U.S. Justice Department's civil suit against the International Brotherhood of Teamsters, brought under the Racketeer Influenced and Corrupt Organization Act (RICO) in June 1988, sought to end mob influence or control of the union. But mob-control per se cannot push wages up much beyond competitive levels, particularly in the largely unregulated intrastate segment of the trucking industry. In fact, mobsters sometimes negotiate "sweetheart" contracts with employers—lower than market wage rates and fringes—in return for payoffs.

**24.** George A. Akerloff and Janet L. Yellin, eds., *Efficiency Wage Models of the Labor Market* (New York: Cambridge University Press, 1986), esp. the introduction and the chapter by Robert M. Solow, "Another Possible Source of Wage Stickiness."

**25.** Martin L. Weitzman, *The Share Economy: Conquering Stagflation* (Cambridge: Harvard University Press, 1984). For Weitzman's theoretical underpinnings, see his: "Increasing Returns and the Foundations of Unemployment Theory," *Economic Journal,* December 1982; "Some Macroeconomic Implications of Alternative Compensation Systems," *Economic Journal,* December 1983; and "The Simple Macroeconomics of Profit Sharing," *American Economic Review,* December 1985. See also James E. Meade, *Alternative Systems of Business Organization and of Workers' Remuneration* (London: Allen & Unwin, 1985), and *Different Forms of Share Economy* (London: Public Policy Centre, 1986). Meade was a 1977 Nobel Prize winner.

**26.** Weitzman, *The Share Economy,* p. 35. Italics in the original.

**27.** This point is supported by Sushil B. Wadhwani of the London School of Economics whose article "The Macroeconomic Implications of Profit Sharing: Some Empirical Evidence," *Economic Journal* Conference 1987, pp. 171–83, I read after reaching my judgment. Wadhwani tested to determine whether the Japanese economy, with its heavy reliance on bonus payments, is more stable—less prone to stagflation—than others. He concludes that "profit sharing might be one factor that can explain Japan's spectacular growth performance," even though "there is nothing in the empirical evidence discussed to suggest that profit sharing has desired macroeconomic effects for the reasons given by Weitzman."

**28.** "Face-to-Face: Economist Martin Weitzman," interview in *INC.,* March 1986, p. 40.

**29.** Amanda Bennett, "Top Dollar: Corporate Chiefs' Pay Far Outpaces Inflation and the Gains of Staffs," *The Wall Street Journal,* March 28, 1988.

**30.** Frederick Rose, "Unocal's Chief, Fred L. Hartley, Resigns Position," *The Wall Street Journal,* June 7, 1988.

**31.** "Who Made the Most—and Why," *Business Week,* cover story, May 2, 1988.

**32.** Graef S. Crystal, "The Wacky, Wacky World of CEO Pay," *Fortune,* June 6, 1988, box "In Search of John Reed's Pay," p. 76. On Citicorp: "Notice of 1988 Annual Meeting of Stockholders and Proxy Statement," pp. 25, 38 n. and 42. For Reed's 1986 pay, see "The Corporate Elite," *Business Week,* October 26, 1987.

**33.** David R. Meredith, "Getting the Right Bang for the Buck: Are CEO's Paid What They Are Worth?" *Chief Executive,* September/October 1987, and Crystal, "The Wacky, Wacky World."

Meredith, a corporate-compensation consultant who heads the Personnel Corporation of America, used *Business Week*'s "Top 100" data for 1986 and ran industry group regressions to determine "competitive pay," which he then compared with actual pay, the difference between them being the "pay factor." Under a rational CEO compensation system—one that rewards success and punishes failure—there should have been high correlations between positive or plus pay factors and high performance or returns to shareholders. But there wasn't.

Crystal, a professor in the University of California at Berkeley, looked at CEO pay in the top 170 companies of the *Fortune* 500. He calculated a "rational" pay level for each by regressing such variables as company size, performance, company risk, government regulation, the CEO's tenure and the company's location. His article highlighted the outlyers, those CEOs whose pay far exceeded "rational" levels and those—notably founders with large equity interests, such as Laurence A. Tisch of Loews, Kenneth H. Olsen of Digital Equipment, and Leon Hess of Amerada Hess—with far less than "rational" pay.

My objections to the Meredith-Crystal approach are spelled out in the text.

**34.** Herbert Joseph Davenport, *The Economics of Enterprise* (New York: Macmillan Company, 1916), pp. 107–108.

**35.** Quoted by Bennett, "Top Dollar."

**36.** For a recent survey of that industry—in which the top fourteen were paid fees totaling more than $360 million in 1987—see Heidi S. Fiske, "The Headhunters' Changing Jungle," *Fortune,* May 9, 1988.

**37.** Crystal, "The Wacky, Wacky World," pp. 76, 72.

**38.** Kevin J. Murphy, "Corporate Performance and Managerial Remuneration: An Empirical Analysis," *Journal of Accounting and Economics,* April 1985, pp. 11–42; George Baker, "Compensation and Hierarchies," Harvard Business School, January 1986.

**39.** Donald R. Katz, *The Big Store: Inside the Crisis and Revolution at Sears* (New York: Viking, 1987), pp. 26–29, 37–41. Philip Purcell, who heads Sears's troubled financial services operations, came to the company from Hay Associates. He was a member of the team, the "Hay Committee," that, beginning in 1975, laid the groundwork for future acquisitions and disasters.

**40.** T. Boone Pickens, Jr., *Boone* (Boston: Houghton Mifflin Company, 1987), pp. 219–20; Jeff Madrick, *Taking America: How We Got from the First Hostile Takeover to Megamergers, Corporate Raiding, and Scandal* (New York: Bantam Books, 1987), p. 269.

**41.** Federal Aviation Administration, *Statistical Handbook of Aviation,* 1975–1988. Table 8.1 gives a breakdown of aircraft in service by primary use. The number of executive aircraft reached a peak of more than 17,000 in 1983 and the subsequent decline reflects tax changes and a tightening up on costly corporate perquisites.

For a good account of the current executive-jet scene—full of self-serving justifications—see "Business May Cut Back, but Not on Its Private Jets," *The New York Times,* January 25, 1989.

**42.** On the Chrysler jet and the Treasury, see Paul H. Weaver, "Lee Since *Iacocca:* The Sequel," *The Wall Street Journal,* July 11, 1988; Lee Iacocca, *Talking Straight* (New York: Bantam Books, 1988), p. 113.

**43.** Anthony Lewis, "Getting Even: An Amazing Decision in the Post Case," *The New York Times,* April 11, 1985.

**44.** William C. Symonds, "Big Trouble at Allegheny," *Business Week,* August 11, 1986. I have drawn on the *BW* story, conversations with my friend Horace De Podwin, and newspaper accounts.

**45.** Clare Ansberry, "Allegheny International Gives Details of Acts Leading to Ex-Chairman's Ouster"; Bruce Ingersoll and Clare Ansberry, "Allegheny International Sued by SEC"; Clare Ansberry, "Plan

Approved by Allegheny International," *The Wall Street Journal,* June 10, 1987, September 10, 1987, and June 20, 1988, respectively.

**46.** *The Dialogues of Plato,* trans. Benjamin Jowett, 3rd ed. (Oxford: Clarendon Press, 1892), vol. 5, p. 127. Aristotle says that Plato "allows a man's whole property to be increased fivefold," *The Politics of Aristotle* trans. Ernest Barker (Oxford: Clarendon Press, 1952), II, 15, p. 59. On J. P. Morgan, Sr., Crystal, "The Wacky, Wacky World," p. 78, cites an unnamed Drucker source. For the average pay of CEOs of corporations with more than $1 billion of revenues, David Kirkpatrick, "Abroad, It's Another World," *Fortune,* June 6, 1988, p. 78.

**47.** Kirkpatrick, "Abroad, It's Another World"; *Business Week,* "Who Made the Most—And Why."

**48.** Crystal, *Wacky, Wacky World,* p. 78. On the Senate action, see stories in *The Wall Street Journal* and *The New York Times,* June 22, 1988.

## 5. DIMENSIONS OF POWER:
### Boardrooms, Markets, Ideas, and Politics

**1.** John Locke, *Two Treatises of Government* (New York: Dutton, 1977), bk. 1, chap. 9, sect. 106, p. 73.

**2.** *Business Week,* July, 7, 1986, cover story, pp. 57–58. Black is quoted in Connie Bruck, *The Predators' Ball: The Junk-Bond Raiders and the Man Who Staked Them* (New York: The American Lawyer/Simon and Schuster, 1988), p. 149.

**3.** Much of what follows is based on Sarah Bartlett, "Power Investors: Now Wall Street Firms Want to Own the Company—Not Just Its Shares," *Business Week,* June 20, 1988; and Bartlett, "New Type of Owner Emerges in Wave of Company Buyouts, *The New York Times,* November 8, 1988; and on Carol J. Loomis, "Buyout Kings," *Fortune,* July 4, 1988.

**4.** Donald P. Kelly, "A Big Raider Gets the Last Laugh," *Fortune,* July 4, 1988, p. 69. What is presented as a monologue began with an interview by an editor.

**5.** Loomis, "Buyout Kings," p. 53.

**6.** Loomis, "Buyout Kings," p. 60.

**7.** Matthew Wald, "Icahn Loss on Texaco Conceded," *The New York Times,* June 20, 1988; Caleb Solomon and Carolyn Phillips, "Icahn

Concedes Defeat in Fight for Texaco Seats," *The Wall Street Journal,* June 20, 1988.

It was later revealed that six weeks before the proxy vote, Texaco's management contributed $10,000 to Regan's reelection campaign for comptroller. See Jack Newfield and Tom Robbins, who broke the story, "Hitched to Texaco Star," *New York Daily News,* August 31, 1988, and Elizabeth Kolbert, "Regan Bans Staff from Any Fund-Raising Role," *The New York Times,* September 8, 1988. Not astonishingly, Regan denied that the contribution influenced his vote.

Allanna Sullivan and James A. White, "Texaco, Pressured by Pension Funds, Accepts Brademas as Nominee for Board," *The Wall Street Journal,* January 24, 1989.

**8.** On J. P. Morgan, Sr.: Louis Galambos and Joseph Pratt, *The Rise of the Corporate Commonwealth: U.S. Business and Public Policy in the Twentieth Century* (New York: Basic Books, 1988), chaps. 1 and 2; and Vincent P. Carosso, *The Morgans: Private International Bankers, 1854–1913* (Cambridge: Harvard University Press, 1987), chaps. 7 and 10. On Rathenau: Count Harry Kessler, *Walther Rathenau, His Life and Work* (New York: Harcourt, Brace, 1930). On the *zaibatsu:* G. C. Allen, "The Concentration of Economic Control in Japan," *Economic Journal,* June 1937; Neil Skene Smith, "Japan's Business Families," *The Economist,* June 18, 1938; and Robert A. Brady, *Business as a System of Power* (New York: Columbia University Press, 1943), chap. 3. The literal meaning of *zaibatsu* is "money clique."

**9.** Bartlett, "New Type of Owner Emerges," p. 117. Her "total funding target" numbers are as follows: Morgan Stanley, $1.8 billion; Prudential-Bache, $1.8 billion; Merrill Lynch, $1.6 billion; Shearson Lehman Hutton, $1.25 billion; Blackstone Group, $1 billion; Wasserstein Perella, $1 billion; Ranieri Wilson, $.6 billion; Lodestar Group, $.5 billion; Vector Capital, $.3 billion. Total: $9.4 billion.

**10.** "Experts estimate that at least $25 billion is now targeted for making leveraged buyouts investments. And because of the 10-1 leverage typically used in these deals—that is for every $1,000 of purchase price, investors put up only $100 of their own money and borrow the rest—the investment funds have the muscle to make acquisitions totaling $250 billion." (Anise C. Wallace, "All Dressed Up and No Place to Go?," *The New York Times,* August 7, 1988.)

A later estimate puts buyout power at $150 billion, reflecting greater caution in the autumn of 1988 and a demand for greater equity that reduces leverage. See Christopher Farrell, "Learning to Live with Leverage," *Business Week,* November 7, 1988, p. 138. Leverage is the most volatile factor in the equation. Once institutions are committed to partnerships, the equity total is pretty much fixed.

**11.** Rankings of market values as of March 18, 1988, taken from *Business Week,* "The *Business Week* Top 1000," April 15, 1988.

**12.** See Judith H. Dobrzynski, "Was RJR's Ross Johnson Too Greedy for His Own Good,?" *Business Week,* November 21, 1988, p. 95; Benjamin J. Stein, "A New Low? The RJR LBO Makes a Travesty of Fiduciary Responsibility," *Barron's,* November 14, 1988; John Helyar and Bryan Burrough, "Buyout Bluff: How Underdog KKR Won RJR Nabisco With Highest Bid," *The Wall Street Journal,* December 2, 1988; and James Sterngold, "Nabisco Battle Redefines Directors' Role," *The New York Times,* December 5, 1988.

**13.** Anise C. Wallace, "Institutions Proxy Power Grows," *The New York Times,* July 5, 1988.

A question-begging *Business Week* editorial, July 4, 1988, p. 128, opines that the "benefits" of putting institutions on corporate boards "would include closer, hands-on scrutiny of management and less churning of investment portfolios . . . It's time institutions started acting like owners rather than traders." But how can they act like owners without the means of exercising power?

**14.** Bruce Ingersoll and Clare Ansberry, "Allegheny International Sued by SEC," *The Wall Street Journal,* September 10, 1987; William C. Symonds, "Big Trouble at Allegheny," *Business Week,* August 11, 1986. Also, conversations with my good friend, Horace J. De Podwin.

**15.** A Washington raconteur who suffered his abuse in the State Department tells this story about Haig. A Henry Kissinger protégé, Haig underwent coronary bypass surgery in the early 1980s. Later Kissinger was faced with a cardiac problem, and while being wheeled into surgery for his bypasses was asked whether he had any last questions. *"Ja,"* replied Henry the K. "Vill it make me as kraazy as Al Haig?"

**16.** Laurie Baum, "The Job Nobody Wants: Outside Directors Find That Hassles and Risks Aren't Worth It," *Business Week,* September 8, 1986; and Irving Kristol, "The War Against the Corporation," *The Wall Street Journal,* January 24, 1989.

**17.** Constance Mitchell, "Mellon's Chairman Pearson Says Extent of Bad Loans Shocked Outside Directors," *The Wall Street Journal,* April 21, 1987. During the following year the Mellon Bank, under its new CEO, Frank Cahouet, was negotiating an agreement with Drexel Burnham under which participation in a portfolio of about $1 billion of its bad loans would be sold to the public at large discounts from their face values. See Sarah Bartlett, "Mellon Set to Shift Bad Loans," *The New York Times,* July 26, 1988; Linda Sandler, "Mellon's Good/Bad Bank Realignment Plan Invites Analyses of Odds for Success, Imitation," *The Wall Street Journal,* July 26, 1988.

**18.** Baum, "The Job Nobody Wants," p. 59, box entitled, " 'Professional' Directors: So Many Boards, So Little Time."

**19.** Douglass C. North and Robert Paul Thomas, *The Rise of the Western World. A New Economic History* (Cambridge: Cambridge University Press, 1973), esp. pp. 1–8.

**20.** W. R. Vance, "Alienation of Property," *Encyclopedia of the Social Sciences* (New York: Macmillan Company, 1930), vol. 1, p. 640. Vance quotes the U.S. Supreme Court to the effect that alienation "is an inherent attribute of the property itself" (p. 639).

**21.** Perhaps the most important feudal exception in the eastern part of the country was the land tenure system of New York's upper Hudson River valley in which descendants of the original Dutch patroons, seventeenth century proprietors of vast tracts, levied rents on lands which were leased long-term to families of farmers, who over generations made many improvements and by the nineteenth century believed fervently in their claims to unencumbered ownership. When attempts were made by the Van Rensselaer family to collect back rents in 1839, an effort in which other landholders soon joined, there were outbreaks of violence and much political agitation in what came to be known as the Antirent War, a development that brought the Whig party to power. Passions subsided when the legislature in Albany took measures to relieve tenants, and future long-term leases were finally outlawed by the state constitution of 1846.

**22.** See *Moran* v. *Household Internatl.* (490 A2d 1059 Del. Ch. 1985; affirmed 500 A2d 1346 Del. Ch. 1985).

**23.** Irving Kristol, *Two Cheers for Capitalism* (New York: New American Library, 1979), pp. 19–20. Italics in original.

**24.** Kristol, *Two Cheers,* p. 21.

**25.** Irving Kristol, "A Cure for Takeovers' Social Ills," *The Wall Street Journal,* May 13, 1988. He first wrote about Potlatch's four-year holding requirement in the *Journal,* March 2, 1987.

**26.** Felix Rohatyn, "The Blight on Wall Street," *The New York Review of Books,* March 12, 1987.

**27.** Lee Iacocca, *Talking Straight* (New York: Bantam Books, 1988), pp. 121–22. For press coverage of the revelation, *The New York Times,* June 1, 1988.

**28.** Linda Sandler, "Class Struggle: Dual Stock Categories Spur Powerful Debate Over Stability vs. Gain," *The Wall Street Journal,* May 17, 1988.

**29.** On common and B shares oustanding as of December 31, 1987, see the Ford Annual Report for 1987, pp. 28 and 34, note 10. The voting power provisions are spelled out in the company's certificate of incorporation, as amended in December 1987.

**30.** Dow Jones & Company, Inc., Notice of 1984 Annual Meeting and Proxy Statement, pp. 12–21, appendix A, pp. 1–7; The New York Times Company, 1987 Annual Report, pp. 52, 55–56, and form 10-K for 1987, cover page.

**31.** Sandler, "Class Struggles." Sugarman also lost a proxy fight.

**32.** Quoted in Sandler, "Class Struggles."

**33.** When Hershey Foods, the big chocolate maker, gave its shareholders a choice between ordinary voting shares and non-voting shares with a bigger dividend, they chose the bigger dividend. Wang Laboratories, the computer manufacturer, gave its shareholders the same options.

Thomas Ricks, "SEC Adopts Narrow Rule to Eliminate Extremely Unequal Voting Rights," *The Wall Street Journal,* July 8, 1988; and Nathaniel C. Nash, "Share Vote Proposal Approved: S.E.C. Bars Classes of Stock Granting 'Supervoting Rights,' " *The New York Times,* July 8, 1988.

**34.** For a generally critical view of the rule, see Oliver Hart, "SEC May Kill Shareholders with Kindness," *The Wall Street Journal,* July 14, 1988. An MIT economist, Hart argues that dual issues often accomplish the same end as leveraged buyouts—putting the insiders in control—and therefore enhance efficiency. But dual issues would only be equivalent to an LBO that is highly unfavorable to outsiders, the sort of abuse discussed in chapter 3, pp. 96–97, 112. In my view, the benefits of barring dual issues as an antitakeover device outweigh any efficiency losses.

**35.** For a classic but still fresh insight into the Japanese society and economy, read Thorstein Veblen's essay "The Opportunity of Japan," first published in 1915 and reprinted in his *Essays in Our Changing Social Order* (New York: Viking Press, 1943), pp. 246–66. Other works that have shaped my view are: Ruth Benedict, *The Chrysanthemum and the Sword* (Boston: Houghton Mifflin, 1946); David Bergamini, *Japan's Imperial Conspiracy* (New York: Pocket Books, 1972); and The Pacific War Research Society's compilation, *Japan's Longest Day* (Tokyo: Kodansha International, 1968), an account of the surrender on August 15, 1945, as seen through the eyes of the leading participants.

A fascinating Japanese perspective on the current trade rivalry with the United States—and much more, all in an adult comic book format—is Shotaro Ishinomori, *Japan Inc.: An Introduction to Japanese Economics* (*The Comic Book*) (Berkeley: University of California Press, 1988).

**36.** Shotaro, *Japan Inc.,* pp. 30, 33, 53, and 56.

**37.** For graphs and tables based on industry data, see Arthur Way, "A Survey of the Motor Industry," *The Economist,* October 15, 1988, pp. 6, 8.

**38.** John Holusha, "The Taurus: Big Sales, Big Repairs. Ford's New Way of Making Cars Brings Profits and Many Problems," *The New York Times,* June 19, 1988.

**39.** See the following articles in *The Wall Street Journal:* Clyde Prestowitz, "In Defense of the Semiconductor Pact," September, 26, 1986; Brenton R. Schlender and Stephen Kreider Yoder, "Falling Chips: Semiconductor Accord With Japan Fails to Aid U.S. Firms, as Intended," February 12, 1987; Peter Waldman and Brenton R. Schlender, "Falling Chips: Is a Big Federal Role the Way to Revitalize Semiconductor Firms?" February 17, 1987; Michael S. Malone, "Fear and Xenophobia in Silicon Valley," February 23, 1987; Art Pine, "Chips Fight: Reagan's Tariff Move May Be Turning Point in Japanese Relations," March 30, 1987; George Gilder, "Chip Sense and Nonsense," April 2, 1987; Michael S. Malone, "Chip Consortium: Before Congress Antes Up," November 17, 1987; Brenton R. Schlender, "Chip Prices Fall; Easing of Shortage Seen," July 18, 1988; Brian S. Westbury, "Letters to the Editor," July, 19, 1988; Carrie Dolan and Eduardo Lachia, "Sematech Names Intel's Noyce to Head Semiconductor Industry Research Group," July 28, 1988.

See also Malcolm Gladwell, "Silicon Valley Goes to Washington: Semi-Tough," *The New Republic,* May 18, 1987; and Gary Hector, "Competition: The U.S. Chipmakers' Shaky Comeback," *Fortune,* June 20, 1988.

See the following articles in *The New York Times:* Roger Altman and

Gail Zauder, "Rescuing the Semiconductor Industry," March 17, 1987; David Sanger, "Chip Dispute: Reading Between the Lines," March 30, 1987; Andrew Pollack, "Chip Pioneer to Head Consortium," July 28, 1988.

**40.** Louis Galambos and Joseph Pratt, *The Rise of the Corporate Commonwealth: United States Business and Public Policy in the Twentieth Century* (New York: Basic Books, Inc., 1988). The foregoing draws in part on my review, "What's Good for Industry . . ." *The New Leader,* May 2, 1988.

**41.** Alex Taylor, III, "Competition: Japan's Carmakers Take On the World," *Fortune,* June 20, 1988.

**42.** Damon Darlin, "Trade Switch: Japan Getting a Dose of What It Gave U.S.: Low-Priced Imports," *The Wall Street Journal,* July 20, 1988.

**43.** John Maynard Keynes, *The General Theory of Employment, Interest and Money* (New York: Harcourt, Brace and Company, 1936), pp. 383–84.

**44.** Donald R. Katz, *The Big Store: Inside the Crisis and Revolution at Sears* (New York: Viking, 1987), p. 354.

**45.** For a classic analysis by Nobel laureates Milton Friedman and Simon Kuznets, *Income from Independent Professional Practice* (New York: National Bureau of Economic Research, 1945), esp. chaps. 4 and 6.

**46.** Some of what follows first appeared in Harvey H. Segal, "Educating the Managers," *The New Leader,* February 8, 1988.

**47.** John P. Kotter, *The Leadership Factor* (New York: The Free Press, 1988), p. 123.

**48.** Gordon Donaldson, *Managing Corporate Wealth: The Operation of a Comprehensive Financial Goals System* (New York: Praeger, 1984), pp. 22–23. For a fuller account of Donaldson's research, see chap. 1, pp. 23–26 above.

**49.** For a provocative but not critically intelligent account, J. Paul Mark, *The Empire Builders: Inside the Harvard Business School* (New York: William Morrow and Company, 1987), esp. chaps. 13, 15, and 17.

**50.** Amanda Bennett, "MBA May Not Be Worth It for Many Career Switchers," *The Wall Street Journal,* July 20, 1988. She presents a pertinent table that shows how much a career switcher would have to earn to make up for two years' loss of income and the tuition costs of an

MBA. Assuming 5 percent annual increases, the MBA who gets a job with a starting salary of $40,000 or $50,000 annually would never recoup the costs. With 10 percent annual increases, the MBA who gets a $40,000 job would break even in twenty-two years.

**51.** Adam Smith, *An Inquiry into the Nature and Causes of the Wealth of Nations* (Indianapolis: Liberty Classics, 1981), vol. 1, p. 456. Robin Marris, *The Economic Theory of "Managerial" Capitalism* (New York: Basic Books, 1968), p. 2. Italics in original.

**52.** Michael Kinsley, "Companies as Citizens: Should They Have a Conscience," *The Wall Street Journal*, February 19, 1987; Alix M. Freedman, "Blowing Smoke: Tobacco Firms, Pariahs to Many People, Still Are Angels to the Arts," *The Wall Street Journal*, June 8, 1988.

**53.** Robert Kuttner, *The Life of the Party: Democratic Prospects in 1988 and Beyond* (New York: Viking, 1987), p. 235.

**54.** Stories on Hyatt Clark and the Quincy shipyard were featured on the Public Broadcasting Service's "MacNeil/Lehrer News Hour," July 2, 1987.

## 6. PEERING INTO THE CORPORATE FUTURE:
### Forces, Directions, and Conjectures

**1.** Adam Ferguson, *An Essay on the History of Civil Society* (1767); cited by F. A. Hayek, *Studies in Philosophy, Politics and Economics* (New York: Simon and Schuster, 1969), chap. 6, "The Results of Human Action but Not of Human Design," p. 96.

Ferguson (1732–1815) was a Scottish historian and philosopher who taught at the University of Edinburgh. For a nineteenth-century development of this idea by an Austrian founder of neoclassical economic theory, see Carl Menger, *Problems of Economics and Sociology* (Urbana: University of Illinois Press, 1963), bk. 3, chap. 2, esp. p. 158.

**2.** Quoted by Albert B. Crenshaw, "Taking Some of the Levers Out of Leveraged Buyouts," *The Washington Post* National Weekly Edition, December 19–25, 1988.

**3.** Transcript of George Bush's press conference, January 12, 1989, *The New York Times*, January 13, 1989. Two short deletions were made in the interest of syntax.

**4.** Quoted in Alan Murray, "Bush Indicates He May Favor Reducing Tax Deduction for Junk-Bond Interest," *The Wall Street Journal,* January 13, 1989.

**5.** See Jeffrey H. Birnbaun and Paul Duke, Jr., "Tax Writers Move on Plan to Curb LBOs," *The Wall Street Journal,* January 26, 1989; and Howard Gleckman, "Why Washington May Not Lay a Glove on LBOs," *Business Week,* February 6, 1989.

**6.** Martin Lipton, "Is This the End of Takeovers," memorandum, "To Our Clients," October 28, 1988. Italics added. For a summary and commentaries on Lipton's letter, Laurie P. Cohen, "Lipton Asserts Corporate Boards Can Simply Reject Hostile Bids," *The Wall Street Journal,* November 4, 1988.

**7.** Bryan Burrough, "Interco Defense Against Rales Is Struck Down," *The Wall Street Journal,* November 1, 1988; "Appeal Moot in Interco Case," *The New York Times,* November 19, 1988.

**8.** Martin Lipton, "The Interco Case," memorandum "To Our Clients," November 3, 1988.
   Laurie P. Cohen, "Lipton Tells Clients That Delaware May Not Be a Place to Incorporate," *The Wall Street Journal,* November 11, 1988; Stephen Labaton, "Business and the Law: The 'Poison Pill' Takes a Beating," *The New York Times,* November 14, 1988.

**9.** Fidelity High Income Fund, "Notice of Special Meeting of Shareholders," October 25, 1988, p. 10.

**10.** What follows is based on Lawrence M. Fisher, "Safeway Buyout: A Success Story," *The New York Times,* October 21, 1988.

**11.** Christopher Farrell, "Learning to Live with Leverage," *Business Week,* November 7, 1988, p.139.

**12.** Farrell, "Learning to Live," p. 138.

# INDEX

General Motors (GM):
  consolidation of, 32–35, 36, 38
  decentralization of, 47
  diseconomies of scale in, 48–
    49
  economic importance of, 128–
    129
  as holding company, 7
  market share of, 38, 48–49,
    131, 180
  operating divisions of, 33–34,
    61
  pension plan of, 82
  stock of, 15
  takeover bid for, 175
  wage efficiency in, 145–46
Gephardt, Richard, 184
Germany, Federal Republic of
    (West):
  currency conversions by, 135,
    136
  postwar recovery of, 125–26
Getty, Gordon, 108
Getty Oil, 105, 108
Giannini, Amadeo P., 71
Gibson Greeting Card, 78
Giuliani, Rudolph W., 111
Glass-Steagall Act (1933), 90
GNP (gross national product),
    124–25, 126, 129, 138
"going private," see leveraged
  buyouts (LBOs)
"golden parachutes," 73, 93, 118,
  159
Goldin, Harrison J., 82, 167, 168
Goldman, Henry, 44
Goldman, Sachs, 111
Goldsmith, James, 79, 95
gold standard, 115–16, 132–33,
  135, 136–37
Goodyear Tire & Rubber Com-
  pany, 95
Gould, Jay, 71, 94

Graham, Benjamin, 57, 58
Graham family, 177
Great Britain, economy of, 121–
  122, 123–24, 125
Great Depression, 11, 13–14, 15,
  116–17
Green, Charles, 71
Greene, G. Davis, Jr., 82–83
Greenhill, Robert F., 72
greenmail, 71, 93, 95
Greenspan, Alan, 198
Gulf Oil, 39, 76, 77, 89, 92
Gutfreund, John, 104

Haft, Herbert, 163
Haft, Robert, 163
Haig, Alexander M., Jr., 169
Harcourt Brace Jovanovich, 99
Harley, Robert, 3
Hartford Fire Insurance Com-
  pany, 51, 52, 53
Hartley, Fred L., 150, 155, 197
Hart-Scott-Rodino Antitrust Im-
  provements Act (1976), 80
Harvard Business School, 23, 188
Hay Associates, 154
Hayes, Samuel L., III, 161, 162
headhunters, 151, 153
Hennessy, Edward L., Jr., 83–
  84, 175
Heyman, Samuel J., 88, 97
Hickman, W. Braddock, 86
Hilferding, Rudolf, 9
Hills, Roderick M., 60
Hiss, Donald, 130
Hoffmann-La Roche, 92
holding companies, 6, 7, 196
Household International, 56, 172
Hugel, Charles E., 167
Hughes Aircraft, 61
Hyatt Clark, 191
Hyatt Roller Bearing Company,
  33